Y0-BPW-335

# CONTENTS

Une publication équivalente est disponible en français
sous le titre suivant : *Le curriculum de l'Ontario, de la
1re à la 8e année – Éducation artistique, 2009.*

This publication is available on the Ministry of Education's
website, at http://www.edu.gov.on.ca.

# INTRODUCTION

This document replaces *The Ontario Curriculum, Grades 1–8: The Arts, 1998*. Beginning in September 2009, all arts programs for Grades 1 to 8 will be based on the expectations outlined in this document.

## THE IMPORTANCE OF THE ARTS IN THE CURRICULUM

> *Since arts experiences offer other modes and ways of experiencing and learning, children will have opportunities to think and feel as they explore, problem solve, express, interpret, and evaluate the process and the results. To watch a child completely engaged in an arts experience is to recognize that the brain is on, driven by the aesthetic and emotional imperative to make meaning, to say something, to represent what matters.*
>
> The Arts Go to School, David Booth and Masayuki Hachiya, eds. (Markham, Ontario: Pembroke Publishers, 2004), p.15

Education in the arts is essential to students' intellectual, social, physical, and emotional growth and well-being. Experiences in the arts – in dance, drama, music, and visual arts – play a valuable role in helping students to achieve their potential as learners and to participate fully in their community and in society as a whole. The arts provide a natural vehicle through which students can explore and express themselves and through which they can discover and interpret the world around them. Participation in the arts contributes in important ways to students' lives and learning – it involves intense engagement, development of motivation and confidence, and the use of creative and dynamic ways of thinking and knowing. It is well documented that the intellectual and emotional development of children is enhanced through study of the arts. Through the study of dance, drama, music, and visual arts, students develop the ability to think creatively and critically. The arts nourish and stimulate the imagination, and provide students with an expanded range of tools, techniques, and skills to help them gain insights into the world around them and to represent their understandings in various ways. Study of the arts also provides opportunities for differentiation of both instruction and learning environments.

Participation in the arts and learning about the arts can also broaden students' horizons in various ways. Through study of the arts, students learn about some of the diverse artistic practices, both traditional and contemporary, of a variety of cultures. They learn that they are part of a living and changing culture. They also learn to appreciate the similarities and differences among the various forms of artistic expression of people around the world. The arts offer students unique opportunities to engage in imaginative and innovative thought and action and to develop the ability to communicate and represent their thoughts, feelings, and ideas in numerous ways.

Through interacting with various works of dance, drama, music, and visual arts, including multimedia art works, students deepen their awareness and appreciation of diverse perspectives. They can empathize with the characters in a dance work, a drama, a song, or a visual art work, and can imagine what it would be like to be in the same situation as these people. They can identify common values, both aesthetic and human, in various works of art, and in doing so, increase their understanding of others. The arts can also encourage students to be responsible and critically literate members of society and citizens of the world. Students can learn to approach issues and present ideas and points of view in new ways and to challenge perceptions, while engaging their audience. They can explore and create original "artistic texts" in kinesthetic, visual, spatial, aural, and dramatic ways with attention to both conceptual and aesthetic considerations. Use of current and emerging technologies (e.g., video, multimedia) is integrated in the four disciplines as means of recording, enhancing, communicating, and reinterpreting ideas.

The arts are a way of knowing that provides ways of perceiving, interpreting, organizing, and questioning various aspects of our world through exploration and experimentation. Artistic expression involves clarifying and restructuring personal ideas and experiences. The arts enable individuals and groups to create ideas and images that reflect, communicate, and change their views of the world. An important part of arts literacy is the development of an understanding of the nature of the arts, which includes an understanding of what artists, musicians, actors, and dancers do as individuals and as a community, how ideas are generated in the various arts, and what benefits are associated with these activities. The arts themselves can be regarded as "texts" or commentaries that reflect, record, celebrate, and pass on to future generations the personal and collective stories, values, innovations, and traditions that make us unique. Students may contribute their vision, abilities, and creative energies to the extensive arts and culture sector of Canada, and thus help define, renew, and shape our sense of personal and national identity. The arts broaden young minds and exalt our spirits; they help us understand what it is that makes us human by validating our commonalities and celebrating our differences.

Students will learn to link the study of the arts with the study of a variety of subjects and topics such as history, geography, language, culture, and human interaction. They gain an appreciation of the great importance of the arts as sources of enjoyment and as means of communication in cultures around the world. They also learn to understand that the arts have long served as important media for recording and communicating ideas and feelings. Students will learn that all the arts not only reflect historical and cultural values, but can also be interpreted differently depending on the experiences of the viewer and the perspective presented by the art work. Artistic "texts" (e.g., modern dance, sculptures, shadow plays, songs) carry meaning and require analysis, interpretation, and understanding of their context (for example, how and why the work is created and viewed).

Learning through the arts fosters integration of a student's sensory, cognitive, emotional, and motor capacities. For example, hands-on materials and activities can challenge students to move from the concrete to the abstract, and students can develop ideas while working through the stages of the creative process. The arts can be enjoyable and fulfilling, but they are also intellectually rigorous disciplines involving the use of complex symbols (e.g., choreography, gesture, icons, musical notation) to communicate meaning and understanding. Many of these symbols are rooted in a particular social, historical, and cultural context and therefore may have meanings that are different from what one knows from one's own culture and time.

All of the arts disciplines are distinct, each with its own body of knowledge, and with its own concepts, forms, styles, conventions, techniques, and modes of inquiry, but these disciplines are also linked in various ways and they enrich and are enriched by each other and by other subjects. The world of communication has been affected by the arts in many significant ways, such as the use of body language, music, visuals, and voice in the media. It is important, therefore, that students see and understand the arts in their wider context – as endeavours with important ideas for people – and that they learn to connect their knowledge of the arts to the world beyond the school. In making links between the arts and other areas of the curriculum, students will learn to see how the arts can increase understanding or can give them alternative modes of expression for their ideas. For example, students can use dance to explore feeling and movement in the study of a science topic such as the stages of a natural disaster; through drama, they can explore the point of view of characters whose voice is not heard in a story; they can use their understanding of the power of music to create mood and a sense of time and place in a historical film; or they can use the power of imagery in art work or popular media to influence the viewer.

In producing their own works, students communicate their insights while developing artistic skills and aesthetic judgement. Since artistic activities are closely connected to play and human interaction, students experience a sense of wonder and joy when engaged in the arts, which can motivate them to participate more fully in cultural life and in other educational opportunities. Participation in arts activities helps students develop their ability to listen and observe, and enables them to become more self-aware and self-confident. It encourages them to take risks, to solve problems in creative ways, and to draw on their resourcefulness to build on new ideas. It encourages them to develop a personal voice. Fostering a love of the arts in students, even if they do not intend to be professional artists, will enrich their future experience as audience members. As well, study of the arts expands the ways in which students can express their ideas, feelings, beliefs, and values, as well as their understanding of those of others. It encourages innovative thinking, spontaneity, intuition, divergent thinking, and improvisation. Such learning is vital for communication, understanding, and intellectual and emotional growth. It is also necessary for critically analysing and selecting information in an age when a plethora of information is available instantaneously. The knowledge and skills developed in the study of the arts can therefore be applied in many other endeavours.

## APPROACHES TO EDUCATION IN THE ARTS

The approaches to education in the arts that are briefly discussed below are based on the ideas underlying the arts curriculum that are outlined in the chart on page 6.

**Participation in the Arts.** Learning experiences in the arts include aesthetic experiences, creative engagement, and development of skills of expressive participation, as well as acquisition of knowledge and skills related to specific arts. Arts experiences are unique learning experiences since they combine sensory perception, the affective domain, and the kinesthetic domain with the cognitive domain. Learning experiences in the arts thus provide opportunities for learning that involve the whole person, and participation in the arts provides a context for making wide-ranging and personal connections. In arts education, this is often referred to as "learning in the arts".

**Analysis and Appreciation of the Arts.** Analysis, criticism, and appreciation are integral aspects of an arts program that is concerned with understanding the meaning and "language" of art forms and contemporary and historical artistic products. Learning experiences in analysis and appreciation of the arts may focus on one of the arts or on more than one, or on particular art forms or several forms combined. In arts education, this is often referred to as "learning about the arts".

**Integrated Learning in the Arts.** Various aspects of the arts can also be used to illuminate other aspects of the school curriculum or to help develop students' skills in other subjects. For example, teachers may have students demonstrate their learning in other subjects by using artistic modes of expression. Through integration of the arts with other subjects, students can also develop broader abilities – for example, communication skills. In arts education, this is often referred to as "learning through the arts".

The arts curriculum is based on four central ideas – *developing creativity, communicating, understanding culture*, and *making connections*. Major aspects of these ideas are outlined in the chart below.

| Ideas Underlying the Arts Curriculum | |
|---|---|
| **Developing Creativity** | • developing aesthetic awareness<br>• using the creative process<br>• using problem-solving skills<br>• taking an innovative approach to a challenge |
| **Communicating** | • manipulating elements and forms to convey or express thoughts, feelings, messages, or ideas through the arts<br>• using the critical analysis process<br>• constructing and analysing art works, with a focus on analysing and communicating the meaning of the work<br>• using new media and technology to produce art works and to convey thoughts, feelings, and ideas about art |
| **Understanding Culture** | • understanding cultural traditions and innovations<br>• constructing personal and cultural identity (developing a sense of self and a sense of the relationship between the self and others locally, nationally, and globally)<br>• making a commitment to social justice and dealing with environmental issues |
| **Making Connections** | • making connections between the cognitive and affective domains (expressing thoughts and feelings when creating and responding to art works)<br>• collaborating to create works with others, and performing in ensembles<br>• making connections between the arts and other subjects (e.g., transferring knowledge, skills, and understanding to other subject areas) |

# ROLES AND RESPONSIBILITIES IN ARTS EDUCATION

## Students

Students' responsibilities with respect to their own learning develop gradually and increase over time, as students progress through elementary and secondary school. With appropriate instruction and with experience, students come to see how making an effort can enhance learning and improve achievement. As they mature and develop their ability to persist, to manage their own impulses, to take responsible risks, and to listen with understanding, students become better able to engage with their own learning. Learning to take responsibility for their progress and achievement is an important part of every student's education.

Mastering the concepts and skills connected with the arts curriculum requires work, practice, study, and the development of cooperative skills. It also requires hands-on exploration and a commitment to safety practices. Through ongoing practice and review and revision of their work, students deepen their appreciation and understanding of the arts. In addition, students can learn to use skills that they have developed in the arts in a variety of other contexts and subjects – for example, to help them engage with their learning in other subjects and to revise their ideas. Students can also extend their learning in the arts by participating in school and community arts activities.

## Parents

Parents[1] have an important role to play in their children's learning. Studies show that students perform better in school if their parents are involved in their education. By becoming familiar with the arts curriculum, parents can better appreciate what is being taught in each grade and what their children are expected to learn. This awareness will enhance parents' ability to discuss their children's work with them, to communicate with teachers, and to ask relevant questions about their children's progress. Knowledge of the expectations will also help parents to understand how their children are progressing in school, to interpret teachers' comments on student progress, and to work with teachers to improve their children's learning.

Effective ways in which parents can support their children's learning include the following: attending parent-teacher interviews, participating in parent workshops and school council activities (including becoming a school council member), and encouraging their children to complete their assignments and to practise at home. Parents can also promote and attend artistic events at their children's school. By attending concerts, exhibitions, and arts presentations, parents can demonstrate a commitment to their children's success.

Parents can also provide valuable support for their children's learning by taking an interest in their children's projects in the arts and projects in other subject areas that require the application of knowledge and skills learned in the study of the arts. Such an interest encourages students and promotes a positive attitude to the arts, and the recognition of their achievements helps children develop confidence. The involvement of parents in their children's education also gives parents an opportunity to promote safe techniques in the handling of tools and materials (e.g., musical instruments, paints), and to encourage their children to take proper care of arts materials and instruments.

---

1. In this document, *parent(s)* is used to refer to parent(s) and guardian(s).

In addition to supporting regular school activities, parents may wish to encourage their children to take an active interest in using the arts for meaningful purposes as a regular part of their activities outside school. Parents are encouraged to take their children to art exhibits, theatrical presentations, and musical and dance performances. These events often take place in community centres, places of worship, and public parks or schools, as well as in more formal venues, such as galleries, museums, and concert halls. Such experiences help develop children's appreciation of art works and encourage them to develop their own creativity. The arts curriculum promotes lifelong learning not only for students, but also for their parents and all those with an interest in education.

## Teachers

Teaching is key to student success. Teachers are responsible for developing appropriate instructional strategies to help students achieve the arts curriculum expectations, as well as appropriate methods for assessing and evaluating student learning. Teachers bring enthusiasm and varied teaching and assessment approaches to the classroom, addressing individual students' needs and ensuring sound learning opportunities for every student.

Using a variety of instructional, assessment, and evaluation strategies, teachers provide numerous hands-on opportunities for students to develop and refine their skills and knowledge in creating, presenting, performing, reflecting, analysing, and responding in all of the arts. Through these learning experiences, teachers will enable students to make meaningful connections between what they already know and what they need to know. Teachers are also encouraged to use their knowledge of their students and the curriculum to guide decisions about classroom instruction and activities. Teachers should reflect on the results of the learning opportunities they provide, and make changes to the activities where necessary in order to help students achieve the curriculum expectations to the best of their ability.

Teachers can help students understand that the creative process often requires a considerable expenditure of time and energy and a good deal of perseverance. Teachers can also encourage students to explore alternative solutions and to take the risks necessary to become successful problem-solvers and creators of art work. The arts can play a key role in shaping students' views about life and learning. Since the arts exist in a broader social and historical context, teachers can show students that all of the arts are affected by the values and choices of individuals, and in turn have a significant impact on society.

Teachers provide students with frequent opportunities to practise and apply arts concepts and, through regular and varied assessment, give them the specific and descriptive feedback they need in order to further develop and refine their skills. By assigning tasks that promote the development of creative and thinking skills, teachers also enable students to become thoughtful and effective communicators. Opportunities to relate knowledge and skills in arts learning to wider contexts, both across the curriculum and in the world beyond the school, motivate students to learn and to become lifelong learners.

## Principals

The principal works in partnership with teachers and parents to ensure that each student has access to the best possible educational experience. The principal is also a community builder who creates an environment that is welcoming to all, and who ensures that all members of the school community are kept well informed.

To support student learning, principals ensure that the Ontario curriculum is being properly implemented in all classrooms through the use of a variety of instructional approaches, and that appropriate time, facilities, and resources are made available for teachers to allow all students to participate in all four strands of the arts program. To enhance teaching and student learning in all subjects, including the arts, principals promote learning teams and work with teachers to facilitate teacher participation in professional development activities. Principals are also responsible for ensuring that every student who has an Individual Education Plan (IEP) is receiving the modifications and/or accommodations described in his or her plan – in other words, for ensuring that the IEP is properly developed, implemented, and monitored.

## Community Partners

Community partners can be an important resource for a school's arts program. They can provide models of how the arts relate to life beyond school. These models include partnerships of school boards and individual schools with arts agencies and institutions, social services, community organizations, corporations, and local businesses. Such modelling and mentoring can enrich not only the educational experience of students but also the life of the community.

Schools and school boards can play a role by coordinating efforts with community partners. They can involve community artists and volunteers in supporting arts instruction and in promoting a focus on the arts inside and outside the school. Schools should ensure that partnership initiatives are carried out within the context of strong educational objectives. It is important that schools plan the ways in which visits from artists and other members of the arts community can help students to achieve particular arts learning expectations. It is also important to decide what are the best ways of integrating artists' visits into the sequence of lessons within the unit(s) of instruction. Community partners can be included in arts events held in the school, and can help facilitate educational visits. School boards can collaborate with leaders of existing community-based arts programs for youth, including programs offered in public libraries and community centres. Art galleries, theatres, museums, and concert venues (where available) provide rich environments for field trips and for exploration of the local community and its resources.

In choosing community partners, schools should build on existing links with their local communities and create new partnerships in conjunction with ministry and school board policies. These links are especially beneficial when they have direct connections to the curriculum. Teachers may find opportunities for their students to participate in community arts projects or events. At the elementary level, participation in inclusive exhibitions, concerts, and performances is encouraged. Teachers may have their students participate in festivals that focus on the curriculum, support the units or sequence of instruction, have clear criteria, are designed for educational purposes, and provide descriptive feedback. Teachers may provide ongoing exhibitions and performance opportunities within classrooms, schools, school districts, colleges, universities, and other community venues.

## ATTITUDES IN THE ARTS

The attitudes of everyone involved with students have a significant effect on how students approach the arts. Parents can demonstrate a positive attitude towards the arts at home and in the community, and teachers should ensure that they project a positive attitude towards the arts in their instruction. Teachers should encourage students to use their imagination and their problem-solving and critical-thinking skills in planning, producing, and assessing works of art. They should also help students understand that even the most accomplished artists continue to put a great deal of time and effort into their work.

Teachers can also encourage a positive attitude towards the arts by helping students learn about careers in various areas of the arts industry. By studying art in a variety of forms, learning about artists within and outside the community, and participating in a variety of artistic activities, students will become better informed about the possibilities for active participation in the arts later in life.

Students' attitudes towards the arts can have a significant effect on their achievement of the curriculum expectations. Teaching methods and learning activities that encourage students to recognize the value and relevance of what they are learning will go a long way towards motivating students to work and to learn effectively.

# THE PROGRAM IN THE ARTS

## CURRICULUM EXPECTATIONS

*The Ontario Curriculum, Grades 1–8: The Arts, 2009* identifies the expectations for each grade and describes the knowledge and skills that students are expected to acquire, demonstrate, and apply in their class work and investigations, on tests, and in various other activities on which their achievement is assessed and evaluated.

Two sets of expectations are listed for each grade in each *strand*, or broad area of the curriculum, in the arts for Grades 1 to 8 – overall expectations and specific expectations.

The *overall expectations* describe in general terms the knowledge and skills that students are expected to demonstrate by the end of each grade. There are three overall expectations for each strand in each grade in the arts.

The *specific expectations* describe the expected knowledge and skills in greater detail. The specific expectations are organized under numbered headings, each of which indicates the overall expectation to which the group of specific expectations corresponds. The organization of expectations into groups is not meant to imply that the expectations in any one group are achieved independently of the expectations in the other groups. The numbered headings are used merely to help teachers focus on particular aspects of knowledge and skills as they develop various lessons and learning activities for their students (see the illustration on page 12).

Taken together, the overall and specific expectations represent the mandated curriculum.

Most of the specific expectations are accompanied by examples, given in parentheses, as well as "teacher prompts". The examples and teacher prompts help to clarify the requirements specified in the expectations, and suggest the intended depth and level of complexity of the expectations. They have been developed to model appropriate practice for the grade and are meant to serve as illustrations for teachers. Teachers can choose to use the examples and teacher prompts that are appropriate for their classrooms, or they may develop their own approaches that reflect a similar level of complexity. Whatever the specific ways in which the requirements outlined in the expectations are implemented in the classroom, they must, wherever possible, be inclusive and reflect the diversity of the student population and the population of the province.

Each grade is organized into four **strands**, numbered A, B, C, and D.

A **numbered subheading** introduces each overall expectation. The same heading is used to identify the group of specific expectations that relates to the particular overall expectation (e.g., within the specific expectations, "A1. Creating and Presenting" relates to overall expectation A1 for the Dance strand).

The **overall expectations** describe in general terms the knowledge and skills students are expected to demonstrate by the end of each grade. Three overall expectations are provided for each strand in every grade. The numbering of overall expectations indicates the strand to which they belong (e.g., A1 through A3 are the overall expectations for strand A).

# A. DANCE

## OVERALL EXPECTATIONS

By the end of Grade 3, students will:

**A1. Creating and Presenting:** apply the creative process (see pages 19–22) to the composition of dance phrases, using the elements of dance to communicate feelings and ideas;

**A2. Reflecting, Responding, and Analysing:** apply the critical analysis process (see pages 23–28) to communicate their feelings, ideas, and understandings in response to a variety of dance pieces and experiences;

**A3. Exploring Forms and Cultural Contexts:** demonstrate an understanding of a variety of dance forms and styles from the past and present, and their social and/or community contexts.

The **fundamental concepts** embedded in the expectations for each strand are outlined in this box for each grade.

---

**FUNDAMENTAL CONCEPTS FOR GRADE 3**

Students in Grade 3 will develop or extend understanding of the following concepts through participation in various dance experiences (e.g., exploring movement and pattern forms), with particular emphasis on time and energy.

ELEMENTS OF DANCE
* *body:* body actions, body shapes, locomotor movements (e.g., running, galloping, crawling), non-locomotor movements (e.g., lifting, pulling, marching, waving arms), body bases (e.g., seat as base), use of body zones (e.g., body areas of front and back)
* *space:* levels, pathways, directions, size of movement
* *time:* freeze, tempo (e.g., slow, sustained, fast)
* *energy:* force (e.g., lightness/strength), effort (e.g., pressing, gliding), quality (e.g., smoothly, cautiously, erratically, percussively)
* *relationship:* (e.g., interconnected shapes)

---

The **specific expectations** describe the expected knowledge and skills in greater detail. The expectation number identifies the strand to which the expectation belongs and the overall expectation to which it relates (e.g., A1.1 and A1.2 relate to the first overall expectation in strand A).

## SPECIFIC EXPECTATIONS

### A1. Creating and Presenting

By the end of Grade 3, students will:

**A1.1** imitate movements found in their natural environment in a variety of ways and incorporate them into a dance phrase (*e.g., modify the movements of animals, snow falling to the ground, ice melting, plants growing; connect a series of insect-like movements together to make a phrase*)

*Teacher prompt:* "How would the quality of your movements change if you were first moving like a bee and then moving like a butterfly [erratic, gliding]? Would your movements change to sharp and sudden, or smooth and slow? Would your path be direct and gliding or indirect and meandering?"

**A1.2** use dance as a language to represent ideas from diverse literature sources, with a focus on time and energy (*e.g., interpret stories, poems, and texts from other subject areas through dance; respond to a story about insects by depicting the sustained lifting and pulling actions of ants versus the sustained floating actions of butterflies*)

*Teacher prompts:* "When creating a dance phrase to represent the idea of this poem, consider the poem's punctuation. How would you express the dance equivalent of an exclamation mark for emphasis in the dance?" "Which combination of elements will you choose from the time and energy chart to portray the rest of the insect characters in the story?"

The **examples** help to clarify the requirement specified in the expectation and to suggest its intended depth and level of complexity. The examples are illustrations only, not requirements. They appear within parentheses and are set in italics.

**Teacher prompts** illustrate the kinds of questions teachers might pose in relation to the requirement specified in the expectation. They are illustrations only, not requirements. Teacher prompts always follow the expectation and examples.

In the expectations for each of the strands, some repetition has been necessary to reflect the progressive nature of skill development in the arts. Expectations dealing with skills that continue to be of major importance as students progress from grade to grade are repeated for all relevant grades. Progression is indicated either by means of increasingly complex examples or by changes to the expectations.

It should also be noted that all the skills specified in the early grades continue to be developed and refined as students move on through the grades, whether or not the skills continue to be explicitly mentioned.

## STRANDS IN THE ARTS CURRICULUM

The expectations in the arts curriculum are organized into four strands – Dance, Drama, Music, and Visual Arts. The knowledge and skills described in the expectations in these four strands will enable students to create, understand, respond to, and appreciate a range of works in the arts.

The program in all grades is designed to develop a range of essential skills in each of the arts – dance, drama, music, and the visual arts. These skills will be built on a solid foundation of knowledge of arts concepts and will include creative, analytical, critical thinking, and communication skills. Students learn best when they are encouraged to consciously monitor their thinking as they learn (metacognition), and each strand includes expectations that call for such reflection.

The emphasis in each strand is on developing students' ability to communicate through creating and presenting/performing works in the arts and to communicate their thoughts and feelings about works in the arts. Students' demonstration of understanding of the knowledge and skills specified in each strand must occur through active participation in the various arts. Learning in the arts cannot be viewed as merely the learning of facts, but must focus on developing students' knowledge and skills in hands-on, age-appropriate ways.

The expectations for each strand are grouped under three subheadings, as follows:

*Creating and Presenting/Performing* focuses on the students' creative use of the various art forms to express and communicate feelings and ideas in those forms. Students are required to be actively engaged in the stages of the creative process (described on pages 19–22). When engaged in the creative process, students should be given opportunities to be inventive and imaginative in their thinking, rather than merely to find a prescribed answer. Reflection and feedback, both ongoing and summative, are essential parts of the creative process, allowing students to evaluate their own achievement and to grow in their creative endeavours.

*Reflecting, Responding, and Analysing* focuses on the students' awareness and communication of emotional and intellectual responses to works in the various art forms. Students are required to use the critical analysis process (described on pages 23–28) to analyse, discuss, and interpret their own works and those of others, and to assess their strengths and areas for growth as both creators and audience members. Students learn that all ideas can be expanded upon and revised and can be considered from a variety of perspectives. Practice in using the critical analysis process is intended to help students move beyond quick judgements to develop informed personal points of view and to learn how to articulate their creative and artistic choices.

*Exploring Forms and Cultural Contexts* focuses on the students' awareness and understanding of how the various arts and art forms have developed in various times and places; of the role of the different arts in students' own lives and in the local, national, and global communities; and of the social and economic factors that influence how the arts are perceived and valued. This component also encompasses the study of contemporary media and art forms. It is intended to help students understand that the arts are an important means of recording and expressing cultural history and identity and are also an essential aspect of living for all people. The focus should not be on the learning of facts, but rather on a meaningful extension of creating and learning in the arts.

The three groups of expectations are closely interrelated, and the knowledge and skills described in the expectations in each group are interdependent and complementary. Teachers should plan activities that blend expectations from these three groups in order to provide students with the kinds of experiences that promote meaningful learning and that help them understand the interrelationships between creative and practical work, critical analysis, and learning about the sociocultural and historical context of the arts.

Teachers should be aware that dance, drama, music, and the visual arts are separate disciplines, each with its own body of knowledge, artistic "language" or symbols, and modes of investigation. They each have a history and heritage, and they have structures in which ideas and experiences may be developed. Each discipline therefore provides unique opportunities through which students can develop their ability to communicate and to interpret meaning – for example, through visual, auditory, or kinesthetic forms or symbols. The arts can have a powerful influence on the way we think and communicate, and students can benefit from opportunities to interpret meaning and develop their communication skills in a variety of expressive forms in the arts.

## Dance

The dance curriculum is intended to help students to develop an understanding and appreciation of dance, as well as the ability to create works using the elements and the choreographic forms of the discipline. Through exploring dance and movement, students will develop an understanding of the art form, themselves, and others, and will learn about the lives of people in different times, places, and cultures. They will develop practical artistic skills, critical analysis skills, and a variety of communication skills.

Dance is expressive movement with purpose and form. All dance communication is transmitted through movement – that is, through the body movements and gestures of the dancer. A dancer is, therefore, both the performer and the instrument through which dance is expressed. It is not recommended that students at the elementary level be given instruction in formal dance techniques (e.g., ballet, Graham, Límon techniques). Instead, students will develop their own movement vocabularies that they will use to create dance pieces that communicate their feelings, ideas, and understandings. This approach to dance, as outlined in this curriculum, is based on dance pedagogies (e.g., Laban), and focuses on the use of movement and the elements of dance instead of rote repetition of dance steps.

In all grades, students will draw upon a variety of sources – such as literature, media texts, images, historical and current events, and topics and themes from across the curriculum, particularly the other arts – in order to create dance pieces in which they communicate their interpretation of personal ideas and feelings, social justice issues, themes, situations, and the motives of various characters. Dance is a physical and non-verbal medium for learning about the self and the world; it offers the opportunity to participate in learning in kinesthetic, cognitive, and imaginative ways. It is important that movement skills be developed within students' ongoing dance explorations and creations, rather than be focused on isolated, repetitive exercises.

As students engage in creating and responding to dance works, they will develop their awareness of aesthetic issues and explore various ways a dance piece can be interpreted. The meaning each person derives from a work of art is different and is based on the connections the observer makes between the dance and personal experience, the dance and other works of art, or the dance and the world. Students should also reflect on the meaning they communicate through their own dance. They will also learn to use technology both for observing performances by accomplished artists (e.g., DVDs, videos) and in creating their own presentations (e.g., lighting, musical recordings, projected images). The dance program should provide opportunities for students to view and be exposed to a variety of dance performances and works by local, multicultural, and professional Canadian artists both within and outside the school. Emphasis should be placed on understanding that dance is continually evolving and that innovations develop alongside or out of traditional forms or practices.

The Dance strand has three overall expectations, one for each of Creating and Presenting; Reflecting, Responding, and Analysing; and Exploring Forms and Cultural Contexts.

## Drama

The drama curriculum is intended to help students to develop an understanding and appreciation of drama, as well as the ability to create works using the forms, concepts, elements, and conventions of the discipline. Through exploring drama, students will develop an understanding of the art form, themselves, and others, and will learn about the lives of people in different times, places, and cultures. As they work in role in a context, they will come to understand particular situations, texts, ideas, and stories. In addition to role playing, students will use their growing understanding of drama forms, conventions, and elements to develop process drama with others, explore issues through improvisation, or develop or interpret scenes. It is not recommended that students at the elementary level be given instruction in formal drama or theatre techniques (e.g., memorizing scripts or interpreting mannerisms of a specific character using the Stanislavski method). Instead, students will expand their thinking, solve problems, and develop their ability to express ideas and feelings through aspects of the art form such as contextual or process drama and role play. Students should explore dramatic situations episodically and should assume different roles using various drama conventions. They will also develop practical artistic skills, critical analysis skills, and a variety of communication skills that will enable them to clarify and articulate their own point of view.

Drama provides many opportunities for students to practise communicating with different audiences for a variety of purposes, through moving, speaking and writing in role. Role playing is a key component of the drama curriculum. Pretending to be someone else involves an act of the imagination that is of central importance in the development of the ability to understand others. As students "live through" experiences of others in imagined situations, they learn to understand a variety of points of view and motives and to empathize with others. This exploration of the "as if" in roles and worlds will help students deepen their understanding of humanity and issues of equity and social justice. Students will also learn to use language effectively to communicate a character's emotional state and point of view.

In all grades, students will draw upon a variety of sources – such as literature, personal stories and experiences, historical and current events, and topics and themes from across the curriculum – to create a meaningful context for their drama explorations. Students can also draw on previous instruction and prior experience with other art forms – including visual arts, writing, dance, and music – to enhance and extend their drama work. As students engage in creating and critiquing works of drama, they will develop their awareness of aesthetic issues, not only in drama but in the arts generally, and will learn about ways in which the arts are interconnected. They will also learn to use a variety of existing and emerging technologies both for observing performances by accomplished artists (e.g., DVDs, videos) and in creating their own presentations (e.g., lighting, projections, musical recordings). In the higher grades, students will also use various technologies for research. The drama program should provide opportunities for students to view and be exposed to a variety of drama performances/media and works by local, multicultural, and professional Canadian artists both within and outside the school.

The Drama strand has three overall expectations, one for each of Creating and Presenting; Reflecting, Responding, and Analysing; and Exploring Forms and Cultural Contexts.

## Music

The music curriculum is intended to help students develop an understanding and appreciation of music, as well as the ability to create and perform it, so that they will be able to find in music a lifelong source of enjoyment and personal satisfaction. Emphasis should be placed on encouraging students to become active participants in composing music, exploring ideas through music, responding to music, and performing.

An interesting and challenging program in music not only develops practical artistic skills but also enables students to sharpen their ability to reason, to think critically, and to explore their emotional responses to the music. Students develop musical literacy through singing, playing, moving, performing, creating, and listening actively. It is therefore essential that a balanced music program be offered – one that includes listening and responding, performing, interpreting, and creating and that may appeal to a wide variety of students. Children learn to love music when they have opportunities to experience it in the context of a rich and varied curriculum.

As students engage in creating and performing music, they will learn to generate and focus their thoughts in a musical form; explore and experiment with instruments, found or environmental sounds, and compositional forms and techniques that are appropriate for their developmental stage; revise and refine their work; and present and share their composition or performance with others. Through creating and performing, students will experience the joy of making music, create compositions that express and communicate their ideas and feelings, learn to identify and solve problems, and apply their knowledge of the elements of music both independently and in cooperation with others.

Students will learn to use the critical analysis process to respond to, analyse, and interpret music they experience or hear. As they express their initial thoughts, feelings, and ideas about music, analyse the musical choices that are made, and explore the context in which music was created, they will build the knowledge and language they need to communicate *about* music as well as *through* music.

Students will further their understanding of the music of various cultures by studying a wide range of music and musicians from different time periods and cultures, including Aboriginal, local, national, and global societies.

The Music strand has three overall expectations, one for each of Creating and Performing; Reflecting, Responding, and Analysing; and Exploring Forms and Cultural Contexts.

## Visual Arts

The visual arts include a broad range of forms, genres, and styles that include the traditional arts of drawing, painting, sculpting, printmaking, architecture, and photography, as well as commercial art, traditional and fine crafts, industrial design, performance art, and electronic and media arts. The visual arts curriculum is intended to help students develop their creativity, as well as the ability to communicate their understanding of the world around them through visual arts. In learning to express themselves in visual ways, students will sharpen their powers of observation, imagination, and invention. In developing the ability to respond to, analyse, and describe works of art, they will learn to interpret art works and to communicate their understanding of the meaning and intentions they see in the works. The development of visual literacy skills and knowledge will therefore prepare students to investigate and understand images, media, and art works, and will equip them to interpret the complex contemporary visual world.

The visual arts curriculum is rooted in the experience of art making. Visual arts provide ways of describing, exploring, and responding, and can be used to express ideas, experiences, and feelings. In order to make visual art works, students need to acquire a range of skills and some specific knowledge. It is essential for students to be engaged in meaningful, open-ended art-making activities that enable them to express personal feelings, experiences, and ideas and develop the skills to use art tools, materials, and techniques that are appropriate for the grade. When students become familiar with the possibilities and limitations of a variety of tools, materials, and techniques and can demonstrate control of these resources, they will be expected to apply their knowledge and skills in making artistic choices in their own work.

The works of art to which students are exposed should represent various topics, themes, and styles (e.g., representational or realistic, stylized, Impressionist, abstract works) and different historical periods, including contemporary art by living artists, and should also include conceptual and fine art, traditional art, and artefacts. Teachers are expected to use a range of high-quality art reproductions so that students have high-quality materials to observe and learn from. It should be noted that the art works cited in the curriculum are only examples and are not meant to limit teachers' choices. The works selected for study should include the works of both men and women and should reflect the cultural diversity of Canada and the world, including the contributions of Aboriginal, Métis, and Inuit artists. Through experiencing a wide variety of art works, students will also learn to understand and appreciate the range and significance of artistic expression. Wherever appropriate, the study of the visual arts should be linked to the other arts disciplines and other subject areas.

The Visual Arts strand has three overall expectations, one for each of Creating and Presenting; Reflecting, Responding, and Analysing; and Exploring Forms and Cultural Contexts.

## Media Arts and Multimedia Technology

Although media arts does not represent a separate strand, the arts curriculum must take it into account. There has been a global transformation of culture, as new and emerging media forms have blurred the boundaries between the arts, leading to the creation of new art forms and new ways of looking at the arts.

A new aesthetic sensibility has arisen from the technological revolution, allowing young people to view the world through multiple modalities. Multisensory and cross-disciplinary approaches are challenging fixed forms and categories as means for interpreting human experience. Traditional definitions of the arts do not sufficiently take these forces into account.

New technologies are increasingly being used in teaching, learning, and creating in the arts. These technologies are contributing to the emergence of new art forms. Moreover, the use of multimedia technology also gives students opportunities to develop collaborative skills, since creating a multimedia project in the arts often involves a number of learners. Such collaborative and interactive activities foster holistic learning, the integration of skills and knowledge, and the development of transferable skills. Students also need to develop the ability to think critically when creating and viewing print and electronic media so that they are aware of the effect of media on their perceptions and experience of the world.

## FUNDAMENTAL CONCEPTS IN THE ARTS

In this document, fundamental concepts are listed separately for each of the arts – dance, drama, music, and visual arts. These concepts represent essential aspects of each of the arts. They consist of *elements* in the Dance, Drama, and Music strands and *elements* and *principles* in the Visual Arts strand. The elements and principles used in this document are listed in the table below.

| Fundamental Concepts | |
|---|---|
| Dance | *Elements:* body, space, time, energy, and relationship |
| Drama | *Elements:* role/character, relationship, time and place, tension, and focus and emphasis |
| Music | *Elements:* duration, pitch, dynamics and other expressive controls, timbre, texture/harmony, and form |
| Visual Arts | *Elements:* line, shape and form, space, colour, texture, and value<br>*Principles:* contrast, repetition and rhythm, variety, emphasis, proportion, balance, unity and harmony, and movement |

In the Fundamental Concepts tables for each grade and strand, the requirements emphasized in the expectations for that grade and strand are listed under the appropriate element or principle. As students progress through the curriculum from grade to grade, they extend and deepen their understanding of these fundamental concepts and learn to apply their understanding with increasing sophistication. They also continue to build on the skills related to these concepts that they have learned in earlier grades.

It should be noted that students should not learn about the concepts of the various arts in isolation but through meaningful, creative activities. Teachers must also determine the extent to which the students have prior knowledge of the concepts in each strand and grade; they may need to provide differentiated instruction to ensure that students are given support, for example, in reviewing and applying the concepts and skills introduced in previous grades. For this reason, teachers should be familiar with the curriculum expectations for at least the grades that immediately precede and follow the grade that they are teaching.

## THE CREATIVE PROCESS

Students are expected to learn and use the creative process to help them acquire and apply knowledge and skills in the arts. Use of the creative process is to be integrated with use of the critical analysis process (described on pages 23–28) in all facets of the arts curriculum as students work to achieve the expectations in the four strands.

All children have the ability to be creative. Education in the arts builds upon this ability and deepens children's capacity for artistic expression and representation. Awareness of one's inner feelings and thoughts is a prerequisite to making art. Inspiration and innovative thinking spring from this awareness and provide us with new answers and solutions, and new questions to pursue. Through the creation and presentation of art works, students express and communicate their creative insights in a range of forms and with varying degrees of concreteness and abstraction.

Creativity involves the invention and the assimilation of new thinking and its integration with existing knowledge. Sometimes the creative process is more about asking the right questions than it is about finding the right answer. It is paradoxical in that it involves both spontaneity and deliberate, focused effort. Creativity does not occur in a vacuum. Art making is a process requiring both creativity and skill, and it can be cultivated by establishing conditions that encourage and promote its development. Teachers need to be aware that the atmosphere they create for learning affects the nature of the learning itself. A setting that is conducive to creativity is one in which students are not afraid to suggest alternative ideas and take risks.

The creative process comprises several stages:
- challenging and inspiring
- imagining and generating
- planning and focusing
- exploring and experimenting
- producing preliminary work
- revising and refining
- presenting, performing, and sharing
- reflecting and evaluating

The creative process is intended to be followed in a flexible, fluid, and cyclical manner. As students and teachers become increasingly familiar with the creative process, they are able to move deliberately and consciously between the stages and to vary their order as appropriate. For example, students may benefit from exploring and experimenting before planning and focusing; or in some instances, the process may begin with reflecting. Feedback and reflection can happen throughout the process.

### The Creative Process

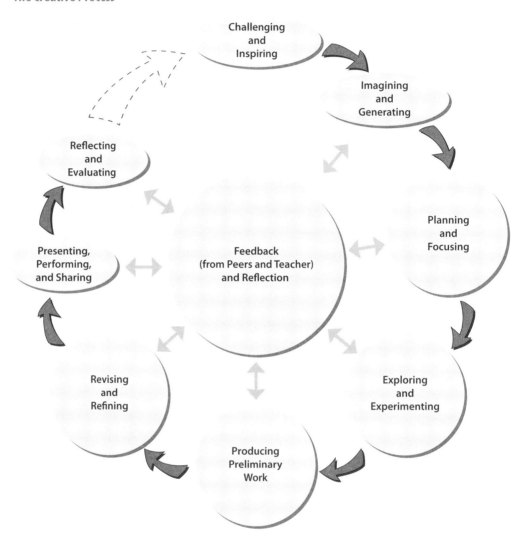

The creative process will sometimes take students through the complete cycle, beginning with a contextualized challenge or inspiration and resulting in a final product to be evaluated and/or reflected upon. At other times, the process may only be followed through to the exploration and experimentation phase. Research clearly shows that the exploration and experimentation phase is a critical phase in the creative process. Students should be encouraged to experiment with a wide range of materials, tools, techniques, and conventions and should be given numerous opportunities to explore and manipulate the elements within each art form.

Ongoing feedback and structured opportunities for students to engage in reflection and metacognition – for example, reflecting on strengths, areas for improvement, and alternative possibilities, and setting goals and identifying strategies for achieving their goals – are woven into each stage of the creative process. In this way, assessment by both teacher and student is used to inspire students' creativity and support their development and achievement in the arts. The communication and reflection that occur during and after the process of problem solving help students not only to articulate and refine their thinking but also to see the problem they are solving from different perspectives. Descriptive feedback to the students on their work can occur throughout the stages of the creative process. Drafts and other first attempts at creation or production may be works in progress assessed by the student, his or her peers, or the teacher. These sketches and drafts or preliminary recordings and videos may be housed in each student's working portfolio. Students might periodically select items or exhibits from their working or process portfolios to place in a presentation portfolio. Both types of portfolios are to be included in the assessment process.

The stages of the creative process are outlined in the chart that follows. Various activities that are characteristic of each stage are listed, and the role of the teacher at each stage is described.

| THE CREATIVE PROCESS | | |
|---|---|---|
| **Stage of the Process** | **The Student** | **The Teacher** |
| *Challenging/Inspiring* | – uses creative ideas inspired by the stimulus for creation<br>– uses research, takes inventory, makes choices<br>– participates in the development of a plan or description of criteria for evaluating success | – introduces the initial idea, challenge, stimulus, inspiration, experience<br>– provides models, examples, and/or learning goals<br>– establishes expectations, defines parameters, and helps develop criteria for evaluating success |
| *Imagining/Generating* | – uses ideas inspired by the stimulus: brainstorms, "bodystorms", lists, sketches, discusses, poses questions, draws on prior knowledge and experience<br>– defines the problem in a unique way | – observes, listens, prompts with questions, and provides choices |
| *Planning/Focusing* | – gathers information, storyboards ideas, discusses, determines a focus for exploration, uses a variety of tools for recording plans (e.g., inquiry, research)<br>– states what he or she is trying to do, or articulates the idea to be developed<br>– makes choices about the art forms, tools, strategies, and formal concepts (e.g., elements) | – provides a rich variety of materials and resources<br>– strategically asks questions and/or models planning strategies<br>– shares a variety of samples of plans<br>– structures planning and provides choices (e.g., assigns group management roles to students) |

| THE CREATIVE PROCESS (continued) | | |
|---|---|---|
| **Stage of the Process** | **The Student** | **The Teacher** |
| *Exploring/Experimenting* | – uses a range of arts elements, techniques, conventions, and/or principles (as appropriate for each strand) in response to the challenge, stimulus, or inspiration introduced by the teacher or teaching artist or set by the student | – continues to provide a rich variety of materials and resources for open-ended activities<br>– continues to ask questions and provide direct instruction strategically<br>– provides reference charts of the elements, techniques, conventions, and/or principles (as appropriate for each strand)<br>– provides positive reinforcement for risk taking; expects focus; encourages incubation<br>– provides time to practise |
| *Producing Preliminary Work* | – commits to artistic choices and works to make his or her meaning clear for an intended audience<br>– creates the work (i.e., the embodiment of the idea) | – asks questions about meaning and intended audience<br>– observes aspects of the work and provides descriptive feedback (e.g., verbal, written)<br>– encourages students to reason, communicate ideas, make connections, and apply knowledge and skills |
| *Revising/Refining* | – shares preliminary work with peers; invites outside opinions; develops and refines the formal concepts (elements, techniques, conventions, principles, as appropriate for each strand)<br>– reworks the piece, building on strengths and incorporating feedback<br>– develops and modifies initial idea; makes choices, adapts, and shapes | – continues to ask questions about meaning and intended audience<br>– continues to provide numerous learning opportunities that are varied, and supports the learning needs and experiences of the students<br>– observes and provides descriptive feedback; encourages students to look for alternatives and give reasons for decisions<br>– provides time and opportunities for reflection and revision |
| *Presenting/Performing/Sharing* | – identifies an audience (e.g., teacher, parents, peers, community) and prepares a space for sharing the work; finalizes his or her production | – promotes student talk about the arts<br>– makes necessary arrangements to ensure that performers/exhibitors are sharing with an appropriate audience<br>– promotes the collaborative sharing of ideas and strategies; helps structure the sharing for students<br>– is supportive |
| *Reflecting/Evaluating* | – reflects on the process and the degree of success, and identifies further learning goals and opportunities and next steps | – encourages reflection<br>– links evaluation to criteria and the lessons taught<br>– provides a variety of methods of evaluation to accommodate the learning styles of a variety of students<br>– provides descriptive feedback<br>– evaluates on the basis of a body of evidence collected over time |

## THE CRITICAL ANALYSIS PROCESS

The critical analysis process is a central part of the arts curriculum. Students need to be guided through the stages of this process. As they learn the steps of the process they will become increasingly independent in their ability to develop and express an informed response to a work of dance, drama, music, visual art, or media/multimedia art. They will also become more sophisticated in their ability to critically analyse the works they are studying or responding to. Students learn to approach works in the arts thoughtfully by withholding judgement until they have enough information to respond in an informed manner.

It should be emphasized that the critical analysis process is not used in isolation, since aspects of the critical analysis process are often also used during the creative process (e.g., during the revising/refining and reflecting/evaluating stages). The critical analysis process and the creative process are therefore inextricably linked. Although students need to continually develop their critical abilities, creative work is at the heart of the arts program, and most of the students' time will be spent in creating and presenting/performing.

Using the critical analysis process will enable students to:

- respond knowledgeably and sensitively to their own and others' dance, drama, music, and visual art works;
- make connections between their own experiences and works in the arts, between different art forms, and between art works and the lives of people and communities around the world
- perceive and interpret how the elements of each art form contribute to meaning in dance, drama, music, and visual art works;
- develop, share, and justify an informed personal point of view about works in the arts;
- demonstrate awareness of and appreciation for the importance of dance, drama, music, and visual arts in society;
- demonstrate appreciation appropriately as audience members in formal and informal settings (e.g., peer performances in the classroom; excursions to arts institutions, galleries, concert halls, theatres).

Teachers can set the stage for critical response and analysis by creating a reassuring learning environment in which students feel free to experiment with new or alternative approaches and ideas. This is a good opportunity to remind students that different people may respond to the same work in different ways. Each person brings a particular cultural perspective and a unique personal history to experiences in the arts. Responding to the arts is, in part, a discovery process. While students may lack specific background information about the artists, the history of the arts, or contemporary artistic practices, their own life experience, intuition, ideas, and critical and creative thinking abilities are important and relevant aspects of their interaction with works of all types in the arts.

The critical analysis process includes the following aspects:

- initial reaction
- description
- analysis and interpretation
- expression of an informed point of view
- consideration of cultural context

The process is intended to be used in a flexible manner, taking into account students' prior experiences and the context in which the various art forms and works are experienced. The cultural context of the work should be taken into consideration throughout the critical analysis process.

*The Critical Analysis Process*

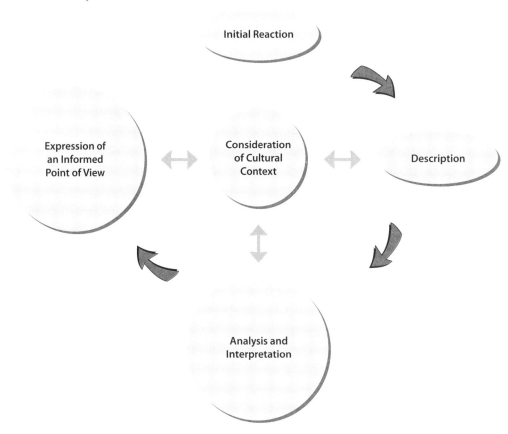

## Initial Reaction

Students are encouraged to express their first reaction to a work. This first impression is the starting point for further investigation and discovery. First impressions may provide a useful benchmark for later evaluations of how students have grown through the process of critiquing a work. This initial reaction may be expressed through a variety of approaches, including active approaches (e.g., a drama response to visual art works). Teachers can elicit students' first impressions by asking questions such as those listed below. If students cannot easily explain why they are making a judgement, these questions can help them move beyond overly simple value judgements such as "good" or "bad". Students should be reminded that there are no wrong answers if their responses are sincere.

Sample guiding questions might include:

- What is your first impression?
- What does this work bring to mind?
- What does this work remind you of?
- What do you feel? What emotions does this work evoke?
- What puzzles you? What are your questions?
- What connections can you make between this work and your own experience or other art forms?

## Description

Students are asked to brainstorm and list everything they see or hear in the work. They can describe the ideas, images, elements, or effects they observe in the work (e.g., blue; organic shape; a low, outstretched starting position; high, fast notes or high voice). Students should keep the list of descriptions simple at this stage.

It is not necessary in this stage for students to try to figure out how the dancer, musician, dramatist, or visual artist organized the elements or achieved the effects they observe. Students are simply describing their observations. It is premature at this stage to assign meaning to what is seen or heard. If a student seems to be focusing on one idea, image, or element, he or she should be encouraged to make a note of it for later.

The description stage should not be lengthy. Its purpose is limited; it is simply a way to get students to note as much as they can before moving on to analysis and interpretation.

Sample guiding questions might include:

- What do you see when you examine the work closely?
- What grabs your attention in the work?
- What do you sense (e.g., see, hear, smell, feel, taste) when you examine the work?
- What stands out for you? What do you notice (e.g., elements)?
- What "qualities" do you hear or see in this work (e.g., strong, repeated rhythm; rapid and slow movements of the upper body; vibrant paint colours; bold brush-strokes or lines; a performer speaking in role with clarity and conviction)?
- What do you think the artist worked particularly hard at while he or she created this work?

## Analysis and Interpretation

Students try to figure out what the artist has done to achieve certain effects. Students can discuss the artist's use of the elements, materials, and concepts specific to the art form. Students might want to refer back to their first impressions (e.g., analyse how the various elements in the work contributed to a first impression of liveliness). Initially, students should be encouraged to identify how the individual elements have been used and how they relate to each other. They can also analyse the overall characteristics and compositional features of the work (e.g., how the artist uses and manipulates various elements, sounds, movements, words, images, or ideas).

As students move towards personal interpretation (e.g., "This dance is about feeling lonely"), they connect their own perspectives, associations, and experiences with the characteristics found in the work. As in the "initial reaction" stage of the formal criticism approach, there are no wrong answers. However, students should be able to provide evidence for their interpretations. This stage requires some use of higher-order thinking skills; students should begin to go beyond free association to combine associations based on evidence found in the work.

Students may also address cultural studies information in this stage. Culturally specific information about the designs, the dances, the people, the music, the themes, and the symbolism enhances students' understanding of the work and of its cultural context. Students can discuss and share their understanding of cultural perspectives.

Activities such as discussing interpretations in a small group, writing an artist's statement, reflective journal writing, working independently on a written analysis, or preparing notes for an oral presentation may all be part of this stage.

Sample guiding questions might include:

- What elements and conventions of the art form are used in this work?
- How are the elements organized, combined, or arranged?
- How does the work evoke ideas, feelings, and images?
- What do you think is the theme or subject of the work? (i.e., What is the artist trying to communicate, and why? or, in reflecting on their own work: What did you intend to communicate, and why?)
- Why do you think the choreographer, composer, playwright, or visual artist created this work?
- What message or meaning do you think the work conveys?
- In your opinion, what is the artist's view of the world?
- How does this view match or contrast with your own view of the world?

The types of questions asked will vary with the type of art works being discussed.

## Expression of an Informed Point of View

Students compare their point of view after reflection and analysis to their initial reaction and make connections to other works of art they have seen or heard. They also reflect on whether they have learned anything that they can apply to their own work.

Sample guiding questions might include:

- How effectively does the artist select and combine elements to achieve an intended effect in this work? (i.e., What works?)
- What doesn't work and why?
- Has your point of view shifted from your initial reaction? If so, how has it changed?
- Have your thoughts or feelings about the work changed since your first impressions? If so, how have they changed?
- What made you change your mind?
- If you have not changed your mind, can you now explain your first reaction more fully or precisely?
- Is this an important work? Why?

Sample guiding questions to help students in reflecting on their own work might include:

- In what ways do you feel the work is successful?

- How did it affect the audience? Was it the way you intended?

- How would you alter this work for a different audience, or to send a different message?

## Consideration of Cultural Context

Everyone views the world through various lenses, and our views of the world and our life experiences inform our understanding of works in the arts. Students need to be taught that the arts are not created in a vacuum; they reflect the personal, social, and historical context of the artists. This is true for works created by professional artists and by the students in the classroom.

Teachers may find that while formal critical analysis and interpretation are highly effective and appropriate for some works, other works are best approached through examination of their social, cultural, historical, or contemporary context. In the latter case, the critical analysis process can help students understand how personal, sociocultural, historical, and political frames of reference have a bearing on the creation and interpretation of particular works in the arts. Knowing something about the context in which a work was created can shed valuable light on the meaning of signs and symbols used in the work. The arts not only reflect social reality but contribute to its creation; people shape and are shaped by cultural interactions and works.

There are many ways to build contextual understanding with students. Teachers can discuss with students the importance of understanding cultural and historical context when viewing or listening to a work of art. They can ask students to consider why artists in different historical periods and in different cultural environments created the works they did. For example, does the work have a specific purpose, convey a message, represent a school of thought, or evoke particular feelings?

The contextual approach can provide opportunities for teachers to incorporate authentic cultural information and inquiry-based research that can add depth and meaning to students' creating and learning. Students might begin by finding out about a work's historical, social, or artistic environment, or by examining how an artist's background or personal history influenced his or her work, or by creating a web or concept map listing multiple connections suggested by the work. This type of investigation can help students understand an artist's intentions and may also lead them to engage in further exploration and discovery. In such investigations, it is also important to avoid stereotypical expressions or judgements. Teachers are reminded that learning to analyse works in the arts is not intended to be a substitute for making works in the arts; it is a complementary component to hands-on work.

Students may conduct their own inquiry-based research, or teachers can support them in discussions of and investigations into:

- events in the artist's life;

- the social, political, and cultural climate at the time in which a work was created;

- the similarities and differences between specific works in the past and present;

- the way in which a work in the arts represents the perspective of individuals within a specific group (e.g., social, cultural);

- examples of other works created in the same period or a comparison of works on a similar topic or theme created by a variety of artists in different times and places;

- the expectations and artistic preferences of audiences at the time the work was created;

- the initial critical reception of the work;

- the responsibilities of an audience, including basic points of audience etiquette and the individual's responsibility to acknowledge any personal biases that may influence his or her response to a work (e.g., cultural biases or past experiences with the arts).

In order to guide students, teachers might ask questions such as:

- What interesting things did you learn about the artist's life and work? Is there something important that we need to know in order to understand the meaning of his or her work?

- Were working conditions for people in the arts more or less favourable at the time this artist lived than they are today? Why, and in what way? Are there viewpoints or voices that are left out or never heard in the works?

- In what ways do you agree or disagree with what the artist or critics said about the work? Also, were there competing beliefs and practices at the time?

- Why might different audiences view a work in a way that is different from the artist's intention (e.g., parents and a teenage audience might understand something different from seeing or hearing the same work)?

- How might the work be understood differently by different people in the same time period or by people in the past and in the present?

- Were you surprised by anything you discovered? If so, what?

Teachers and students need to be aware that the context of a work is constantly shifting, and that the nature of the audience and the time period in which a work is seen or heard have a significant impact on the way in which a work is perceived and understood. Because of these factors, there is no single meaning or truth in a work in the arts and no single way of responding to a work.

Studies of the context in which an artist lived and worked do not always need to be carried out in the form of written assignments. Teachers could also suggest that one student, who is acting in role as a reporter, interview another student, who is acting in role as a painter, composer, playwright, or choreographer, about cultural, social, economic, and political conditions at the time the artist lived. The goal of the analytical and contextual work is to develop students' literacy in the arts, to show them possibilities for their own creative work and creative goals, and to expand their repertoire of artistic strategies. Teachers need to ensure that students are engaged in meaningful activities in the arts, and should not ask students merely to memorize facts such as artists' names or titles and dates of works.

Where students are investigating a traditional work of art, use of cross-cultural studies may be appropriate. It is important for teachers and students to carefully and critically assess the cultural information sources to determine their merit and to consult a range of reputable authorities where possible.

# ASSESSMENT AND EVALUATION OF STUDENT ACHIEVEMENT

## BASIC CONSIDERATIONS

The primary purpose of assessment and evaluation is to improve student learning. Information gathered through assessment helps teachers to determine students' strengths and weaknesses in their achievement of the curriculum expectations in each subject in each grade. This information also serves to guide teachers in adapting curriculum and instructional approaches to students' needs and in assessing the overall effectiveness of programs and classroom practices.

Assessment is the process of gathering information from a variety of sources (including assignments, day-to-day observations, conversations or conferences, demonstrations, projects, performances, and tests) that accurately reflects how well a student is achieving the curriculum expectations in a subject. As part of assessment, teachers provide students with descriptive feedback that guides their efforts towards improvement. Evaluation refers to the process of judging the quality of student work on the basis of established criteria, and assigning a value to represent that quality. In Ontario elementary schools, the value assigned will be in the form of a letter grade for Grades 1 to 6 and a percentage grade for Grades 7 and 8.

Assessment and evaluation will be based on the provincial curriculum expectations and the achievement levels outlined in this document.

In order to ensure that assessment and evaluation are valid and reliable, and that they lead to the improvement of student learning, teachers must use assessment and evaluation strategies that:

- address both what students learn and how well they learn;
- are based both on the categories of knowledge and skills and on the achievement level descriptions given in the achievement chart on pages 34–35;
- are varied in nature, administered over a period of time, and designed to provide opportunities for students to demonstrate the full range of their learning;
- are appropriate for the learning activities used, the purposes of instruction, and the needs and experiences of the students;
- are fair to all students;

- accommodate students with special education needs, consistent with the strategies outlined in their Individual Education Plan;
- accommodate the needs of students who are learning the language of instruction;
- ensure that each student is given clear directions for improvement;
- promote students' ability to assess their own learning and to set specific goals;
- include the use of samples of students' work that provide evidence of their achievement;
- are communicated clearly to students and parents at the beginning of the school year and at other appropriate points throughout the school year.

## Evaluation of Achievement of Overall Expectations

All curriculum expectations must be accounted for in instruction, but evaluation focuses on students' achievement of the overall expectations. A student's achievement of the overall expectations is evaluated on the basis of his or her achievement of related specific expectations. The overall expectations are broad in nature, and the specific expectations define the particular content or scope of the knowledge and skills referred to in the overall expectations. Teachers will use their professional judgement to determine which specific expectations should be used to evaluate achievement of the overall expectations, and which ones will be covered in instruction and assessment (e.g., through direct observation) but not necessarily evaluated.

## Levels of Achievement

The characteristics given in the achievement chart (pages 34–35) for level 3 represent the "provincial standard" for achievement of the expectations. A complete picture of achievement at level 3 in the arts can be constructed by reading from top to bottom in the shaded column of the achievement chart, headed "Level 3". Parents of students achieving at level 3 can be confident that their children will be prepared for work in the next grade.

Level 1 identifies achievement that falls much below the provincial standard, while still reflecting a passing grade. Level 2 identifies achievement that approaches the standard. Level 4 identifies achievement that surpasses the standard. It should be noted that achievement at level 4 does not mean that the student has achieved expectations beyond those specified for a particular grade. It indicates that the student has achieved all or almost all of the expectations for that grade, and that he or she demonstrates the ability to use the knowledge and skills specified for that grade in more sophisticated ways than a student achieving at level 3.

The Ministry of Education has provided teachers with materials that will assist them in improving their assessment methods and strategies and, hence, their assessment of student achievement. These materials include samples of student work (exemplars) that illustrate achievement at each of the four levels. (Adaptations can be made in the exemplar documents to align them with the revised curriculum.)

# THE ACHIEVEMENT CHART FOR THE ARTS

The achievement chart that follows on pages 34–35 identifies four categories of knowledge and skills in the arts. The achievement chart is a standard province-wide guide to be used by teachers. It enables teachers to make judgements about student work that are based on clear performance standards and on a body of evidence collected over time.

The achievement chart is designed to:

- provide a framework that encompasses all curriculum expectations for all grades and subjects represented in this document;
- guide the development of assessment tasks and tools (including rubrics);
- help teachers to plan instruction for learning;
- assist teachers in providing meaningful feedback to students;
- provide various categories and criteria with which to assess and evaluate student learning.

## Categories of Knowledge and Skills

The categories, defined by clear criteria, represent four broad areas of knowledge and skills within which the subject expectations for any given grade are organized. The four categories should be considered as interrelated, reflecting the wholeness and interconnectedness of learning.

The categories of knowledge and skills are described as follows:

*Knowledge and Understanding.* Subject-specific content acquired in each grade (knowledge), and the comprehension of its meaning and significance (understanding).

*Thinking.* The use of critical and creative thinking skills and/or processes.

*Communication.* The conveying of meaning through various forms.

*Application.* The use of knowledge and skills to make connections within and between various contexts.

Teachers will ensure that student work is assessed and/or evaluated in a balanced manner with respect to the four categories, and that achievement of particular expectations is considered within the appropriate categories.

## Criteria

Within each category in the achievement chart, criteria are provided, which are subsets of the knowledge and skills that define each category. The criteria for each category are listed below:

### Knowledge and Understanding
- knowledge of content (e.g., facts, genres, terms, definitions, techniques, elements, principles, forms, structures, conventions)
- understanding of content (e.g., concepts, ideas, procedures, processes, themes, relationships among elements, informed opinions)

### Thinking

- use of planning skills (e.g., formulating questions, generating ideas, gathering information, focusing research, outlining, organizing an arts presentation or project, brainstorming/bodystorming, blocking, sketching, using visual organizers, listing goals in a rehearsal log, inventing notation)

- use of processing skills (e.g., analysing, evaluating, inferring, interpreting, editing, revising, refining, forming conclusions, detecting bias, synthesizing)

- use of critical/creative thinking processes (e.g., creative and analytical processes, design process, exploration of the elements, problem solving, reflection, elaboration, oral discourse, evaluation, critical literacy, metacognition, invention, critiquing, reviewing)

### Communication

- expression and organization of ideas and understandings in art forms (dance, drama, music, and the visual arts), including media/multimedia forms (e.g., expression of ideas and feelings using visuals, movements, the voice, gestures, phrasing, techniques), and in oral and written forms (e.g., clear expression and logical organization in critical responses to art works and informed opinion pieces)

- communication for different audiences (e.g., peers, adults, younger children) and purposes through the arts (e.g., drama presentations, visual arts exhibitions, dance and music performances) and in oral and written forms (e.g., debates, analyses)

- use of conventions in art forms (e.g., allegory, narrative or symbolic representation, style, articulation, drama conventions, choreographic forms, movement vocabulary) and arts vocabulary and terminology in oral and written forms

### Application

- application of knowledge and skills (e.g., performance skills, composition, choreography, elements, principles, processes, technologies, techniques, strategies, conventions) in familiar contexts (e.g., guided improvisation, performance of a familiar work, use of familiar forms)

- transfer of knowledge and skills (e.g., concepts, strategies, processes, techniques) to new contexts (e.g., a work requiring stylistic variation, an original composition, student-led choreography, an interdisciplinary or multidisciplinary project)

- making connections within and between various contexts (e.g., between the arts; between the arts and personal experiences and the world outside the school; between cultural and historical, global, social, and/or environmental contexts; between the arts and other subjects)

## Descriptors

A "descriptor" indicates the characteristic of the student's performance, with respect to a particular criterion, on which assessment or evaluation is focused. In the achievement chart, *effectiveness* is the descriptor used for each criterion in the Thinking, Communication, and Application categories. What constitutes effectiveness in any given performance task will vary with the particular criterion being considered. Assessment of effectiveness may therefore focus on a quality such as appropriateness, clarity, accuracy, precision, logic, relevance, significance, fluency, flexibility, depth, or breadth, as appropriate for the particular criterion. For example, in the Thinking category, assessment of effectiveness might focus on the degree of relevance or depth apparent in an analysis; in the Communication category, on clarity of expression or logical organization of information and ideas; or in the Application category, on appropriateness or breadth in the making of connections. Similarly, in the Knowledge and Understanding category, assessment of knowledge might focus on accuracy, and assessment of understanding might focus on the depth of an explanation. Descriptors help teachers to focus their assessment and evaluation on specific knowledge and skills for each category and criterion, and help students to better understand exactly what is being assessed and evaluated.

## Qualifiers

A specific "qualifier" is used to define each of the four levels of achievement – that is, *limited* for level 1, *some* for level 2, *considerable* for level 3, and *a high degree* or *thorough* for level 4. A qualifier is used along with a descriptor to produce a description of performance at a particular level. For example, the description of a student's performance at level 3 with respect to the first criterion in the Thinking category would be: "The student uses planning skills with considerable effectiveness".

The descriptions of the levels of achievement given in the chart should be used to identify the level at which the student has achieved the expectations. Students should be provided with numerous and varied opportunities to demonstrate the full extent of their achievement of the curriculum expectations, across all four categories of knowledge and skills.

# THE ACHIEVEMENT CHART FOR THE ARTS: GRADES 1–8

| Categories | Level 1 | Level 2 | Level 3 | Level 4 |
|---|---|---|---|---|
| **Knowledge and Understanding** – Subject-specific content acquired in each grade (knowledge), and the comprehension of its meaning and significance (understanding) | | | | |
| | The student: | | | |
| **Knowledge of content** *(e.g., facts, genres, terms, definitions, techniques, elements, principles, forms, structures, conventions)* | demonstrates limited knowledge of content | demonstrates some knowledge of content | demonstrates considerable knowledge of content | demonstrates thorough knowledge of content |
| **Understanding of content** *(e.g., concepts, ideas, procedures, processes, themes, relationships among elements, informed opinions)* | demonstrates limited understanding of content | demonstrates some understanding of content | demonstrates considerable understanding of content | demonstrates thorough understanding of content |
| **Thinking** – The use of critical and creative thinking skills and/or processes | | | | |
| | The student: | | | |
| **Use of planning skills** *(e.g., formulating questions, generating ideas, gathering information, focusing research, outlining, organizing an arts presentation or project, brainstorming/bodystorming, blocking, sketching, using visual organizers, listing goals in a rehearsal log, inventing notation)* | uses planning skills with limited effectiveness | uses planning skills with some effectiveness | uses planning skills with considerable effectiveness | uses planning skills with a high degree of effectiveness |
| **Use of processing skills** *(e.g., analysing, evaluating, inferring, interpreting, editing, revising, refining, forming conclusions, detecting bias, synthesizing)* | uses processing skills with limited effectiveness | uses processing skills with some effectiveness | uses processing skills with considerable effectiveness | uses processing skills with a high degree of effectiveness |
| **Use of critical/creative thinking processes** *(e.g., creative and analytical processes, design process, exploration of the elements, problem solving, reflection, elaboration, oral discourse, evaluation, critical literacy, metacognition, invention, critiquing, reviewing)* | uses critical/creative thinking processes with limited effectiveness | uses critical/creative thinking processes with some effectiveness | uses critical/creative thinking processes with considerable effectiveness | uses critical/creative thinking processes with a high degree of effectiveness |

| Categories | Level 1 | Level 2 | Level 3 | Level 4 |
|---|---|---|---|---|
| **Communication** – The conveying of meaning through various forms | | | | |
| | The student: | | | |
| **Expression and organization of ideas and understandings in art forms** (dance, drama, music, and the visual arts), including media/multimedia forms *(e.g., expression of ideas and feelings using visuals, movements, the voice, gestures, phrasing, techniques),* and in oral and written forms *(e.g., clear expression and logical organization in critical responses to art works and informed opinion pieces)* | expresses and organizes ideas and understandings with limited effectiveness | expresses and organizes ideas and understandings with some effectiveness | expresses and organizes ideas and understandings with considerable effectiveness | expresses and organizes ideas and understandings with a high degree of effectiveness |
| **Communication for different audiences** *(e.g., peers, adults, younger children)* and purposes through the arts *(e.g., drama presentations, visual arts exhibitions, dance and music performances)* and in oral and written forms *(e.g., debates, analyses)* | communicates for different audiences and purposes with limited effectiveness | communicates for different audiences and purposes with some effectiveness | communicates for different audiences and purposes with considerable effectiveness | communicates for different audiences and purposes with a high degree of effectiveness |
| **Use of conventions in dance, drama, music, and the visual arts** *(e.g., allegory, narrative or symbolic representation, style, articulation, drama conventions, choreographic forms, movement vocabulary)* and arts vocabulary and terminology in oral and written | uses conventions, vocabulary, and terminology of the arts with limited effectiveness | uses conventions, vocabulary, and terminology of the arts with some effectiveness | uses conventions, vocabulary, and terminology of the arts with considerable effectiveness | uses conventions, vocabulary, and terminology of the arts with a high degree of effectiveness |
| **Application** – The use of knowledge and skills to make connections within and between various contexts | | | | |
| | The student: | | | |
| **Application of knowledge and skills** *(e.g., performance skills, composition, choreography, elements, principles, processes, technologies, techniques, strategies, conventions)* in familiar contexts *(e.g., guided improvisation, performance of a familiar work, use of familiar forms)* | applies knowledge and skills in familiar contexts with limited effectiveness | applies knowledge and skills in familiar contexts with some effectiveness | applies knowledge and skills in familiar contexts with considerable effectiveness | applies knowledge and skills in familiar contexts with a high degree of effectiveness |
| **Transfer of knowledge and skills** *(e.g., concepts, strategies, processes, techniques)* to new contexts *(e.g., a work requiring stylistic variation, an original composition, student-led choreography, an interdisciplinary or multidisciplinary project)* | transfers knowledge and skills to new contexts with limited effectiveness | transfers knowledge and skills to new contexts with some effectiveness | transfers knowledge and skills to new contexts with considerable effectiveness | transfers knowledge and skills to new contexts with a high degree of effectiveness |
| **Making connections within and between various contexts** *(e.g., between the arts; between the arts and personal experiences and the world outside the school; between cultural and historical, global, social, and/or environmental contexts; between the arts and other subjects)* | makes connections within and between various contexts with limited effectiveness | makes connections within and between various contexts with some effectiveness | makes connections within and between various contexts with considerable effectiveness | makes connections within and between various contexts with a high degree of effectiveness |

# SOME CONSIDERATIONS FOR PROGRAM PLANNING IN THE ARTS

When planning a program in the arts, teachers must take into account considerations in a number of important areas, including those discussed below.

## INSTRUCTIONAL APPROACHES AND TEACHING STRATEGIES

*The mind is not a vessel to be filled but a fire to be kindled.*

*Plutarch, 45–125 A.D.*

One of the primary objectives of elementary arts curricula is to encourage children's natural inclination to express their ideas through the arts. Students come to school with a natural desire for a wide variety of outlets for their creativity. Students also bring with them individual interests and abilities, as well as diverse personal and cultural experiences, all of which have an impact on their prior knowledge about arts and about the world in which they live. The arts curriculum, particularly for students in the primary grades, should be enjoyable for students, and should be designed to encourage them to take a lifelong interest in the arts.

High-quality instruction is a key to student success in arts education. It is based on the belief that all students can be successful in arts learning. Teachers who provide high-quality instruction respect students' strengths, capture their interest, identify their learning needs, and use ongoing feedback and assessment to plan instruction. They clarify the purpose for learning, help students activate prior knowledge, scaffold instruction, and differentiate instruction for individual students and small groups according to need. High-quality instruction motivates students and instils positive habits of mind, such as a willingness and determination to explore and persist, to develop their thinking skills, to represent and communicate their ideas with clarity, to take responsible risks, and to observe, listen, ask questions, and pose problems.

Students learn best by doing. Teachers can stimulate and encourage all students by establishing environments where students have plenty of time and opportunities to explore the arts in ways that are meaningful to them. Teachers should provide as many hands-on activities as possible, since many of the skills emphasized in this curriculum are best taught and learned through participatory, creative experiences with concrete materials. Time, space, and a wide variety of tools and materials are necessary for supporting effective learning in the arts. In such an environment, students are free to explore abstract ideas in rich, varied, and concrete ways. Students need to have frequent opportunities to explore and to practise and apply new learning. Through regular and varied assessments, teachers can give them the specific feedback they need to further develop and refine their skills.

Students should be given a wide range of activities and assignments that foster mastery of the basic fundamental concepts and development of inquiry and research skills as well as opportunities for self-expression. In effective arts programs, teachers provide a variety of activities based on assessment of students' individual needs, proven learning theory, and best practices. Effective activities integrate expectations and enable both direct teaching and modelling of knowledge, skills, and learning strategies that encourage students to express their thinking and learning processes. Teachers should also be models for life-long learning in the arts, showing a willingness to participate in the arts, to appreciate unfamiliar art forms, to attempt new approaches, and to engage in new experiences.

Effective teaching approaches promote the development of higher-order thinking skills. In this way, teachers enable students to become thoughtful and effective communicators. In addition, teachers encourage students to think out loud about their own artistic choices and processes, and support them in developing the language and techniques they need to assess their own learning. As well, teachers encourage students to relate the knowledge and skills gained to issues and themes that are relevant to them.

Teaching approaches should be informed by the findings of current research related to creativity and arts education. These include approaches based on constructivist learning theory, which argues that humans construct knowledge and meaning from their experiences. For example, teachers should be both co-learners and facilitators, and should always aim to provide students with learning experiences that interest them. Such experiences include learning through inquiry, through initiating their own projects, and through engaging in arts projects with other students to develop a sense of community through teamwork. A well-planned curriculum should be at the students' level, but should also push them a little further than their comfort level, still keeping within their "zone of proximal development" (that is, within the range of things they can do on their own and with guidance). Teachers should also create a classroom environment for the arts that is focused not only on activities but on creative activities that involve exploration of ideas. It is instructive to note that creativity is now within the highest levels of thinking skills in the revised edition of Bloom's taxonomy.

Teachers also need to provide options to accommodate different learning styles and intelligences. The arts contribute to student engagement in school by addressing multiple intelligences, which can be used to differentiate instruction.

Teachers need to provide direct instruction in the arts. It is particularly important for young children to have a balanced program that provides for direct instruction in content, and to have opportunities to use their knowledge and skills in structured, as well as unstructured, activities. Teachers should also plan ways to engage students through shared and guided practice so that they can gradually move towards a greater level of independence and a greater level of comfort with risk-taking in the arts.

When exploring the cultural contexts of the arts, teachers need to avoid marginalizing groups or following stereotypes when planning lessons. For example, teachers should avoid focusing on art forms from only one place or that reflect only one style; avoid judging some art forms as "better" than others; avoid teaching by artistic movement or period; and avoid choosing only male artists' work or only European works for study. To put this in positive terms, teachers should include consideration of arts from around the world and from a variety of times, including contemporary works by living artists; comparisons of a variety of art works by theme, topic, and purpose; and study of both male and female artists. In short, teachers should plan to develop and extend students' awareness by using a wide variety of sources as a springboard and by helping them ask meaningful questions about the artists and their work.

When planning the use of classroom space, teachers should organize the learning environment in a way that facilitates activity and stimulates creativity – for example, ensuring that there is sufficient open space for dance activities, drama circles, or musical activities, or for groups to work at tables on visual arts projects. Likewise, it is important to plan routines for students to move from one arts activity to another, including use of materials, tools, and instruments, and to support routines with the use of visuals. Teachers should create a classroom environment that is comfortable, colourful, and stimulating; that allows for flexible groupings; that displays student work in meaningful and engaging ways; and that highlights the learning and creative process by displaying such items as sketches, as well as finished works, and students' reflective statements. Much of the work at the elementary level should encourage students to use the arts to explore and understand the process of learning, and to express ideas and feelings through the arts for a small audience of their peers in the classroom.

Teachers should keep in mind that the intention of the arts curriculum is to give all students the opportunity to discover and develop their ability in different artistic forms and media and to learn to appreciate works of art. In other words, the classroom needs to be inclusive of all students. The arts curriculum is not intended to provide the intensive instruction that students with special abilities need. The abilities of such students can be developed through other means (e.g., private lessons), which support the development of talents to a high level.

Teachers should also keep in mind that instruction in the arts needs to take place on a regular basis and in a variety of large and small blocks of time in order to allow skills to develop. Students should not be given isolated experiences – for example, engaging in a one-time craft activity on a Friday afternoon.

Descriptions of some strategies that are effective in teaching the arts can be found below.

***Analysis of Bias and Stereotype.*** Teachers can use this critical thinking strategy to help students examine inequities based on race, ethnicity, gender, class, point of view or perception, and any number of physical or mental attributes of individuals. Students can examine their own prejudices, as well as systemic discrimination, and learn to understand how social, political, economic, organizational, and cultural structures contribute to these perceptions. Students learn the skills to make critical assessments with respect to their reading, listening, and viewing in order to be aware of biases and stereotypes reflected therein. Students consider how the variety of motivations, controls, and constraints related to media directly influence our perceptions and views.

*Brainstorming.* Teachers can use brainstorming as a thinking strategy to help students generate questions, ideas, and examples and to explore a central idea or topic. During brainstorming, students share ideas that come to mind and record these ideas without making judgements about them. When introducing a topic, teachers can use brainstorming sessions to determine what students already know or wish to learn, and to provide direction for learning and reflection. Brainstorming stimulates fluent and flexible thinking and can also be used to extend problem-solving skills.

*Conference.* During a student–teacher conference, students can report on their progress, consider problems and solutions, and note strengths and areas for improvement. Teachers can discuss students' work with pairs or small groups of students in order to facilitate learning. Conferences therefore require an inviting and supportive atmosphere to encourage open discussion, as well as a high level of trust between participants. Conferences provide teachers with an opportunity to guide and support learners and a forum for students to demonstrate their learning through discussion, sketchbooks, or portfolios.

*Cooperative Learning.* Cooperative-learning techniques allow students to work as a team to accomplish a common learning goal. For example, a group of students may work together to prepare a drama, dance, or music performance, to create an art work, or to complete a research project.

In addition to the final product produced by the group, an important aspect of the cooperative-learning process is having each group member examine how the group functioned in its task and evaluate his or her own contribution to the group process. Discussions, journal entries, and self-evaluation checklists are some ways in which students can reflect on the group work process and their part in it.

*Discussion.* Discussion is a cooperative strategy through which students explore their thinking, respond to ideas, process information, and articulate their thoughts in exchanges with peers and the teacher. Discussion can be used to clarify understanding of concepts, ideas, and information. Emphasis is placed on talking and listening to each other. Through discussion, students can make connections between ideas and experience, and reflect on a variety of meanings and interpretations of texts and experiences.

*Experimenting.* Experimenting is central to the arts, and is frequently used in making connections between the concrete and the abstract. Experimenting requires that students investigate, test, explore, manipulate, solve problems, make decisions, and organize information in hands-on ways. Experimenting also encourages students to use cooperative skills effectively in interpreting and communicating findings. Experimenting enhances student motivation, understanding, and active involvement and can be initiated by the teacher or the student.

*Focused Exploration.* This is a method of instruction in which students use the materials and equipment available in the classroom in ways of their choosing. The teacher observes and listens while students are exploring, and provides guidance as needed, using information gathered from assessment. For example, the teacher may pose a question, prompt deeper thinking, or introduce new vocabulary.

*Free Exploration.* This is a key instructional activity that is initiated by students, using the materials available in the classroom in ways of their choosing. Teachers observe and listen as part of ongoing assessment while students are exploring freely, but do not guide the exploration as they do during focused exploration.

*Graphic or Visual Organizers.* The use of visual supports is an especially powerful teaching strategy. Graphic organizers, often also referred to as key visuals, allow students to understand and represent relationships visually rather than just with language, providing helpful redundancy in making meaning from a text. Graphic organizers can be used to record, organize, compare, analyse, and synthesize information and ideas. They can assist students in accessing prior knowledge and connecting it to new concepts learned as well as consolidating their understanding. Examples of common graphic organizers include the following: timeline, cycle diagram, T-chart, Venn diagram, story map, flow chart, grid, web, and problem-solution outline.

The use of a graphic organizer is extremely helpful when carried out initially as a class or group brainstorming activity. The graphic organizer provides a way of collecting and visually presenting information about a topic that will make it more comprehensible for students.

When using different graphic organizers, teachers should point out and model for students the usefulness of particular graphic organizers. For example, the T-chart provides an ideal framework for visually representing comparison and contrast, while the flow chart is well suited to illustrating cause-and-effect relationships.

*Guided Activity.* This is a key instructional activity that is initiated by the teacher. On the basis of assessment information, the teacher may pose a series of questions, provide prompts to extend thinking, ask students to demonstrate a familiar concept in a new way, encourage students to try a new activity, and so on.

*Guided Exploration.* The teacher models a concept or skill that is part of a larger set of skills or knowledge, and guides the students as they practise this first step. The process is repeated until the students master the expected knowledge and skills of the lesson. This strategy is particularly useful for introducing new skills that are developed sequentially.

*Jigsaw.* Jigsaw is a cooperative group activity in which a different segment of a learning task is assigned to each member of a small group (the "home" group). All home group members then work to become an "expert" in their aspect of the task in order to teach the other group members. Jigsaw activities push all students to take equal responsibility for the group's learning goals. In the arts, jigsaw activities can be done in creating/performing, listening, and reading formats.

In a jigsaw activity in creating/performing, each student becomes a member of an "expert" group, which learns a particular arts skill. Experts then return to their home groups to share information and demonstrate the skill. Each expert must ensure that all members of the home group understand the information and the method of performing the skill. A similar procedure can be followed for a jigsaw listening activity or a jigsaw reading activity.

*Lateral Thinking.* This is a thinking process first described by Edward di Bono, who recognized that the mind can perceive issues from many angles and is thus able to generate many creative solutions, even unorthodox ones. Lateral thinking involves reviewing a problem or challenge from multiple perspectives, often breaking up the elements and recombining them in different ways, even randomly. Use of lateral thinking methods develops skills in bringing positive and negative aspects of a problem to the fore and evaluating the whole picture.

*Media Analysis.* Media analysis is a critical literacy strategy in which commercial media works are examined for the purpose of "decoding" the work – that is, determining the purpose, intended audience, mood, and message of the work, and the techniques used to create it. Through media analysis, students evaluate everyday media, maintaining a critical distance and resisting manipulation by media producers, and they learn about media techniques that they can then use to create or enhance their own works. Key concepts of media analysis include recognition that media construct reality, have commercial implications, contain ideological and value messages, and have social and political implications.

*Modelling.* Teachers can demonstration a task or strategy to students, and may "think aloud" while doing it to make the process clearer. By imitating the model, students become aware of the procedures needed to perform the task or use the strategy.

*Multiple Points of View.* Teachers can encourage students to adopt another point of view in order to develop their ability to think critically and to look at issues from more than one perspective. In this activity, students identify which person's point of view is being considered and the needs and concerns of the person. They also locate and analyse information about the person and summarize the person's position. They learn to examine issues and characters and to form conclusions without letting personal bias interfere. This strategy can be used in both creating and viewing activities in the arts.

*Oral Explanation.* Students may use oral explanation to clarify thinking, to justify reasoning, and to communicate their understanding in any of the arts.

*Panel Discussion.* A panel discussion provides opportunities for students to examine controversial issues from different perspectives. A moderator introduces the topic, and the panel members then each present to an audience a prepared statement of three to five minutes that elucidates a particular viewpoint. The moderator facilitates audience participation and allows panel members to clarify previous statements or provide new information. After the discussion period, the moderator asks each panel member for some general conclusions or summary statements. Topics chosen for a panel discussion should engage students intellectually and emotionally, allowing them to use higher-order thinking skills as they make reasoned and logical arguments.

*Role Play.* Role play allows students to simulate a variety of situations, using language for different purposes and audiences. Through role plays, students can practise and explore alternative solutions to situations outside the classroom. The role-play strategy also allows students to take different perspectives on a situation, helping them to develop sensitivity and understanding by putting themselves in the shoes of others. An important phase in any role-playing activity is the follow-up. Debriefing after a role play allows students to analyse the role-play experience and the learning in the activity.

*Simulation.* Through simulation, students can participate in a replication of real or hypothetical conditions and respond and act as though the situation were real. Simulation is useful when students are learning about complex processes, events, ideas, or issues, or when they are trying to understand the emotions and feelings of others. Simulation requires the manipulation of a variety of factors and variables, allowing students to explore alternatives and solve problems and to take values and attitudes into consideration when making decisions and experiencing the results. Simulation can take a number of forms, including role playing, dramatizations, and enactments of historical events.

*Sketching to Learn.* Through making quick sketches, students can represent ideas and their responses to them during or immediately following a presentation or lesson. They can also take notes in pictorial or graphic form while reading a story for a dance or drama project. Sketching to learn is often used during a listening or viewing experience in order to help students understand new or complex concepts or techniques.

*Think-Aloud.* In the think-aloud strategy, the teacher models out loud a thinking or learning process while using it. It is particularly useful when students are learning a difficult concept or reinforcing learning. Think-alouds can also be done by students on their own as they learn a skill, with a peer, or with the teacher for assessment purposes.

*Think-Pair-Share.* During a think-pair-share activity, students individually consider an issue or problem and then discuss their ideas in pairs or in a small group. A few students are then called on by the teacher to share their thoughts and ideas with the whole class.

*Visualization.* Visualization is a process of making an object, an event, or a situation visible in one's imagination by mentally constructing or recalling an image. Teachers can use visualization with students as an exercise in image creation prior to creating an art work. Visualization allows students to draw on their own prior experience and extend their thinking creatively. Teachers can also make use of a variety of visual stimuli (e.g., illustrations, photographs, reproductions, videos, real objects, graphics) to assist students in generating ideas for various kinds of works in all the arts.

## CROSS-CURRICULAR AND INTEGRATED LEARNING

In cross-curricular learning, students are provided with opportunities to learn and use related content and/or skills in two or more subjects. For example, all subjects, including the arts, can be related to the language curriculum. In the arts, students use a range of language skills: they build subject-specific vocabulary, read stories for inspiration for their art works, and respond to and analyse art works using language. Teachers can also use reading material about the arts in their language lessons, and can incorporate instruction in critical literacy in their arts lessons by, for instance, having students develop alternative illustrations for advertisements or fiction texts that use colour or angle of view to modify the message (e.g., a spoof advertisement criticizing commercial propaganda) or to show a different point of view (e.g., that of a child in the situation). Students can also use drama conventions to bring to life the motivations of minor characters who have other perspectives on the story.

In integrated learning, students are provided with opportunities to work towards *meeting expectations from two or more subjects* within a single unit, lesson, or activity. By linking expectations from different subject areas, teachers can provide students with multiple opportunities to reinforce and demonstrate their knowledge and skills in a range of settings. The arts can be used to provide other ways of learning and making connections. Through integrated learning, exploration of topics, issues, experiences, or themes can provide students with a stimulus both for engaging in artistic creation and for developing understanding in another subject area. For example, teachers can create a unit linking expectations from the arts curriculum and the social studies curriculum. Connections can be made between these curricula in a number of areas, including the relationship between art forms and their social and cultural context at various times and places around the world, the importance of the arts in Canada, and the impact of changes in technology on the arts (e.g., improvements to musical instruments, use of multimedia technology). In such a unit, students can gain insights into the importance of the arts for a range of people. They can also, for instance, work with drama or dance movement to express their understanding of a historical character or a visual art work, and through that activity develop imagery that reflects their own ideas, time, and place.

In integrated learning, teachers need to ensure that the *specific knowledge and skills for each subject are taught*. For example, if they ask students to draw an illustration for their story, they need to give not only language instruction, but instruction in creating the images; the teacher could instruct the students in using compositional concepts, such as creating sight lines that make use of lines, shapes, and colours to lead the eye to a particular point for emphasis. Likewise, in dance, the teacher could instruct the students in using elements of dance (e.g., body, level, tempo, space) and not simply assign a set dance routine to use to accompany the story. In drama, the teacher could instruct the students in using dramatic conventions to explore the possible motivations of a character in the story and not simply ask them to recreate the scene. In music, the teacher could instruct the students in elements of music and musical forms so that they could create a mood piece to accompany the story, not merely select an existing piece.

Integrated learning can also be a solution to fragmentation and isolated skill instruction – that is, in integrated learning, students can learn and apply skills in a meaningful context, not merely learn how to mix colours or play technical musical exercises. In such contexts, students can also develop their ability to think and reason and to transfer knowledge and skills from one subject area to another.

## PLANNING ARTS PROGRAMS FOR STUDENTS WITH SPECIAL EDUCATION NEEDS

Classroom teachers are the key educators of students who have special education needs. They have a responsibility to help all students learn, and they work collaboratively with special education resource teachers, where appropriate, to achieve this goal. They commit to assisting every student to prepare for living with the highest degree of independence possible.

*Education for All: The Report of the Expert Panel on Literacy and Numeracy Instruction for Students With Special Education Needs, Kindergarten to Grade 6, 2005* describes a set of beliefs, based in research, that should guide all program planning for students with special education needs. Teachers planning arts programs need to pay particular attention to these beliefs, which are as follows:

- All students can succeed.
- Universal design and differentiated instruction are effective and interconnected means of meeting the learning or productivity needs of any group of students.

- Successful instructional practices are founded on evidence-based research, tempered by experience.
- Classroom teachers are key educators for a student's literacy and numeracy development.
- Each student has his or her own unique patterns of learning.
- Classroom teachers need the support of the larger community to create a learning environment that supports students with special education needs.
- Fairness is not sameness.

In any given classroom, students may demonstrate a wide range of strengths and needs. Teachers plan programs that recognize this diversity and give students performance tasks that respect their particular abilities so that all students can derive the greatest possible benefit from the teaching and learning process. The use of flexible groupings for instruction and the provision of ongoing assessment are important elements of programs that accommodate a diversity of learning needs.

In planning arts programs for students with special education needs, teachers should begin by examining both the curriculum expectations for the appropriate grade level of the individual student and his or her strengths and learning needs to determine which of the following options is appropriate for the student:

- no accommodations[2] or modifications; or
- accommodations only; or
- modified expectations, with the possibility of accommodations; or
- alternative expectations, which are not derived from the curriculum expectations for a grade and which constitute alternative programs.

If the student requires either accommodations or modified expectations, or both, the relevant information, as described in the following paragraphs, must be recorded in his or her Individual Education Plan (IEP). More detailed information about planning programs for students with special education needs, including students who require alternative programs,[3] can be found in *The Individual Education Plan (IEP): A Resource Guide, 2004* (referred to hereafter as the *IEP Resource Guide, 2004*). For a detailed discussion of the ministry's requirements for IEPs, see *Individual Education Plans: Standards for Development, Program Planning, and Implementation, 2000* (referred to hereafter as *IEP Standards, 2000*). (Both documents are available at www.edu.gov.on.ca.)

## Students Requiring Accommodations Only

Some students with special education needs are able, with certain accommodations, to participate in the regular curriculum and to demonstrate learning independently. (Accommodations do not alter the provincial curriculum expectations for the grade level.) The accommodations required to facilitate the student's learning must be identified in his or her IEP (see *IEP Standards, 2000*, page 11). A student's IEP is likely to reflect the same accommodations for many, or all, subject areas.

Providing accommodations to students with special education needs should be the first option considered in program planning. Instruction based on principles of universal

---

2. *Accommodations* refers to individualized teaching and assessment strategies, human supports, and/or individualized equipment.

3. Alternative programs are identified on the IEP form by the term "alternative (ALT)".

design[4] and differentiated instruction[5] focuses on the provision of accommodations to meet the diverse needs of learners.

There are three types of accommodations:

- *Instructional accommodations* are changes in teaching strategies, including styles of presentation, methods of organization, or use of technology and multimedia.
- *Environmental accommodations* are changes that the student may require in the classroom and/or school environment, such as preferential seating or special lighting.
- *Assessment accommodations* are changes in assessment procedures that enable the student to demonstrate his or her learning, such as allowing additional time to complete tests or assignments or permitting oral responses to test questions (see page 29 of the *IEP Resource Guide, 2004* for more examples).

If a student requires "accommodations only" in the arts, assessment and evaluation of his or her achievement will be based on the appropriate grade-level curriculum expectations and the achievement levels outlined in this document. The IEP box on the student's Provincial Report Card will not be checked, and no information on the provision of accommodations will be included.

## Students Requiring Modified Expectations

In the arts, for most students with special education needs, modified expectations will be based on the regular grade-level curriculum, with changes in the number and/or complexity of the expectations. Modified expectations must represent specific, realistic, observable, and measurable achievements, and must describe specific knowledge and/or skills that the student can demonstrate independently, given the appropriate assessment accommodations.

Modified expectations must indicate the knowledge and/or skills the student is expected to demonstrate and have assessed in each reporting period (*IEP Standards, 2000*, pages 10 and 11). Modified expectations should be expressed in such a way that the student and parents can understand exactly what the student is expected to know or be able to do, on the basis of which his or her performance will be evaluated and a grade or mark recorded on the Provincial Report Card. The student's learning expectations must be reviewed in relation to the student's progress at least once every reporting period, and must be updated as necessary (*IEP Standards, 2000*, page 11).

If a student requires modified expectations in the arts, assessment and evaluation of his or her achievement will be based on the learning expectations identified in the IEP and on the achievement levels outlined in this document. On the Provincial Report Card, the IEP box must be checked for any subject in which the student requires modified expectations, and the appropriate statement from the *Guide to the Provincial Report Card, Grades 1–8, 1998* (page 8) must be inserted. The teacher's comments should include relevant information on the student's demonstrated learning of the modified expectations, as well as next steps for the student's learning in the subject.

---

4. The goal of Universal Design for Learning (UDL) is to create a learning environment that is open and accessible to all students, regardless of age, skills, or situation. Instruction based on principles of universal design is flexible and supportive, can be adjusted to meet different student needs, and enables all students to access the curriculum as fully as possible.

5. Differentiated instruction is effective instruction that shapes each student's learning experience in response to his or her particular learning preferences, interests, and readiness to learn.

## PROGRAM CONSIDERATIONS FOR ENGLISH LANGUAGE LEARNERS

*[English language learners] each have a language, a culture, and background experiences. Effective teachers draw on these resources and build new concepts on this strong experiential base.*

Y. S. Freeman and D. E. Freeman, *Closing the Achievement Gap: How to Reach Limited-Formal-Schooling and Long-Term English Learners* (2002), p. 16

Ontario schools have some of the most multilingual student populations in the world. The first language of approximately 20 per cent of the children in Ontario's English-language schools is a language other than English. Ontario's linguistic heritage includes several Aboriginal languages and many African, Asian, and European languages. It also includes some varieties of English – also referred to as dialects – that differ significantly from the English required for success in Ontario schools. Many English language learners were born in Canada and have been raised in families and communities in which languages other than English, or varieties of English that differ from the language used in the classroom, are spoken. Other English language learners arrive in Ontario as newcomers from other countries; they may have experience of highly sophisticated educational systems, or they may have come from regions where access to formal schooling was limited.

When they start school in Ontario, many of these children are entering a new linguistic and cultural environment. All teachers share in the responsibility for these students' English-language development.

English language learners (students who are learning English as a second or additional language in English-language schools) bring a rich diversity of background knowledge and experience to the classroom. These students' linguistic and cultural backgrounds not only support their learning in their new environment but also become a cultural asset in the classroom community. Teachers will find positive ways to incorporate this diversity into their instructional programs and into the classroom environment.

Most English language learners in Ontario schools have an age-appropriate proficiency in their first language. Although they need frequent opportunities to use English at school, there are important educational and social benefits associated with continued development of their first language while they are learning English. Teachers need to encourage parents to continue to use their own language at home in rich and varied ways as a foundation for language and literacy development in English. It is also important for teachers to find opportunities to bring students' languages into the classroom, using parents and community members as a resource.

During their first few years in Ontario schools, English language learners may receive support through one of two distinct programs from teachers who specialize in meeting their language-learning needs:

*English as a Second Language (ESL)* programs are for students born in Canada or newcomers whose first language is a language other than English, or is a variety of English significantly different from that used for instruction in Ontario schools.

*English Literacy Development (ELD)* programs are primarily for newcomers whose first language is a language other than English, or is a variety of English significantly different from that used for instruction in Ontario schools, and who arrive with significant gaps in their education. These children generally come from countries where access to education is limited or where there are limited opportunities to develop language and literacy skills in any language. Some Aboriginal students from remote communities in Ontario may also have had limited opportunities for formal schooling, and they also may benefit from ELD instruction.

In planning programs for children with linguistic backgrounds other than English, teachers need to recognize the importance of the orientation process, understanding that every learner needs to adjust to the new social environment and language in a unique way and at an individual pace. For example, children who are in an early stage of English-language acquisition may go through a "silent period" during which they closely observe the interactions and physical surroundings of their new learning environment. They may use body language rather than speech or they may use their first language until they have gained enough proficiency in English to feel confident of their interpretations and responses. Students thrive in a safe, supportive, and welcoming environment that nurtures their self-confidence while they are receiving focused literacy instruction. When they are ready to participate, in paired, small-group, or whole-class activities, some students will begin by using a single word or phrase to communicate a thought, while others will speak quite fluently.

With exposure to the English language in a supportive learning environment, most young children will develop oral fluency quite quickly, making connections between concepts and skills acquired in their first language and similar concepts and skills presented in English. However, oral fluency is not a good indicator of a student's knowledge of vocabulary or sentence structure, reading comprehension, or other aspects of language proficiency that play an important role in literacy development and academic success. Research has shown that it takes five to seven years for most English language learners to catch up to their English-speaking peers in their ability to use English for academic purposes. Moreover, the older the children are when they arrive, the more language knowledge and skills they have to catch up on, and the more direct support they require from their teachers.

Responsibility for students' English-language development is shared by the classroom teacher, the ESL/ELD teacher (where available), and other school staff. Volunteers and peers may also be helpful in supporting English language learners in the arts classroom. Teachers must adapt the instructional program in order to facilitate the success of these students in their classrooms. Appropriate adaptations for the arts program include:

- modification of some or all of the subject expectations so that they are challenging but attainable for the learner at his or her present level of English proficiency, given the necessary support from the teacher;
- use of a variety of instructional strategies (e.g., extensive use of visual cues, images, diagrams, visual representations of key ideas, graphic organizers, scaffolding; manipulation of images to find solutions to a design problem; pre-teaching of key vocabulary; peer tutoring; use of music, movement, and gestures; strategic use of students' first languages);
- use of a variety of learning resources (e.g., simplified text, graphic novels, arts-specific word walls, songs that teach language, bilingual dictionaries; visual material, displays, art work, diagrams that show how to use materials, graphical information from textbooks, manipulatives, modelling clay; music, plays, dances, materials to be used in open-ended activities, and materials that reflect cultural diversity);

- use of assessment accommodations (e.g., granting of extra time; use of oral interviews and presentations; participation in dance or physical drama; participation in songs or chants; use of portfolios, demonstrations, visual representations or models (e.g., sketches, drawings, paintings, sculptures), or tasks requiring completion of graphic organizers instead of essay questions and other assessment tasks that depend heavily on proficiency in English).

In general, the arts provide English language learners with multiple modes of expression beyond written and oral texts, and support achievement for these learners across the curriculum.

Although the degree of program adaptation required will decrease over time, students who are no longer receiving ESL or ELD support may still need some program adaptations to be successful. If a student's program has been modified, a checkmark must be placed in the ESL/ELD box on the student's report card. If the student requires modified expectations, the appropriate statement from the *Guide to the Provincial Report Card, Grades 1–8, 1998* (page 8) must be inserted.

For further information on supporting English language learners, refer to the following documents:

- *Supporting English Language Learners in Grades 1 to 8: A Practical Guide for Ontario Educators, 2008*

- *Supporting English Language Learners with Limited Prior Schooling: A Practical Guide for Ontario Educators, Grades 3 to 12, 2008*

- *English Language Learners – ESL and ELD Programs and Services: Policies and Procedures for Ontario Elementary and Secondary Schools, Kindergarten to Grade 12, 2007*

- *Supporting English Language Learners in Kindergarten: A Practical Guide for Ontario Educators, 2007*

- *Many Roots, Many Voices: Supporting English Language Learners in Every Classroom – A Practical Guide for Ontario Educators, 2005*

## ENVIRONMENTAL EDUCATION AND THE ARTS

*Environmental education is education about the environment, for the environment, and in the environment that promotes an understanding of, rich and active experience in, and an appreciation for the dynamic interactions of:*

- *The Earth's physical and biological systems*

- *The dependency of our social and economic systems on these natural systems*

- *The scientific and human dimensions of environmental issues*

- *The positive and negative consequences, both intended and unintended, of the interactions between human-created and natural systems.*

*Shaping Our Schools, Shaping Our Future: Environmental Education in Ontario Schools* (June 2007), p. 6

As noted in *Shaping Our Schools, Shaping Our Future: Environmental Education in Ontario Schools*, environmental education "is the responsibility of the entire education community. It is a content area and can be taught. It is an approach to critical thinking, citizenship, and personal responsibility, and can be modelled. It is a context that can enrich and enliven education in all subject areas, and offer students the opportunity to develop a deeper connection with themselves, their role in society, and their interdependence on one another and the Earth's natural systems" (page 10).

There are many opportunities to integrate environmental education into the teaching of the arts. Nature often provides an inspirational starting point for creativity in both representational and more abstract art forms. Indeed, a sense of connection to the immediate environment and the natural world is frequently reflected in the arts – for example, Paleolithic cave paintings of animals, traditional dances and performances that evoke aspects of nature, landscape painting, and Impressionist music. To facilitate these connections, arts teachers are encouraged to take students out of the classroom and into the world beyond the school to help students observe, explore, and investigate nature, and to design activities that allow students to integrate natural materials into their creative works.

The arts can also be used as powerful forms of expression for students to use to explore and articulate the social and political impact of issues related to the environment. They can also serve as effective media to advocate protection of and respect for the environment. As well, the actual use of arts materials can be related to environmental education. Many safety guidelines are followed to reduce harmful effects arising from the interaction of potentially hazardous substances with the environment. The safe handling and disposal of substances used in the arts provides opportunities for students to explore how everyday human interactions with the environment can have significant consequences.

## ANTIDISCRIMINATION EDUCATION IN THE ARTS PROGRAM

The implementation of antidiscrimination principles in education influences all aspects of school life. It promotes a school climate that encourages all students to work to high standards, affirms the worth of all students, and helps students strengthen their sense of identity and develop a positive self-image. It encourages staff and students alike to value and show respect for diversity in the school and the wider society. It requires schools to adopt measures to provide a safe environment for learning, free from harassment, violence, and expressions of hate. Antidiscrimination education encourages students to think critically about themselves and others in the world around them in order to promote fairness, healthy relationships, and active, responsible citizenship.

Schools also have the opportunity to ensure that school–community interaction reflects the diversity in the local community and wider society. Consideration should be given to a variety of strategies for communicating and working with parents and community members from diverse groups, in order to ensure their participation in such school activities as plays, concerts, and teacher interviews. Families new to Canada, who may be unfamiliar with the Ontario school system, or parents of Aboriginal students may need special outreach and encouragement in order to feel comfortable in their interactions with the school.

In an inclusive arts program, learning resources and art work presented for analysis reflect the broad range of both female and male students' interests, backgrounds, cultures, and experiences. Teachers routinely use materials that reflect the diversity of Canadian and world cultures, including those of contemporary First Nation, Métis, and Inuit peoples, and ensure that students have access to such material. At the same time, the creation of various forms of art, inspired by styles from diverse cultures, provides opportunities for students to explore issues relating to their self-identity.

Students should be made aware of the historical, cultural, and political contexts of both the traditional and non-traditional gender and social roles represented in the material they are studying. Attention should be drawn to the ways in which minority groups are represented. In visual arts, for instance, examples can be taken from traditional art forms and crafts, which in the past were largely the purview of women, as well as from fine arts. In music, male and female students should be encouraged to play instruments of their choice without facing gender bias. In dance, same-sex partnering and grouping should be supported, and opportunities to explore non-stereotypical social roles in dance forms should be provided. The dramatic arts provide opportunities for teachers and students to examine the work of Aboriginal storytellers and playwrights and those from other minority groups.

Outside the classroom, the work of women and many minority groups is underrepresented in public galleries, theatres, dance and music concert halls, and the world of popular culture. As a result, women's and minority perspectives and viewpoints in drama, film, dance, music, and the visual arts are limited. Changes are occurring, however. For example, many instrumental music groups hold auditions for new members behind a screen so that the evaluators cannot tell whether they are assessing female or male instrumentalists. Nevertheless, there are few female conductors of major orchestras in the world, and in the dance world, the works of male choreographers predominate. Teachers should make students aware of these equity issues and ensure that the work of a socio-culturally and historically diverse range of both women and men is valued and explored. As well, teachers should provide positive role models for both male and female students in the areas they are exploring, both to engage the students and to help students consider the possibility of careers in those areas.

The arts give both students and teachers a unique way to explore positive ways of dealing with the social and emotional impact of various forms of discrimination, such as racism, sexism, homophobia, and religious intolerance, as well as the effects of bullying, harassment, and other expressions of violence and hatred. Teachers can help students link the understanding they gain in this regard to messages conveyed through the school's antibullying and violence-prevention programming.

Participation in the arts can also benefit students who have not had educational or economic advantages. By being actively engaged in arts activities, students become motivated and can develop the ability to be persistent in tasks; through their successes, they develop self-confidence. In addition, participation in the arts gives them opportunities to develop social skills, such as skills in conflict resolution, self-control, and collaboration, as well as social tolerance and empathy. They can also learn to take creative risks in a safe environment.

## LITERACY, NUMERACY, AND INQUIRY IN THE ARTS

Literacy, numeracy, and inquiry and research skills are critical to students' success in all subjects of the curriculum and in all areas of their lives.

> *Literacy is defined as the ability to use language and images in rich and varied forms to read, write, listen, view, represent, and think critically about ideas. It involves the capacity to access, manage, and evaluate information; to think imaginatively and analytically; and to communicate thoughts and ideas effectively. Literacy includes critical thinking and reasoning to solve problems and make decisions related to issues of fairness, equity, and social justice. Literacy connects individuals and communities and is an essential tool for personal growth and active participation in a cohesive, democratic society.*
>
> *Reach Every Student: Energizing Ontario Education* (2008), p. 6

"Literacy instruction must be embedded across the curriculum. All teachers of all subjects… are teachers of literacy" (*Think Literacy Success, Grades 7–12: The Report of the Expert Panel on Students at Risk in Ontario*, 2003, p. 10). This instruction takes different forms of emphasis in different subjects and needs to be explicitly taught.

In the arts, literacy includes writing artistic statements and storyboards, connecting illustrations and text, role playing to make meaning from stories, learning songs, researching, discussing, listening, viewing media, and – especially important for kinesthetic learners – participating in action and physical activity. Students use language to record their observations, to describe their critical analyses in both informal and formal contexts, and to present their findings in presentations and reports in oral, written, graphic, and multimedia forms. Understanding in the arts requires the use and understanding of specialized terminology. In all arts programs, students are required to use appropriate and correct terminology, and are encouraged to use language with care and precision in order to communicate effectively.

Fostering students' communication skills is an important part of the teacher's role in the arts classroom. Students need to be able to use aural, oral, physical, and visual communication as well as reading, writing, and media literacy skills to gain new learning in the arts and to communicate their understanding of what they have learned.

Oral communication skills are fundamental to the development of arts literacy and are essential for thinking and learning. Through purposeful talk, students not only learn to communicate information but also explore and come to understand ideas and concepts, identify and solve problems, organize their experience and knowledge, and express and clarify their thoughts, feelings, and opinions.

To develop their oral communication skills, students need numerous opportunities to listen to information and talk about a range of subjects in the arts. The arts program provides opportunities for students to engage in various oral activities in connection with expectations in all the strands, such as brainstorming to identify what they know about a new topic they are studying, discussing strategies for solving a problem, presenting and defending ideas or debating issues, and offering critiques or feedback on an art work and expressed opinions of their peers.

Students' understanding is revealed through both oral and written communication, but it is not necessary for all critical analysis in arts learning to involve a written communication component. Students need opportunities to focus on their oral communication without adding the additional responsibility of writing.

Whether students are talking or writing about their arts learning, teachers can prompt them to explain their thinking and reasoning behind a particular solution, design, or strategy, or to reflect on what they have done, by asking questions. Because a rich, open-ended question provides the starting point for an effective inquiry or for addressing a problem, it is important that teachers model such questions for their students and allow students multiple opportunities to ask, and find answers to, their own questions.

When reading texts related to the arts, students use a different set of skills than they do when reading fiction. They need to understand vocabulary and terminology that are unique to the various arts disciplines, and must be able to interpret symbols, charts, and diagrams. To help students construct meaning, it is essential that teachers of the arts model and teach the strategies that support learning to read while students are reading to learn in this subject area.

The Ministry of Education has facilitated the development of materials to support literacy instruction across the curriculum. Helpful advice for integrating literacy instruction in the arts may be found in the following resource materials:

- *A Guide to Effective Literacy Instruction, Grades 4 to 6, Volume Seven: Media Literacy, 2008*
- *Me Read? No Way! A Practical Guide to Improving Boys' Literacy Skills, 2004*
- *Think Literacy: Cross-Curricular Approaches, Grades 7–12, 2003*
- *Think Literacy: Cross-Curricular Approaches, Grades 7–12 – Subject-Specific Examples: Drama and Dance, Grades 7–10, 2005*
- *Think Literacy: Cross-Curricular Approaches, Grades 7–12 – Subject-Specific Examples: Music, Grades 7–9, 2004*
- *Think Literacy: Cross-Curricular Approaches, Subject-Specific Examples: Music, Grades 1–6, 2008*
- *Think Literacy: Cross-Curricular Approaches, Grades 7–12 – Subject-Specific Examples: Visual Arts, Grades 7–12, 2005*
- *Webcasts for Educators: Critical Literacy, November 29, 2007* (available through http://www.edu.gov.on.ca or on DVD)

In addition to providing opportunities for literacy development, the arts program also builds on, reinforces, and enhances mathematical literacy. For example, clear, concise communication often involves the use of diagrams, charts, tables, and graphs, and many components of the arts curriculum emphasize students' ability to interpret and use symbols and graphic texts.

Inquiry is at the heart of learning in all subject areas. In the arts program, students are encouraged to develop their ability to ask questions and to explore a variety of possible answers to those questions. As they advance through the grades, they acquire the skills to locate relevant information from a variety of sources, such as books, periodicals, dictionaries, encyclopedias, interviews, videos, and the Internet. The questioning they practised in the early grades becomes more sophisticated as they learn that all sources of information have a particular point of view and that the recipient of the information has a responsibility to evaluate it, determine its validity and relevance, and use it in appropriate ways. The ability to locate, question, and validate information allows a student to become an independent, lifelong learner.

## CRITICAL THINKING AND CRITICAL LITERACY IN THE ARTS

Critical thinking is the process of thinking about ideas or situations in order to understand them fully, identify their implications, make a judgement, and/or guide decision making. Critical thinking includes skills such as questioning, predicting, hypothesizing, analysing, synthesizing, examining opinions, identifying values and issues, detecting bias, and distinguishing between alternatives. It involves an inquiry process of exploring questions about and solutions for issues that are not clearly defined and for which there are no clear-cut answers. Students who are taught these skills become critical thinkers who do not merely accept the obvious as a given.

Students use critical thinking skills in the arts when they assess, analyse, and/or evaluate the impact of something and when they form an opinion about something and support that opinion with a rationale. In order to do these things, students need to examine the opinions and values of others, detect bias, look for implied meaning, and use the information gathered to form a personal opinion or stance, or a personal plan of action with regard to making a difference.

As they work to achieve the arts expectations, students frequently need to identify the possible implications of choices. As they gather information from a variety of sources, they need to be able to interpret what they are listening to, reading, or viewing; to look for instances of bias; and to determine why that source might express that particular bias.

In developing critical thinking skills in the arts, students must ask good questions to interpret information, detect bias, and consider the values and perspectives of a variety of groups and individuals.

Critical literacy is the capacity for a particular type of critical thinking that involves looking beyond the literal meaning of a text to determine what is present and what is missing, in order to analyse and evaluate the text's complete meaning and the author's intent. Critical literacy goes beyond conventional critical thinking by focusing on issues related to fairness, equity, and social justice. Critically literate students adopt a critical stance, asking what view of the world the text advances and whether they find this view acceptable, who benefits from the text, and how the reader is influenced.

In the arts, students who are critically literate are able, for example, to actively analyse art works and texts to identify possible meanings. They are able to determine what biases might be contained in an art work and why that might be, how the content of the art work was determined and by whom, and whose perspectives might have been left out and why. These students would then be equipped to produce their own interpretation of the issue. Opportunities should be provided for students to engage in a critical discussion of "texts", which can include television programs, movies, web pages, advertising, music, gestures, oral texts, visual art works, and other means of expression. This discussion empowers students to understand how the authors of texts are trying to affect and change them as members of society. Language and communication are never neutral: they are used to inform, entertain, persuade, and manipulate.

Critically literate students understand that meaning is not found in texts in isolation. People make sense of a text, or determine what a text means, in a variety of ways. Students therefore need to be aware of points of view (e.g., those of parents and students), the context (e.g., the beliefs and practices of the time and place in which a text is read), the background of the person interacting with the text (e.g., upbringing, friends, school and other communities, education, experiences), intertextuality (e.g., information that a viewer brings to a film from other films viewed previously), gaps in the text (e.g., information that is left out and that the reader must fill in), and silences in the text (e.g., voices of a person or group not heard).

## MULTIPLE LITERACIES IN THE ARTS

*The arts disciplines … are basic: as means of communication, as historical components of civilization, and as providers of unique forms of knowledge. As such, they need no other justification as essential components of education. While study in the arts disciplines may enhance other skills, encourage personal development, or lead to a stronger economic base for professional presentation of the arts, these are not and should not be the primary reasons for their study.*

*The goal of all education in the arts should be the development of basic literacy in dance, music, theater, and the visual arts. Such literacy is grounded in the study of the language and grammar of each art form as they are related directly to creation, performance, or exhibition. Studies in the history, literature, and analysis of the arts at the appropriate time are equally important in the development of artistic literacy.*

Thomas A. Hatfield, "The Future of Art Education: Student Learning in the Visual Arts", *NASSP Bulletin* 82/597 (1998), pp. 11–12

In developing their understanding of the world, young children respond to gesture and movement before they react to the spoken word. They understand and explore the use of sound before they learn to speak. They draw pictures before they form letters. They dance and role-play stories before they learn to read. Gestures, movement, sound, and images are symbol systems for forms of thinking and communication that allow children, as students, to formulate ideas and express observations and understandings.

Literacies in the arts are developed as students learn in, through, and about different art forms within the arts disciplines and as they learn to use the "languages" of these disciplines to communicate and to interpret meaning. There are many ways of knowing and of communicating what we know and understand, and the arts provide multiple avenues for expression. These include the visual (e.g., still and animated images, layout, design, hypermedia, three-dimensional forms), oral (e.g., timbre and tone of voice), gestural (e.g., body language, kinesthetic movement), and aural (e.g., music, sound effects) – in fact, anything that can be "read", whether it uses print or other symbol systems to communicate. Visual, auditory, or kinesthetic signs and symbols are used by artists, choreographers, composers, dancers, dramatists, and musicians as part of the language of their discipline.

Because the arts offer various ways of knowing and different forms of communication, they provide students with relevant options for developing and representing their understanding. Education in arts programs is relevant to learning in all subjects because it offers students different means of expression while strengthening linguistic literacy, and it offers teachers various ways of differentiating instruction and engaging students in learning. In addition, since art forms, genres, styles, and techniques are rooted in a cultural context, students have an opportunity to develop an understanding of the meaning of the artistic languages used in art forms from various cultures by studying art forms in their cultural context.

The various arts disciplines are therefore a vital component of literacy education. The arts disciplines promote literacies that contribute to students' ability to explore, negotiate, communicate, interpret, and make sense of the changing realities of contemporary culture, technology, and society. Since technological advances continue to develop at an unprecedented rate, educators should promote the learning of multiple literacies as crucial to living successfully in an age in which communication and change have so much importance. Education in the arts prepares students not only to adapt to change but also to be active participants in bringing about change.

## THE ROLE OF THE SCHOOL LIBRARY IN ARTS PROGRAMS

The school library program can help to build and transform students' knowledge to support a lifetime of learning in an information- and knowledge-based society. The school library program supports student success across the arts curriculum by encouraging students to read widely, teaching them to read many forms of text for understanding and enjoyment, and helping them to improve their research skills and to use information gathered through research effectively. The school library program enables students to:

- develop a love of reading for learning and for pleasure;
- develop a critical appreciation of works of art;
- acquire an understanding of the richness and diversity of artistic and informational texts produced in Canada and around the world;
- obtain access to programs, resources, and integrated technologies that support all curriculum areas;
- understand and value the role of public library systems as a resource for lifelong learning.

The school library program plays a key role in the development of information literacy and research skills. In collaboration with classroom or content-area teachers, teacher-librarians design, teach, and provide students with authentic information and research tasks that foster learning, including the ability to:

- access, select, gather, process, critically evaluate, create, and communicate information;
- use the information obtained to explore and investigate issues, solve problems, make decisions, build knowledge, create personal meaning, and enrich their lives;
- communicate their findings for different audiences, using a variety of formats and technologies;
- use information and research with understanding, responsibility, and imagination.

In addition, teacher-librarians can work with teachers of the arts to help students to:

- develop literacy in using non-print forms, such as the Internet, CDs, DVDs, and videos, in order to access images of art works, critical reviews, and a variety of performances;
- design inquiry questions for research for arts projects;
- create and produce art works in dance, drama, music, and the visual arts, including media/multimedia works, that communicate their experiences.

Teachers of the arts are also encouraged to collaborate with both local librarians and teacher-librarians on collecting digital, print, and visual resources for arts projects (e.g., storybooks on a theme or topic to inspire role play, picture books for artistic inspiration, culture-specific and large-format image collections, informational and performance videos). Librarians may also be able to assist in accessing a variety of online resources and collections (e.g., professional articles, image galleries, videos).

In addition to resource materials in the school library, teachers may be able to access specialized libraries of plays, musical scores, and copyright-free music collections for use in video editing. Teachers need to discuss with students the concept of ownership of work and the importance of artists' copyright in all forms of art.

## THE ROLE OF INFORMATION AND COMMUNICATIONS TECHNOLOGY IN ARTS EDUCATION

Information and communications technologies (ICT) provide a range of tools that can significantly extend and enrich teachers' instructional strategies and support students' learning in the arts. ICT tools include multimedia resources; databases; Internet websites; digital cameras; notation, sequencing, and accompaniment software; and software for animation, image/video editing, and graphic design. Computer programs can help students to collect, organize, and sort the data they gather, and to write, edit, and present reports on their findings. ICT can also be used to connect students to other schools, at home and abroad, and to bring the global community into the local classroom.

The integration of technology into the arts curriculum represents a natural extension of the learning expectations associated with each art form. An education in the arts will engage students in the use of a wide range of technologies through which artistic expression can be achieved. The most obvious example is the use of multimedia technologies, which primarily involves the process of solving artistic problems through the application of various technologies, such as still and video photography, sound recording, and digital technologies. In the dance curriculum, students are expected to use computer technology as a compositional tool. In drama, students can gain facility in the use of lighting, sound, and other production technologies. Music education includes the use of analog and digital technology. Many visual arts activities engage students in the use of current technologies both as research tools and as creative media. Of particular interest in all of the arts is an analysis of the impact of various technologies on contemporary society.

Whenever appropriate, therefore, students should be encouraged to use ICT to support and communicate their learning. For example, students working individually or in groups can use computer technology and/or Internet websites to gain access to museums and archives in Canada and around the world. Students can also use digital cameras and projectors to design and present multimedia works, as well as to record the process of creating their arts projects.

Although the Internet is a powerful learning tool, all students must be made aware of issues of privacy, safety, and responsible use, as well as of the ways in which the Internet can be used to promote hatred.

ICT tools are also useful for teachers in their teaching practice, both for class instruction and for the design of curriculum units that contain varied approaches to learning to meet diverse student needs. A number of educational software programs to support the arts are licensed through the ministry and are listed on www.osapac.org under the software link.

## GUIDANCE IN ARTS EDUCATION

The guidance and career education program should be aligned with the arts curriculum. Teachers need to ensure that classroom learning across all grades and subjects provides ample opportunity for students to learn how to work independently (e.g., complete homework independently), cooperate with others, resolve conflicts, participate in class, solve problems, and set goals to improve their work.

The arts help students learn and apply skills that will be useful throughout their lives – for example, the ability to use a range of modes of communication and representation; to make qualitative judgements; to act on the awareness that problems can have more than one solution and that there are many ways to see and interpret the world; and to take circumstances into account when solving problems. Research shows that learning about and participating in the arts improves self-esteem, empathy, confidence, and self-motivation. As well, learning through participation in the arts can benefit students across the spectrum of ability, achievement, and interests. Research also shows that, when the arts are an integral part of the school environment, students have better attendance, are more motivated to learn, have improved multicultural understanding, and are more likely to stay in school and graduate.

The arts and cultural industries are among the largest sectors of the Canadian economy. In fact, the work force in the culture sector has increased over a recent twenty-year period at a much faster rate than the total work force in Canada.[6] Educational and career opportunities related to the arts are consequently many and varied. The arts program can offer opportunities for a variety of career exploration activities, including career mentorships and visits from a wide variety of guest speakers in the arts – for example, actors, animators, architects, artists, audio and video technicians, choreographers, comedians, composers, critics, dancers, designers, directors, educators, gallery or museum curators, graphic artists, illustrators, music arrangers, musicians, photographers, recording engineers, sculptors, video and recording editors, web designers, and individuals working in film, television, special effects, and interactive media (such as game designers and programmers).

---

6. Paul Sereda, "Culture Employment in a North American Context: 1981 to 2001" (Ottawa: Statistics Canada, 2007), p. 18.

# HEALTH AND SAFETY IN ARTS EDUCATION

Teachers must model safe practices at all times and communicate safety expectations to students in accordance with school board and Ministry of Education policies.

To carry out their responsibilities with regard to safety, it is important that teachers have concern for their own and their students' safety, and that they ensure that safe practices are followed at all times when using tools, materials, and equipment and when participating in performance tasks. The following are some ways of ensuring that classes in the arts are safe:

- Ensure that all tools are used safely – for example, scissors, linoleum cutters, and other sharp tools, and hot glue guns. *Note:* Teachers supervising students who are using power tools, such as drills, sanders, and saws, need to have *specialized training* in handling such tools.

- Choose non-toxic materials for students to use, such as non-toxic glues, glazes, and paints. Avoid toxic materials, such as solvent-based markers or painting materials, and avoid choosing substances that are hazardous if inhaled, such as aerosol paints or fixatives. Also ensure that students follow safe practices when using any materials – for example, washing their hands after handling art materials and not putting materials or tools in their mouths.

- Ensure that students take precautions when using materials that are in a powdered state and that therefore can be inadvertently inhaled. For example, instruct students not to sand plaster or clay when it is in a dry state; not to use paint pigments or wallpaper paste in a powdered state; and not to "blow" chalk pastel off an art work but rather tap the work onto damp newsprint. They should also wet-mop and wipe surfaces after using clay or any other art media that create dust.

- Ensure that all equipment is safe and that it is also handled safely. Props need to be safe – for example, costumes should be short enough so that students will not trip when wearing them, and masks should permit clear vision. Secure sound and lighting equipment. Ensure that kilns are properly ventilated. Instruct students not to play musical instruments close to others' ears. Make sure that musical instruments are sterilized after use (e.g., brass and woodwind mouthpieces).

- Ensure that safe practices are followed in all performance tasks. For example, have students do warm-up exercises before dance activities, drama activities, and singing. Have them wear appropriate footwear for movement activities (or have them do the activities in bare feet, if appropriate). Choose songs that fall within an appropriate range for the students, and ensure that primary students use their voices in a way that is appropriate for their high, light voices. Ensure that students use proper playing techniques. Also, ensure that ladders are used safely when setting up stages; manage the pace of activities; and manage the use of space (e.g., move obstacles to allow for creative movement or performance).

- Ensure that students feel comfortable emotionally and psychologically. For example, discuss emotional roles in drama; encourage sensitivity to others' cultural values; and encourage students to be aware of the personal space of others, emphasizing that touching required for a dance or drama activity needs to be respectful.

It is also important that parents ensure that appropriate school staff members are informed of any allergies their children may have, especially in the case of younger children – for example, an allergy to latex. Teachers should take those allergies into consideration when preparing arts lessons – for example, having them use non-latex gloves and masks and other forms of glue and make-up.

Students demonstrate that they have the knowledge, skills, and habits of mind required for safe participation in arts activities when they:

- maintain a well-organized and uncluttered work space;
- follow established safety procedures;
- identify possible safety concerns;
- suggest and implement appropriate safety procedures;
- carefully follow the instructions and example of the teacher;
- consistently show care and concern for their safety and that of others.

It is recommended that teachers not use donated art materials *unless* the ingredients are clearly labelled and known to meet current safety standards. New materials should also be clearly labelled or have a written product description to accompany them (e.g., information on the box or a material safety data sheet describing the contents of a paint tube).

# OVERVIEW OF GRADES 1 TO 3

Children's early learning experiences have a profound effect on their development. The arts program for Grades 1 to 3 focuses on the foundational knowledge and skills students need in order to learn through and about the arts. The expectations build on students' prior knowledge and experience to strengthen their oral language, understanding of concepts about movement, capacity for imagining and pretending, vocabulary knowledge, visual and musical tonal awareness, higher-order thinking skills, and capacity for reflection.

The emphasis in the primary grades should be on exploration of the student's self, family, personal experiences, and world. Through guided practice students begin to develop the ability to use the creative process (see pages 19–22) and the critical thinking process (see pages 23–28) in their explorations. Young children are naturally curious and ask many questions about things that catch their attention, and arts programs should capitalize on this natural desire to learn and absorb information. Since young children learn best by doing, it is especially important to provide opportunities for them to engage in open-ended, hands-on activities. Teachers should plan learning experiences that promote integrated learning and that allow children to handle, explore, and experiment with familiar materials in a learning environment that is safe, secure, and inviting. A developmentally appropriate arts program for young children provides opportunities for child-initiated individual expression. It allows children freedom to make choices and to use their observations, experiences, and background knowledge to engage in a wide range of arts activities. It recognizes that there is no one way to create, and that every child's interpretation is to be valued. It promotes risk taking. It provides blocks of time to allow students' skills to develop, and it encourages them to revisit projects rather than focusing only on one-time art experiences.

Most of what primary students know about the arts comes from listening and speaking with adults; experiences in the home, school, and community; and interacting with media such as advertisements, television programs, video games, songs, photographs, two- and three-dimensional art works, and films. The expectations for the arts build upon the prior knowledge and experience that students from diverse cultural and linguistic backgrounds bring to Ontario classrooms. Because this base of knowledge, experience, and skills varies from student to student, and because students will have varying levels of prior exposure to the elements, skills, forms, genres, and traditions of the arts, it is important for instruction to be differentiated to meet the needs of individuals and small groups of students. Exposure to a broad range of stimuli that reflect diversity is also crucial: efforts should be made to honour the cultural traditions of students from all groups in the community.

Students create, view, and experience the arts for a variety of purposes, both formal and informal. They develop an understanding of appropriate listening, speaking, viewing, and collaborative behaviours and identify strategies they can use to understand what they hear, view, and experience and to communicate what they want to say. In all four strands, teachers should explicitly teach and model the use of the knowledge, skills, and strategies most relevant to the particular strand. Initially, students engage in learning through shared and guided practice; eventually, they demonstrate independently their achievement of the learning expectations through multiple, diverse learning opportunities and activities.

Primary students should have access to and opportunities to create works of dance, drama, music, and visual art on familiar topics. Teachers need to use a variety of means to motivate and engage students, including songs, poems, teacher read-alouds or simple readers' theatre, large- and small-group discussions, storytelling activities, one-on-one conversations, role play, self-directed pretend play, stories in children's first language, soundtracks, posters or signs, photographs, collages, digital and print images, recorded music, sculptures, cartoons, movies, and television shows. Through participating in classroom arts experiences, students learn to identify the arts as part of everyday life and recognize that they serve a variety of purposes. By attending exhibitions and performances, students begin to learn that representational art forms can communicate meaning symbolically. Students investigate the purposes of the arts in past and present cultures and the contexts in which they were or are made, viewed, and valued. They also experience what it is to be both an audience member, viewing the work of others, and a presenter, sharing their own work in an informal classroom setting.

## Dance

In the primary grades, students should be moving creatively every day. Students begin to use personal experience, imagination, and familiar movements to develop a movement vocabulary, to respond to prompts and express ideas, and to communicate their thoughts and feelings in various situations. Through a balance of free exploration and guided exploration, students develop awareness of their bodies and of the many different ways they can move. Through modelling and guided movement explorations, they expand their movement vocabulary to include some of the elements of dance. In particular, students begin to travel through pathways, use gesture to communicate feelings, and explore a range of levels, shapes, and locomotor and non-locomotor movements. Students also develop their ability to move and control their bodies in space and time and begin to create short dance pieces using the elements of dance.

## Drama

Dramatic play and whole-group role play are foundational components of learning in drama in the primary grades. By assuming different roles in dramatic play with a partner, or in a small group or whole group in a process drama, students begin to differentiate between the real world and the imagined or fictional contexts of drama. They learn to step into role in order to live through the imagined context of the drama, and to step out of role to reflect upon and make personal connections to the drama experience. Some opportunities for independent and self-directed pretend play should be provided as a bridge to more structured learning experiences. As well, students should be introduced to some of the elements, conventions, and forms of drama that allow them to shape and communicate their thoughts, feelings, and ideas. In Grades 1 to 3, pretend play, personal stories and experiences, nursery rhymes, poetry, and folk tales and stories from around the world should be used to stimulate the imagination and encourage social interaction. Primary students should be encouraged to explore a variety of texts and to represent their understandings in multiple ways. As well, because drama is a highly social art form, teachers should explicitly teach and model effective group skills to help primary students learn to work well with others.

## Music

In the primary grades, students experience and explore the elements of music through singing, listening to, and moving to a variety of songs, rhymes, and chants. Their experiences should include a wide variety of recorded and live music. In Grade 1, they make connections with the role of music in their lives, sing and play in unison, create simple accompaniments, and experiment with found sounds and instruments. In Grade 2, they continue to sing in unison, and learn to use patterns of sound found in speech to create simple accompaniments and explore simple and invented notation. In Grade 3, they perform simple rounds, create and perform soundscapes and melodies based upon the pentatonic scale, and begin to identify and appreciate the role of music in their lives. During the primary grades, students also learn how to use and care for musical instruments properly, become familiar with acceptable audience behaviour, and develop the ability to work with others.

## Visual Arts

The study of visual arts begins with the introduction of skills and concepts that may be new for many of the children. Because of the children's different developmental levels when entering Grade 1, it is expected that this year will emphasize joyful exploration and discovery. The program should expose children to many manipulative materials and encourage exploration with them in a wide variety of open-ended ways. Mass-produced stereotypical images (e.g., identical jack-o'-lanterns pre-cut by adults) have no place in the program. Such materials provide no or limited opportunities for self-expression and the development of a sense of creative empowerment. Similarly, colouring-in activities and photocopied patterns to cut out limit creativity and are developmentally inappropriate. Primary students work with colour emotionally or randomly. They should have opportunities to look at, feel, and interact with stimuli and to create an individualized response based on their own observations. In Grades 1, 2, and 3, students begin to explore art in the world around them, to understand that people all over the world create and enjoy art, and to develop the ability to communicate about their immediate environment and interests through visual images. They engage in a variety of drawing, painting, print-making, and sculpting activities and are introduced to and learn to use a variety of art tools, materials, and techniques. They learn about some of the elements and principles of design and begin to describe how the elements are used by artists. They generate and develop visual ideas, using imagination, observation, and experiments with materials. And they apply their knowledge of design elements and principles to create works of art that tell stories and express thoughts, feelings, and insights.

# GRADE 1

# A. DANCE

## OVERALL EXPECTATIONS

By the end of Grade 1, students will:

**A1. Creating and Presenting:** apply the creative process (see pages 19–22) to the composition of simple dance phrases, using the elements of dance to communicate feelings and ideas;

**A2. Reflecting, Responding, and Analysing:** apply the critical analysis process (see pages 23–28) to communicate their feelings, ideas, and understandings in response to a variety of dance pieces and experiences;

**A3. Exploring Forms and Cultural Contexts:** demonstrate an understanding of a variety of dance forms and styles from the past and present, and their social and/or community contexts.

---

### FUNDAMENTAL CONCEPTS FOR GRADE 1

Students in Grade 1 will develop understanding of the following concepts through participation in various dance experiences (e.g., connecting and altering familiar movements), with particular emphasis on body and space.

ELEMENTS OF DANCE

- *body:* body awareness (e.g., awareness of where one is in space in relation to objects in class, awareness of position), use of body zones (e.g., whole body [versus various body parts], upper body only, lower body only), use of body parts (e.g., arms, legs, head), body shapes (e.g., big, small, angular, twisted, curved, straight, closed), locomotor movements (e.g., galloping, skipping, rolling), non-locomotor movements (e.g., arm movements such as swimming/waving, hopping on one foot, jumping on two feet, kicking, bending knees, melting to the ground, stretching, growing, spinning, folding, bowing), body bases (e.g., feet as body base, hands and knees as body base)

- *space:* levels (e.g., low to high by reaching; high to low by falling, crouching), directions (e.g., forwards, backwards, sideways), general and personal

- *time:* tempo (e.g., fast/slow, movement versus freeze), rhythm (e.g., even, uneven)

- *energy:* quality (e.g., melting, twitching, slumping, percussive, sustained [as in a held stretch])

- *relationship:* with a partner (e.g., slow-motion mirroring)

---

## SPECIFIC EXPECTATIONS

### A1. Creating and Presenting

By the end of Grade 1, students will:

**A1.1** use movements that are part of their daily experience in a variety of ways in dance phrases *(e.g., alter and exaggerate movements based on even rhythms such as walking, galloping, and swimming, and on uneven rhythms such as skipping and jumping; amplify and modify percussive movements such as the movement of a clock ticking or the sustained hold of a cat stretching)*

*Teacher prompts:* "What everyday movements do you do throughout the day?" "When you wave hello to a friend who is close by, is your wave bigger or smaller than when the friend is far away? How might you change the action of waving by making the movement bigger/smaller or faster/slower? Will the speed or rhythm of the movement change when you make it bigger or smaller?"

**A1.2** use dance as a language to express feelings and ideas suggested by songs, stories, and poems, with a focus on the element of body, particularly body shapes *(e.g., use the entire body [crouch, slump] and body parts [folded arms, bowed head] to express an idea such as deep thought)*

*Teacher prompts:* "Show me with your body how the ogres felt when they encountered the dragon (e.g., depict courage)." "How can you position your body, head, arms, and legs so we can better understand the ideas you want to express?"

**A1.3** create dance phrases using a variety of ways to connect movements (*e.g., connect a melt and a spin using a non-locomotor movement; connect a walk and a skip [locomotor movements] with a circle [pathway]*)

*Teacher prompts:* "If you are at a low level and you want to go to a high level (or if you want to go from a high level to a low level), how are you going to get there? Are you going to spin, grow, reach up, melt, rise, or wiggle?" "If you were a seed in the ground, how would you grow into a tree? Would you grow with fast movements or slow?" "In your performance, how can you connect a skip, a fall, and a spin to create a movement sentence (or phrase)?"

**A1.4** use varied and/or contrasting body shapes to communicate different types of messages (*e.g., a high level and open, expansive shape to show dominance; a closed huddled shape to show that you are holding a treasured or secret object*)

*Teacher prompt:* "What body shapes can you use to show you like something? Dislike something? Are there other body shapes to express the same ideas?"

## A2. Reflecting, Responding, and Analysing

By the end of Grade 1, students will:

**A2.1** describe differences they observe when various movements from daily life are used as the basis or stimulus for movements in a dance phrase (*e.g., describe ways in which every-day actions and movements such as skipping on the playground, walking to school, brushing their teeth, or getting dressed are changed when they are used in a dance phrase*)

*Teacher prompt:* "How are actions and gestures used to communicate in daily life different from movements that are used to communicate in dance? What would dances be like if the movements were always the same as movements you see in daily life?"

**A2.2** identify and describe how the element of body is used in contrasting ways to communicate ideas in their own and others' dance phrases, with teacher support (*e.g., standing versus kneeling body bases can communicate differences in power; curved versus straight shapes can communicate contrasting emotions*)

*Teacher prompts:* "What contrasting levels did Sandeep use to show the difference between happy and sad?" "What was Carmen's body base when she was kneeling? What was she saying with that shape?"

**A2.3** identify and give examples of their strengths and areas for growth as dance creators and audience members (*e.g., using connecting movements; working collaboratively in groups to create dance phrases incorporating everyone's ideas; watching peer performances attentively and asking relevant questions*)

*Teacher prompts:* "How do you come up with ideas for movement?" "How do you incorporate everyone's ideas when working together?" "What makes a good audience member? When you watch your classmates dancing, do you try to behave as you would like others to behave when they are watching your dance work?" "What differences are there between the way you behave when watching dancing in a theatre versus at an outdoor stadium or a cultural event with your family?"

## A3. Exploring Forms and Cultural Contexts

By the end of Grade 1, students will:

**A3.1** describe, with teacher guidance, a variety of dances from different communities around the world that they have seen in the media, at live performances and social gatherings, or in the classroom (*e.g., describe traditional dances they have seen to a partner [Chinese ribbon dance, Highland fling, powwow dance styles]*)

*Teacher prompts:* "When we were watching the Highland dancing, were the dancers using mostly locomotor or non-locomotor movements?" "What body shapes did you see in the video of the Chinese ribbon dance?"

**A3.2** identify and describe dance experiences in their own lives and communities (*e.g., At home: dancing or moving to a favourite song/story; seeing dance on television or in a movie DVD; At school: playing at recess; In the community: dancing or observing dances at weddings, parties, cultural celebrations*)

*Teacher prompt:* "What dances do you and your family participate in at special occasions in your life?"

# B. DRAMA

## OVERALL EXPECTATIONS

By the end of Grade 1, students will:

**B1. Creating and Presenting:** apply the creative process (see pages 19–22) to dramatic play and process drama, using the elements and conventions of drama to communicate feelings, ideas, and stories;

**B2. Reflecting, Responding, and Analysing:** apply the critical analysis process (see pages 23–28) to communicate feelings, ideas, and understandings in response to a variety of drama works and experiences;

**B3. Exploring Forms and Cultural Contexts:** demonstrate an understanding of a variety of drama and theatre forms and styles from the past and present, and their social and/or community contexts.

### FUNDAMENTAL CONCEPTS FOR GRADE 1

Students in Grade 1 will develop an understanding of the following concepts through participation in various drama experiences.

ELEMENTS OF DRAMA

- *role/character:* adopting the attitude, voice, or emotional state of a fictional character
- *relationship:* listening and responding in role to other characters in role
- *time and place:* pretending to be in the established setting of the drama
- *tension:* being aware of a sense of mystery or of a problem to be solved
- *focus and emphasis:* being aware of the main idea or issue in the drama

## SPECIFIC EXPECTATIONS

### B1. Creating and Presenting

By the end of Grade 1, students will:

**B1.1** engage in dramatic play and role play, with a focus on exploring a variety of sources from diverse communities, times, and places (*e.g., retell and enact nursery and other childhood rhymes, stories, or narratives from picture books; use movement and voice to explore the thoughts of a familiar folk tale character in a variety of situations; use guided imagery and descriptive language to explore what a character might feel and experience in a story setting or picture; use group role play to explore alternative endings to stories, fairy tales, and personal experiences; use role play or a tableau at key moments in a story to help the protagonist solve a problem; interview a teacher in the role of a character from a story*)

*Teacher prompts:* "How can you and your friends retell the story using puppets?" "How can you and a partner act out how you think the story will end – but without using any words?"

**B1.2** demonstrate an understanding of the element of character by adopting thoughts, feelings, and gestures relevant to the role being played (*e.g., use facial expressions, body movement, and words to respond in role to scenarios and questions; express different points of view after reading a picture book about issues of belonging and discrimination; work with a partner to create a short scene that shows the importance of acceptance, understanding, and inclusion*)

*Teacher prompts:* "When I ask you a question as Grandma, how might you answer me as the wolf?" "How can you show (e.g., using gestures) what you are thinking and feeling when you are in role? Try to imagine why the wolf acts the way it does."

**B1.3** plan and shape dramatic play by building on the ideas of others, both in and out of role (*e.g., In role: add ideas to the dramatic play that reflect the knowledge and experience of the role that is being played [such as a scientist mentioning an experiment or a journalist mentioning an* *interview]; create and share scenes from their own experiences; Out of role: work in a group to plan and prepare a scene and ask follow-up questions such as "How could we make this clearer? What changes can we make to help our story be understood?"; describe the sort of person who might own a particular found object such as a bag or a coat)*

*Teacher prompts: In role:* "What do I need to know about the situation we find ourselves in?" "How might we convince (the main character) to listen to us?" *Out of role:* "How can you work with your friends to act out a story? What do you think the characters should do?" "Can you introduce a new role in response to ideas emerging in the drama?"

**B1.4** communicate feelings and ideas to a familiar audience (*e.g., classmates*) using a few simple visual or technological aids to support and enhance their drama work (*e.g., use a sheer cloth moved quickly to represent water; use a rainstick or shaker to create a sense of mystery or magic; use a variety of classroom objects to create a play area for specific dramatic play experiences*)

*Teacher prompts:* "How was the character feeling at the end of the story?" "What colours could we use to represent feeling happy? Feeling sad?" "If your character was the weather, what body shapes and props could you use to get into character?"

## B2. Reflecting, Responding, and Analysing

By the end of Grade 1, students will:

**B2.1** express feelings and ideas about a drama experience or performance in a variety of ways, making personal connections to the characters and themes in the story (*e.g., in oral discussion, relate themes about family relationships or friendships to their own lives; after viewing a play or clip of a movie dealing with family issues [such as* Cinderella *or* Princess Mononoke*], contribute to a class journal entry or draw a picture to show the feelings of one or more of the characters – a stepsister, Cinderella, the mice*)

*Teacher prompts:* "Can you explain how you are different from and similar to your favourite character in today's drama/read-aloud?" "Does our drama experience make you think about stories we have read? How did the drama make you feel?" "If you could give advice to this character, what would you like to say to him/her?"

**B2.2** demonstrate an understanding of how the element of character/role is used in shared classroom drama experiences and theatre to

communicate meaning (*e.g., to provide important information in a situation; to represent a particular perspective/point of view; to change the direction of the plot; to symbolize an idea such as friendship*)

*Teacher prompts:* "What would the story be like if the wise woman *didn't* appear to give advice? Should we assume that she is a hero/villain?" "How was the character in the play we saw like a real person?" "How would the story change, if it was told by a different character? Who might be interesting to hear from?"

**B2.3** identify and give examples of their strengths, interests, and areas for improvement as drama participants and audience members (*e.g., using personal experience and imagination to extend ideas in the drama; building on their own or others' ideas*)

*Teacher prompts:* "What part of the drama did you enjoy the most and why?" "How did you use your body and volume and tone of voice to tell us how your character was feeling?" "If we were going to do the drama again, what is something that you could do better?"

## B3. Exploring Forms and Cultural Contexts

By the end of Grade 1, students will:

**B3.1** identify and describe drama and theatre forms, events, and activities that they experience in their home, school, and community (*e.g., favourite television or computer programs and characters, imaginative play with action figures, dramatic play, attending plays and celebrations, interacting with picture books, storytelling*)

*Teacher prompts:* "Tell me about a time when you pretended to be someone or something else." "At what celebrations or events in our communities do we see people dressing up or pretending to be someone else?"

**B3.2** demonstrate an awareness of a variety of roles, themes, and subjects in dramas and stories from different communities around the world (*e.g., contribute to a class scrapbook about characters such as trolls/fairies, trickster themes in Nanabush stories [from Native folklore] and Anansi stories [from West African folklore]*)

*Teacher prompts:* "Let's list the different characters from the play." "Why do you think people will dress up as or pretend to be someone else when they are part of a parade or a play?" "How does this lesson or fable apply to real-life situations?"

# C. MUSIC

## OVERALL EXPECTATIONS

By the end of Grade 1, students will:

**C1. Creating and Performing:** apply the creative process (see pages 19–22) to create and perform music for a variety of purposes, using the elements and techniques of music;

**C2. Reflecting, Responding, and Analysing:** apply the critical analysis process (see pages 23–28) to communicate their feelings, ideas, and understandings in response to a variety of music and musical experiences;

**C3. Exploring Forms and Cultural Contexts:** demonstrate an understanding of a variety of musical genres and styles from the past and present, and their social and/or community contexts.

---

### FUNDAMENTAL CONCEPTS FOR GRADE 1

Students will be introduced to the elements of music and related musical concepts that are appropriate for Grade 1. They will develop understanding of these concepts through participation in various musical experiences (e.g., listening, singing, moving, playing musical instruments). These experiences will include reading simple rhythmic or stick notation while listening to the sounds it represents, interpreting simple visual prompts (e.g., solfège hand signs*), and representing elements with manipulatives (e.g., Popsicle sticks, math cubes).

ELEMENTS OF MUSIC

* *duration:* fast and slow *tempi*; rhythm versus beat; two and four beats per bar ($\frac{2}{4}$ and $\frac{4}{4}$ metres); quarter note (oral prompt: "ta"), eighth note(s) (oral prompt: "ti-ti"), quarter rest; simple rhythmic ostinato (e.g., "ta, ta, ti-ti, ta")

* *pitch:* high and low sounds; unison; melodic contour; simple melodic patterns using the notes "mi", "so", and "la" (e.g., the "so–mi–la–so–mi" pitch pattern in some children's songs)

* *dynamics and other expressive controls:* loud, soft; a strong sound for a note or beat (accent); smooth and detached articulation

* *timbre:* vocal quality (e.g., speaking voice, singing voice), body percussion, sound quality of instruments (e.g., non-pitched and pitched percussion), environmental and found sounds

* *texture/harmony:* single melodic line in unison (monophony)

* *form:* phrase, call and response

---

## SPECIFIC EXPECTATIONS

### C1. Creating and Performing

By the end of Grade 1, students will:

**C1.1** sing songs in unison and play simple accompaniments for music from a wide variety of diverse cultures, styles, and historical periods (*e.g., play a simple rhythmic ostinato on a drum or tambourine to accompany singing; match pitches in echo singing*)

*Teacher prompt:* "To reflect the mood of this song, should the ostinato that's played on the drum be soft or loud? Why?"

**C1.2** apply the elements of music when singing, playing, and moving (*e.g., duration: while singing a familiar song, clap the rhythm while others pat the beat, and on a signal switch roles*)

---

* See the Glossary for an illustration of the hand signs. Note that there are different ways of spelling the seven syllables in the tonic sol-fa, or solfège, system. The spelling (with a pronunciation guide) that is used in this document is as follows: "**do**[doe]–**re**[ray]–**mi**[me]–**fa**[fah]–**so**[so]–**la**[lah]–**ti**[tea]–do".

*Teacher prompts:* "As we sing, show the beat in this song. Now show the rhythm. How are they different?" "Show how this music makes you want to move."

**C1.3** create compositions for a specific purpose and a familiar audience (*e.g., use the notes "mi", "so", and "la" to create a melodic phrase that answers a sung question; use rhythm instruments, body percussion, or everyday objects to create an accompaniment to a story or song; use short rhythmic phrases in improvised answers to clapped questions*)

*Teacher prompts:* "When I play this rhythmic question, create your own rhythmic answer." "What kind of music can you create to show how the main character in our story feels?" "How can we use our rhythm instruments and found sounds to show the mood of this story?"

**C1.4** use the tools and techniques of musicianship in musical performances (*e.g., sing with relaxed but straight posture and controlled breathing; rehearse music to perform with others*)

*Teacher prompts:* "Why do we stand in a certain way when we are singing as a group?" "Which way of standing helps us to get more air when we breathe?"

**C1.5** demonstrate understanding that sounds can be represented by symbols (*e.g., show rhythm and beat with manipulatives such as math cubes or Popsicle sticks; use devised, or invented, forms of musical notation, or simple forms of standard musical notation*)

*Teacher prompt:* "Show the rhythm of this song with Popsicle (or rhythm) sticks by drawing shapes or using your hands."

## C2. Reflecting, Responding, and Analysing

By the end of Grade 1, students will:

**C2.1** express initial reactions and personal responses to musical performances in a variety of ways (*e.g., move like an animal of which the music reminds them*)

*Teacher prompts:* "Describe the colours you see or pictures you imagine as the music is playing." "How does this music make you want to move?"

**C2.2** describe ways in which the elements of music are used for different purposes in the music they perform, listen to, and create (*e.g., the tempo and dynamics of a lullaby, the beat and rhythm of a march, the sound quality of a trumpet in a fanfare*)

*Teacher prompts:* "What is it about this music that would help a baby go to sleep?" "Why is this piece of music good for marching?"

**C2.3** identify and give examples of their strengths and areas for growth as musical performers, creators, interpreters, and audience members (*e.g., singing in unison, providing constructive feedback and suggestions for a classmate's or guest performer's performance*)

*Teacher prompts:* "What could we do to improve our next performance?" "How can we demonstrate good audience behaviour during our school concert?"

## C3. Exploring Forms and Cultural Contexts

By the end of Grade 1, students will:

**C3.1** identify and describe musical experiences in their own lives (*e.g., list the places and times within a day when they hear or perform music; describe various times when they sing, play, and move to music in school, at home, and in the community*)

*Teacher prompts:* "What songs can you sing from the movies you've watched?" "How would our lives be different if there was no music or sound for a day?" "What is your favourite movie or television show? How might it be different if there were no music or soundtrack?"

**C3.2** identify a variety of musical pieces from different cultures through performing and/or listening to them (*e.g., folk songs, songs for celebrations, ceremonial music from Canadian and world sources*)

*Teacher prompts:* "What songs do you sing for Diwali? Kwanzaa? Hanukkah?" "Earth Day is coming in April. What songs could we use to help to celebrate the earth?"

# D. VISUAL ARTS

## OVERALL EXPECTATIONS

By the end of Grade 1, students will:

**D1. Creating and Presenting:** apply the creative process (see pages 19–22) to produce a variety of two- and three-dimensional art works, using elements, principles, and techniques of visual arts to communicate feelings, ideas, and understandings;

**D2. Reflecting, Responding, and Analysing:** apply the critical analysis process (see pages 23–28) to communicate feelings, ideas, and understandings in response to a variety of art works and art experiences;

**D3. Exploring Forms and Cultural Contexts:** demonstrate an understanding of a variety of art forms, styles, and techniques from the past and present, and their social and/or community contexts.

### FUNDAMENTAL CONCEPTS FOR GRADE 1

Students in Grade 1 will develop understanding of the following concepts through participation in a variety of hands-on, open-ended visual arts experiences.

ELEMENTS OF DESIGN
Students will develop understanding of all elements of design.

- *line:* jagged, curved, broken, dashed, spiral, straight, wavy, zigzag lines; lines in art and everyday objects (natural and human-made)

- *shape and form:* geometric and organic shapes and forms of familiar objects (e.g., geometric: circles, blocks; organic: clouds, flowers)

- *space:* depiction of objects in the distance as smaller and closer to the top of the art paper; shapes and lines closer together or farther apart; horizon line; spaces through, inside, and around shapes or objects

- *colour:* mixing of primary colours (red, yellow, blue); identification of warm (e.g., red, orange) and cool (e.g., blue, green) colours

- *texture:* textures of familiar objects (e.g., fuzzy, prickly, bumpy, smooth); changes in texture; a pattern of lines to show texture (e.g., the texture of a snake's skin); transfer of texture (e.g., placing a piece of paper over a textured surface and then rubbing the paper with wax crayon)

- *value:* light, dark

PRINCIPLES OF DESIGN
Students will develop understanding of all principles of design (that is, contrast, repetition and rhythm, variety, emphasis, proportion, balance, unity and harmony, and movement), but the focus in Grade 1 will be on contrast.

- *contrast:* light/dark; large/small; pure/mixed colour

# SPECIFIC EXPECTATIONS

## D1. Creating and Presenting

By the end of Grade 1, students will:

**D1.1** create two- and three-dimensional works of art that express feelings and ideas inspired by personal experiences (*e.g., a tempera painting that communicates their feelings about a special occasion or event such as a fair or a parade; a sculpture of a favourite musical instrument made with found objects; a watercolour painting of a favourite part of the schoolyard; an assemblage in which images and objects from home and school are used to represent special memories*)

*Teacher prompts:* "How does your art work reflect your feelings? Which colours could you use to show happiness or excitement?" "Why did you choose to paint this part of the schoolyard?"

**D1.2** demonstrate an understanding of composition, using principles of design to create narrative art works or art works on a theme or topic (*e.g., a drawing of an approaching storm that uses a variety of lines to create contrast [dashed, jagged, curved, spiral]; a cardboard or papier mâché sculpture of a mythical animal in a dynamic pose that uses surface materials to show a contrast in texture [fuzzy yarn; coarse, prickly sawdust]*)

*Teacher prompts:* "How can you vary your lines to create contrast between the area of the image that is the storm and the area of calm?" "How can you use levels and positioning of your sculpture's limbs and body to compose a sculpture that is visually interesting on all sides and that shows a variety of forms?"

**D1.3** use elements of design in art works to communicate ideas, messages, and personal understandings (*e.g., a pattern of broken, wavy, and zigzag lines to make the bark of a tree look rough in a drawing; size and arrangement of organic shapes in a painting of flowers to create the impression that the various flowers are at different distances from the viewer*)

*Teacher prompts:* "What kinds of lines would you use to show this texture?" "Look carefully at the arrangement of these flowers. How do you have to place them and change their shapes in a painting to show that some of them are closer and some farther away?"

**D1.4** use a variety of materials, tools, and techniques to respond to design challenges (*e.g.,*

- drawing: *use wax crayon or oil pastel lines on coloured paper to express their responses to different kinds of music or rhythm*

- mixed media: *use torn paper and textured materials to create a landscape collage of a playground that includes a horizon line*

- painting: *create paint resists that are made with wax crayon on paper, using rubbing plates that have a variety of textures [e.g., bumpy, wavy] to create imaginary creatures inspired by the artistic style of Eric Carle*

- printmaking: *use cut sponge or cardboard and paint stamping to make a pattern of geometric and organic shapes*

- sculpture: *use glued or taped scrap wood to build a wood block sculpture of an imaginary geometric machine*)

*Teacher prompts:* "When you hear the drumbeat in the music, think about how you could show the beat with different kinds of lines." "What techniques or tools can you use to make the texture (e.g., wood bark) look real on your paper?" "How can you move the pieces in your sculpture to make different openings or spaces in it?"

## D2. Reflecting, Responding, and Analysing

By the end of Grade 1, students will:

**D2.1** express their feelings and ideas about art works and art experiences (*e.g., describe feelings evoked by the use of colours in the painting* Inside the Sugar Shack *by Miyuki Tanobe or* The Starry Night *by Vincent van Gogh; use drama to respond to a community art work viewed during a neighbourhood walk; describe the ways in which an artist's representation of an event relates to their own experiences*)

*Teacher prompts:* "Why might someone want to visit this place? If you could take a walk in this picture, where would you go?" "Where would you place yourself if you were in this picture? Who might live or work here?" "What story does this art work tell?"

**D2.2** explain how elements and principles of design are used to communicate meaning or understanding in their own and others' art work (*e.g., explain how repeated lines and shapes are used to depict the texture of snake, lizard, leopard, or dinosaur skin; classify images on a topic, and, focusing on a dominant element, use the images to explain that there are many different ways of approaching the same subject*)

*Teacher prompts:* "What did you do in your drawing to help people understand what you mean or what you are thinking here?" "What kinds of shapes do you see? How can you use some of these shapes to make a collage that depicts the music, a musical instrument, and the mood of the music?"

**D2.3** demonstrate an awareness of signs and symbols encountered in their daily lives and in works of art (*e.g., green is associated with nature and sometimes with envy or illness in the West; red is associated with stopping [traffic lights] in the West, luck in China, success in Cherokee culture, mourning in South Africa*)

*Teacher prompts:* "What are some examples of special colours used for different festivals?" "Does our school have its own colours or a symbol? Why do you think the school chose those colours or that symbol?"

**D2.4** identify and document their strengths, their interests, and areas for improvement as creators of art (*e.g., discuss what they think is good about works in their art folder during conferences with their teacher; do a think-pair-share on their favourite part of one of their art works*)

*Teacher prompts:* "Tell me something you like about your art work. What did you want to express in it?" "Close your eyes. When you open them, tell me the first place your eye goes. What did you put in that part of the image so your eye will go there? What part would you change if you could?" "What other details can you add to your sculpture to make it look as if it is moving? What did you learn from your work?"

By the end of Grade 1, students will:

**D3.1** identify and describe visual art forms that they see in their home, at school, in their community, and in visual arts experiences (*e.g., illustrations in picture books, designs of various toys, patterns on clothing or other textiles, classroom visits by artists, student displays at their school, visits to galleries*)

*Teacher prompts:* "What do you think about having art on display in the classroom?" "Why do people have art in their homes?" "What reaction do you get from others when you display your art works?" "Who is an artist? What do artists do? What everyday objects do they make or design?"

**D3.2** demonstrate an awareness of a variety of works of art from diverse communities, times, and places (*e.g., iconic architecture they have seen either in pictures or in real life, such as the CN Tower, the Eiffel Tower, the Taj Mahal; comics from different countries; decorations or patterns on crafts or old artefacts; contemporary and ancient clay sculptures; paintings of family or community events from different cultures or from previous eras*)

*Teacher prompts:* "How does the artist show that people in the past played games, had families, and made things that had personal meaning to them?" "What kinds of art have you made to remember a special time, person, or place?" "How can you use some of the ideas that have been used in these objects and images in your own art work?" "How do these art works relate to your own experience and to other works you have studied?"

# GRADE 2

# A. DANCE

## OVERALL EXPECTATIONS

By the end of Grade 2, students will:

**A1. Creating and Presenting:** apply the creative process (see pages 19–22) to the composition of simple dance phrases, using the elements of dance to communicate feelings and ideas;

**A2. Reflecting, Responding, and Analysing:** apply the critical analysis process (see pages 23–28) to communicate their feelings, ideas, and understandings in response to a variety of dance pieces and experiences;

**A3. Exploring Forms and Cultural Contexts:** demonstrate an understanding of a variety of dance forms and styles from the past and present, and their social and/or community contexts.

---

### FUNDAMENTAL CONCEPTS FOR GRADE 2

Students in Grade 2 will develop or extend understanding of the following concepts through participation in various dance experiences (e.g., exploring pathways, directions, and shapes to alter familiar activities), with particular emphasis on body and space.

ELEMENTS OF DANCE
- *body:* body awareness (e.g., awareness of where one is in space in relation to objects in class), use of body zones (e.g., the right side of the body only versus the left side only), use of body parts (e.g., arms, legs, fingertips, torso), shapes, locomotor movements (e.g., running, galloping, crawling, creeping), non-locomotor movements (e.g., jumping, turning), body bases (e.g., knees as base, back as base)
- *space:* levels (e.g., middle level, expanding movements), pathways (e.g., straight, curvy, zigzag), directions (e.g., diagonal), size of movement
- *time:* freeze, tempo (e.g., stop/start, sudden, quick, sustained), rhythm (e.g., even, uneven)
- *energy:* force, quality (e.g., exploding, bouncing, shaking, smooth, delicate)
- *relationship:* (e.g., shadowing with a partner)

---

## SPECIFIC EXPECTATIONS

### A1. Creating and Presenting

By the end of Grade 2, students will:

**A1.1** develop short movement phrases inspired by a variety of activities in their community (*e.g., riding a bike; movements from sports, yoga, or playground games/activities*) and incorporating different pathways (*e.g., straight, curvy*), directions (*e.g., forward, back, sideways, diagonal*), and shapes (*e.g., big/small shapes, shapes created individually and with partners*)

*Teacher prompts:* "What body movements do you make when you are sweeping a floor? Can we make the sweeping action smaller? Can two people come together and use both bodies to create the sweeping motion?" "Can you make the action of washing a window bigger? Can you do it while travelling (locomotor movement)? Can you do the action on a different level?" "How can we do this action travelling in a different direction?"

**A1.2** use dance as a language to represent the main ideas in poems and stories, with a focus on body and space (*e.g., use arm movements to suggest a cheering crowd; use a circle pathway to suggest the relationship among several characters; use a smooth and delicate sequence of expanding movements to suggest a butterfly emerging from a cocoon*)

*Teacher prompt:* "Using what we know about movement, stillness, levels, and pathways, how could we use dance to represent the main idea in the story we just read?"

**A1.3** create distinct beginnings and endings for dance phrases in a variety of ways (*e.g., having a moment of silence at the beginning and end of a dance phrase; freezing at the end of a dance phrase; starting and ending in similar or contrasting shapes; dimming the lights to signal the end of a dance phrase*)

*Teacher prompt:* "What could you do to signal to the audience that your dance work is finished?"

**A1.4** use a variety of locomotor and non-locomotor movements to depict creatures and objects in the world around them (*e.g., depict a large animal with torso, arms, and legs that creeps along at a low level; change movements to interpret the motions of various animals represented by the different musical sections of Camille Saint-Saëns's* Carnival of the Animals)

*Teacher prompts:* "Can you demonstrate what kind of movements a tree makes in the wind?" "What kind of non-locomotor movements can we use to create a picture of a forest environment? What levels would we use? What shapes should our bodies take to create a picture of the trees and the sun and the wind and the animals?"

## A2. Reflecting, Responding, and Analysing

By the end of Grade 2, students will:

**A2.1** describe the similarities between their own dance phrases and those of others (*e.g., similarities in the shapes, pathways, levels, and locomotor or non-locomotor movements used in one another's dance phrases*)

*Teacher prompt:* "Was there anything in the dance phrase we just saw that reminds you of movements you've done in your own dance phrase?"

**A2.2** identify, using dance vocabulary, the elements of dance in their own dance phrases and those of others, and describe how each element is used to communicate meaning (*e.g., describe how various aspects of body [shapes, body parts, locomotor and non-locomotor movements] and space [levels, direction] are used to depict crashing waves*)

*Teacher prompt:* "When we were pretending that our fingertips were the rain in the story we just read, what type of pathway did our arms make? Straight? Wavy? Zigzag? Were we moving our arms quickly or slowly? Why did we use that particular pathway and that speed? How would the rain be different if we used other pathways and a very different speed?"

**A2.3** identify and give examples of their strengths and areas for growth as dance creators and audience members (*e.g., describe to a partner what they do well; identify specific movements, stops, and turns that were effective in their dance*)

*Teacher prompts:* "What dance movements do you like to do most? Why? Show me." "What dance element do you need to practise more?" "Do you think viewing dances makes you a better dancer? Why?"

## A3. Exploring Forms and Cultural Contexts

By the end of Grade 2, students will:

**A3.1** describe, with teacher guidance, a variety of dances from communities around the world that they have seen in the media, at live performances and social gatherings, or in the classroom (*e.g., folk dances, ceremonial dances, dances of worship, theatrical dances, social dances*)

*Teacher prompt:* "When we watched the video of Irish dancing, a few students mentioned that the dancers don't use their arms when they dance. Did anyone notice anything else? Are arms used in some of the other dance forms that we saw?"

**A3.2** identify various reasons why people dance in daily life and various contexts in which they do so (*e.g., to socialize [Bangra], to dance for the earth [at powwows], to celebrate [Jewish wedding ritual], for exercise [hip hop], to tell stories [ballet], to relate history [West African dance]*)

*Teacher prompt:* "In the DVD we viewed of dances from Bali, why do you think the dancers were moving so slowly and smoothly? For whom were the dancers performing?"

# B. DRAMA

## OVERALL EXPECTATIONS

By the end of Grade 2, students will:

**B1. Creating and Presenting:** apply the creative process (see pages 19–22) to dramatic play and process drama, using the elements and conventions of drama to communicate feelings, ideas, and stories;

**B2. Reflecting, Responding, and Analysing:** apply the critical analysis process (see pages 23–28) to communicate feelings, ideas, and understandings in response to a variety of drama works and experiences;

**B3. Exploring Forms and Cultural Contexts:** demonstrate an understanding of a variety of drama and theatre forms and styles from the past and present, and their social and/or community contexts.

---

### FUNDAMENTAL CONCEPTS FOR GRADE 2

Students in Grade 2 will develop or extend understanding of the following concepts through participation in various drama experiences.

ELEMENTS OF DRAMA

- *role/character:* adopting the attitude/point of view of a fictional character (e.g., in dialogue and writing in role); using body language (e.g., posture, gestures, facial expression), costumes, and props appropriate to a character; varying vocal levels, tones, and ranges to support the depiction of a character

- *relationship:* listening and responding in role to other characters in role

- *time and place:* establishing a fictional setting and relating to it in role

- *tension:* being aware of a sense of mystery or a problem to be solved

- *focus and emphasis:* identifying the main idea or central theme of the drama

---

## SPECIFIC EXPECTATIONS

### B1. Creating and Presenting

By the end of Grade 2, students will:

**B1.1** engage in dramatic play and role play, with a focus on exploring main ideas and central characters in stories from diverse communities, times, and places (*e.g., retell and enact a story from different points of view; stop at a dramatic point in a story and adopt roles of the characters in the story; enact a scene between characters in a fairy-tale kingdom, animals in the tundra, or neighbours in a back alley*)

*Teacher prompts:* "How might this story change if we told it from a different character's point of view?" "What is a key moment in this story that you can dramatize? How will you use a freeze, bring it to life for one minute through mime, and then another freeze to communicate the main idea to your audience?"

**B1.2** demonstrate an understanding of the element of role by communicating thoughts, feelings, and perspectives appropriate to the role being played (*e.g., devise and share a group mime showing how characters respond to the tension in a situation of conflict, departure, or anticipation; use voice expressively to convey an interpretation of a character's attitude*)

*Teacher prompts:* "In what ways can you use your body and face (i.e., in a mime) to express how a character feels without using words?" "How would you change your gestures and movement if you were portraying wind or water as a character from the story?" "What words and tone can you use in role that will clearly communicate this character's point of view?"

**B1.3** plan and shape the direction of a dramatic play or role play, building on their own and others' ideas both in and out of role, with support (*e.g., In role: respond to a scientist [role-played by the teacher] who says the class must give up their pet dinosaur because it poses a safety hazard; Out of role: use conventions such as discussion and/or guided imagery to establish the setting, context, and characters for a drama activity*)

*Teacher prompts: In role:* "Because you are all experts, I need you to help me solve this problem. Who can make a suggestion?" *Out of role:* "How shall we use the new information that was introduced when we were in role to determine what should happen next in the drama?"

**B1.4** communicate feelings and ideas to a familiar audience (*e.g., classmates*), using several simple visual or technological aids to support and enhance their drama work (*e.g., act out a familiar story using props instead of words; dim lights to create a spooky mood; use simple objects or props such as fur or feathers to indicate animal or bird characters in an Aboriginal story*)

*Teacher prompts:* "How can you use light and found objects to create different effects? For example, how could you use a soundscape and a flashlight to create a spooky mood?" "How can we use costumes or props to make the meaning of our play clearer?" "What objects can you use to help the audience understand that the main character is going on a journey?"

## B2. Reflecting, Responding, and Analysing

By the end of Grade 2, students will:

**B2.1** express thoughts, feelings, and ideas about drama experiences and performances in a variety of ways (*e.g., use a journal response, a think-pair-share activity, visual art work, or a drama convention such as role on the wall to explore both the inner thoughts and feelings of the character and the perspectives of others who know the character*)

*Teacher prompt:* "What part of the play stood out for you and why? What did the events or characters in the play remind you of?"

**B2.2** identify, using drama terminology, the elements and conventions of drama used in shared drama experiences and theatre and describe how they help communicate ideas and feelings and create interest (*e.g., as a class create a checklist of the elements in a drama and what each element*

contributes and helps communicate; use a tableau to share a moment of importance in the story*)

*Teacher prompts:* "How were the elements of drama used in this presentation?" "How could you tell where the play was taking place?" "Who was the main character? How could you tell?" "In what ways did your role and other roles in the drama work together to help make the message clearer?"

**B2.3** identify and give examples of their strengths, interests, and areas for improvement as drama participants and audience members (*e.g., identify the goals they had in presenting a drama work and communicate how they achieved those goals; generate multiple ideas for improvement in a mapping activity or experiential play experience*)

*Teacher prompts:* "Using two stars and a wish, state two drama skills you are proud of and one thing you want to get better at." "What specific aspects (e.g., voice, gestures) of your work were effective in the drama?"

## B3. Exploring Forms and Cultural Contexts

By the end of Grade 2, students will:

**B3.1** identify and describe a variety of drama and theatre forms they experience in their home, school, and community, and in the media (*e.g., favourite television, film, computer programs; favourite play roles; playing with puppets to enact real-life scenarios; attending plays; listening to stories about family and community traditions*)

*Teacher prompts:* "Why do you think people go to movies and see plays?" "What is your favourite TV program?" "How is TV similar to and different from plays?"

**B3.2** demonstrate an awareness of some drama and theatre traditions of communities around the world (*e.g., describe experiences with festivals, pageants, circuses; explain the use of special objects in ceremonies or celebrations; give examples of the use of a narrator in plays or street theatre*)

*Teacher prompts:* "What are some drama activities that happen in our school? In our community?" "What are some elements of drama that are used in special ceremonies and celebrations in other parts of the world (e.g., Caribbean Carnival, Chinese New Year)?"

# C. MUSIC

## OVERALL EXPECTATIONS

By the end of Grade 2, students will:

**C1. Creating and Performing:** apply the creative process (see pages 19–22) to create and perform music for a variety of purposes, using the elements and techniques of music;

**C2. Reflecting, Responding, and Analysing:** apply the critical analysis process (see pages 23–28) to communicate their feelings, ideas, and understandings in response to a variety of music and musical experiences;

**C3. Exploring Forms and Cultural Contexts:** demonstrate an understanding of a variety of musical genres and styles from the past and present, and their social and/or community contexts.

---

### FUNDAMENTAL CONCEPTS FOR GRADE 2

In Grade 2, students will build on their knowledge of the elements of music and related musical concepts that were introduced in Grade 1. Students will develop understanding of musical concepts through participation in various musical experiences (e.g., listening, singing, moving, playing with musical instruments and manipulatives). These experiences will include reading simple rhythmic notation and interpreting simple visual representations (e.g., long and short lines, contour patterns on a one-line staff or a two-line staff, various icon symbols such as pictures or invented symbols).

#### ELEMENTS OF MUSIC

- *duration:* half note (oral prompt: "ta ah"), half rest, whole note (oral prompt: "ta-ah-ah-ah"), whole rest
- *pitch:* high "do", simple melodic ostinato, melodic patterns, melodic patterns using notes of a pentatonic scale (e.g., "do–re–mi–so–la", "do–re–fa–so–la")
- *dynamics and other expressive controls:* gradations in volume encountered in music listened to, sung, and played (e.g., getting louder [*crescendo*], getting softer [*decrescendo/diminuendo*]); articulation (e.g., smooth [*legato*], detached [*staccato*])
- *timbre:* classification of instruments by listening to their sound (e.g., wind [woodwind, brass], stringed, electronic, membrane, pitched percussion instruments)
- *texture/harmony:* single melodic line in unison song with simple accompaniment (homophony), bordun patterns on "do" and "so"
- *form:* phrase, binary (AB) form, simple verse and chorus

---

## SPECIFIC EXPECTATIONS

### C1. Creating and Performing

By the end of Grade 2, students will:

**C1.1** sing unison songs in tune and/or play simple melodies and accompaniments for music from a wide variety of cultures, styles, and historical periods (*e.g., perform a simple three-note melodic ostinato to support a melody*)

*Teacher prompt:* "Which instruments or found sounds could we use to accompany this song?"

**C1.2** apply the elements of music when singing, playing an instrument, and moving (*e.g., pitch: move the body to show how individual pitches go up, go down, or stay the same, and how they connect to form a melody*)

*Teacher prompts:* "What instrument would you use to accompany this song and why?" "How can you move your body while you sing to show the different phrases of this song?"

**C1.3** create simple compositions for a specific purpose and a familiar audience (*e.g., create accompaniments for songs, stories, or poems; create a simple song using the notes "mi", "so", and "la", or the notes of a pentatonic scale*)

*Teacher prompt:* "What words in our shared reading poem could we use to create a rhythmic ostinato to accompany us as we do our choral reading?"

**C1.4** use the tools and techniques of musicianship in musical performances (*e.g., use controlled breathing and relaxed but straight posture when singing; show awareness of proper playing technique when playing instruments; match pitches within an accessible vocal range; clap back rhythms accurately while keeping a steady beat*)

*Teacher prompt:* "What are the things we can all do to help us sing in tune and all together?"

**C1.5** use symbols to represent sounds and sounds to represent musical symbols (*e.g., match short melody maps with the corresponding phrases in a song; use rhythm syllables such as "ta ti-ti" to represent note values orally*)

*Teacher prompt:* "Perform the melodic pattern we just sang with hand signs. What other ways can we represent the melody?"

## C2. Reflecting, Responding, and Analysing

By the end of Grade 2, students will:

**C2.1** express personal responses to musical performances in a variety of ways (*e.g., use a teacher-directed listening log to record their thoughts, feelings, ideas; write or draw their response*)

*Teacher prompts:* "Draw a facial expression (happy, sad, surprised) on the chart to represent how the music makes you feel." "Which animal would you choose to represent music that is loud – a lion or a kitten? Why?" "How can the lyrics help you understand the meaning of this song? Describe in your own words the meaning of the song."

**C2.2** describe ways in which the elements of music are used for different purposes in the music they perform, listen to, and create (*e.g., duration: an increase in tempo to indicate excitement; dynamics: a decrease in volume to*

*create a feeling of relaxation in the music; timbre: the sound quality of a particular instrument to create a particular mood*)

*Teacher prompts:* "Raise your hand when you hear the music get faster. How does it make you feel?" "How do different versions of 'O Canada' make you feel? Why?" "Why do you think 'Twinkle, Twinkle, Little Star' should be sung softly?"

**C2.3** identify and give examples of their strengths and areas for growth as musical performers, creators, interpreters, and audience members (*e.g., share with a partner what they did well during the last performance, using musical vocabulary*)

*Teacher prompts:* "If you were to have a chance to perform this song again, what would you change and why?" "What parts of the song do you find challenging or interesting to sing? Why?"

## C3. Exploring Forms and Cultural Contexts

By the end of Grade 2, students will:

**C3.1** identify reasons why people make music in their daily lives (*e.g., people sing songs that have special meaning in their family; children can use music to promote environmental awareness at school*), and describe contexts in which they make music (*e.g., family gatherings, seasonal celebrations*)

*Teacher prompt:* "What songs do you and your family sing at special occasions in your life?"

**C3.2** identify, through performing and/or listening, a variety of musical forms or pieces from different communities, times, and places (*e.g., "O Canada", an Iroquoian lullaby, Indian classical music, Obwisana from Ghana*)

*Teacher prompts:* "Which children's film uses this traditional/classical music theme?" "What songs have we learned that originally came from France?"

# D. VISUAL ARTS

## OVERALL EXPECTATIONS

By the end of Grade 2, students will:

**D1. Creating and Presenting:** apply the creative process (see pages 19–22) to produce a variety of two- and three-dimensional art works, using elements, principles, and techniques of visual arts to communicate feelings, ideas, and understandings;

**D2. Reflecting, Responding, and Analysing:** apply the critical analysis process (see pages 23–28) to communicate feelings, ideas, and understandings in response to a variety of art works and art experiences;

**D3. Exploring Forms and Cultural Contexts:** demonstrate an understanding of a variety of art forms, styles, and techniques from the past and present, and their social and/or community contexts.

---

### FUNDAMENTAL CONCEPTS FOR GRADE 2

In addition to the concepts introduced in Grade 1, students will develop understanding of the following concepts through participation in a variety of hands-on, open-ended visual arts experiences.

#### ELEMENTS OF DESIGN
Students will develop understanding of all elements of design.

- *line:* horizontal, vertical, diagonal lines; lines that show motion (e.g., pointy, curvy); lines inside shapes
- *shape and form:* symmetrical shapes and forms (e.g., shapes and forms in buildings)
- *space:* overlapping of objects to show depth
- *colour:* secondary colours (various colours made by mixing equal amounts of primary colours, such as violet, orange, green); mixing of colours with a limited palette
- *texture:* textures of familiar objects (e.g., rough tree bark, smooth plastic plate, ridged corduroy fabric); illusion of texture (e.g., a rough texture created by patterns of lines); impasto (thick, textured paint)
- *value:* mixing of a tint; identification of light and dark

#### PRINCIPLES OF DESIGN
Students will develop understanding of all principles of design (that is, contrast, repetition and rhythm, variety, emphasis, proportion, balance, unity and harmony, and movement), but the focus in Grade 2 will be on repetition and rhythm.

- *repetition and rhythm:* repetition of colour and shape in patterns; random, alternating, and regular patterns in everyday objects (e.g., textiles, ceramics) and in art (e.g., works by M. C. Escher)

# SPECIFIC EXPECTATIONS

## D1. Creating and Presenting

By the end of Grade 2, students will:

**D1.1** create two- and three-dimensional works of art that express feelings and ideas inspired by activities in their community or observations of nature (*e.g., a streetscape collage with children playing, made with paint, pastel, and various kinds of paper [newspaper, magazines]; small glue-line prints in which a variety of curvy and pointy lines show illusory texture or represent a pattern they have seen on insects in the schoolyard or garden*)

*Teacher prompts:* "Let's look at how collage is used to show aspects of community in *Snowballs* by Lois Ehlert, *The Snowy Day* by Ezra Keats, or *The Block* by Romare Bearden. What kinds of details can you see? What materials in these images might you like to use in your neighbourhood collage?" "How can you use a variety of diagonal, vertical, and horizontal lines to show the patterns and body parts on the insect?"

**D1.2** demonstrate an understanding of composition, using principles of design to create narrative art works or art works on a theme or topic (*e.g., use repetition of colour throughout an image that communicates a story; create a painting or series of stamp prints, showing depth, perspective, and contrast of pattern by overlapping fish and vegetation of different sizes and shapes*)

*Teacher prompt:* "When you overlap these shapes, which one looks farthest away? How can you arrange and place shapes of different sizes throughout your pattern to make a more varied image?"

**D1.3** use elements of design in art works to communicate ideas, messages, and understandings (*e.g., use tints of a colour to create light areas for emphasis in a collaborative mural of favourite places in the neighbourhood; use a simple action pose to modify form in a sculpture of a pet or other animal made with modelling clay*)

*Teacher prompts:* "How can you use colour and arrangement in the images and pictures in the mural to emphasize the most important personal landmarks along the way to school?" "If you want to make this painting 'feel' like a hot summer day, what kinds of colours would you need to repeat?" "How could you use squeezing, pinching, and pulling techniques to make the legs and head of the sculpture of the pet look as if they were moving?"

**D1.4** use a variety of materials, tools, and techniques to respond to design challenges (*e.g.,*

- drawing: *make marker or coloured-pencil drawings of trees that are close and far away, using contrasts in size and placement on the paper to show depth of space, and basing the drawings on observations of real trees and trees in a variety of art works [e.g., works by Emily Carr or Tom Thomson]*

- mixed media: *use acrylic paint over textured materials [e.g., burlap, cardboard] to make expressive organic shapes, using a combination of traditional techniques [blending, glazing, sgraffito, scumbling, impasto] and experimental techniques [use of sponges, fingers, sticks, twigs, feathers, masking tape]*

- painting: *make a tempera painting depicting friends playing playground games, using a limited palette of colours*

- printmaking: *make a print of a motif for a storybook about dinosaurs, using polystyrene plate stamps or modelling-clay imprints of dinosaurs and plants*

- sculpture: *make insect shapes and habitat features, using wood, twigs, raffia, corn husks, and other natural materials, to explore science concepts*)

*Teacher prompts:* "What materials could you use for building your bugs? How could you hold the parts together?" "How will the mood of the print change if you print it on different kinds of paper (bond, construction, giftwrap) or colours of paper (warm, cool)?"

## D2. Reflecting, Responding, and Analysing

By the end of Grade 2, students will:

**D2.1** express their feelings and ideas about works of art (*e.g., explain why they prefer a work by one artist over another; explain to a partner how well an art work reflects their personal knowledge and prior experience*)

*Teacher prompts:* "When you look at the painting by Lawren Harris, what personal experiences does it remind you of?" "If the people in the painting could talk, what would they say?" "How is this artist's representation of winter different from (or the same as) your own experience of winter?"

**D2.2** explain how elements and principles of design are used to communicate meaning or understanding in their own and others' art work *(e.g., use of different colours for achieving different effects, such as warm, sunny colours for a beach or cool colours for a wet forest; depiction of various textures, such as rough tree bark, smooth plastics, and ridged corduroy; elaboration and variation to create variety in otherwise symmetrical buildings)*

*Teacher prompts:* "How has the artist used elements of design to express anger, happiness, sadness, or excitement?" "What catches your attention in this painting?" "What do you think is the most important thing in this work? How did the artist use the elements to make you see what is most important to him or her?" "How can you tell if what's in this picture is close or far away?" "How do you feel about this painting? What has the artist done to make you feel this way?"

**D2.3** demonstrate an awareness of signs and symbols encountered in their daily lives and in works of art *(e.g., symbols and shapes related to school, travel, and the arts; sports or institutional logos; symbols from art works or heritage crafts of family or community significance)*

*Teacher prompts:* "What symbols have you seen that are connected to dance, drama, music, or visual arts?" "Let's look at these sports posters. What familiar symbols did the designers use? Why would these particular symbols have attracted your attention or gotten their ideas across?"

**D2.4** identify and document their strengths, their interests, and areas for improvement as creators of art *(e.g., identify what is interesting about a work they have produced; identify what they feel they have done well and what they would do differently next time to improve)*

*Teacher prompts:* "Look at your art work and consider it using a 'one star/one wish' approach: write down one thing you did well as an artist and draw a star beside it and one thing you could have improved on and put the word 'wish' beside it." "Why do some of your art works appeal to you more than others?" "How do you plan an art work? What do you need to think about before you start working on it?"

## D3. Exploring Forms and Cultural Contexts

By the end of Grade 2, students will:

**D3.1** identify and describe a variety of visual art forms they see in their home, at school, in their community, and in visual arts experiences *(e.g., design of everyday items; picture books; artists-in-education; community art works, such as public sculpture, architecture, and murals; Aboriginal designs in dancing regalia; art works in student art exhibitions and community art festivals)*

*Teacher prompts:* "What has the designer done to plan a playground that children will enjoy? Why might someone want to play here?" "Where in our community have you seen works of art? What do they look like? What are they made of? What do they add to our community?" "If you could make a public art work, what would you make and where would you place it?"

**D3.2** demonstrate an awareness of a variety of works of art and artistic traditions from diverse communities, times, and places *(e.g., depictions of nature, of people doing things together, or of people at work; miniature paintings from India; Aboriginal textiles, ceramics, and petroglyphs; contemporary Inuit drawings of life in the North by Annie Pootoogook)*

*Teacher prompts:* "How can you tell if a picture shows a celebration or a quiet moment?" "Which painting reminds you of your life?" "Why do artists paint pictures of people at work or at play?" "What are some special traditions in your family, community, or school? How is art part of these traditions?"

# GRADE 3

# A. DANCE

## OVERALL EXPECTATIONS

By the end of Grade 3, students will:

**A1. Creating and Presenting:** apply the creative process (see pages 19–22) to the composition of dance phrases, using the elements of dance to communicate feelings and ideas;

**A2. Reflecting, Responding, and Analysing:** apply the critical analysis process (see pages 23–28) to communicate their feelings, ideas, and understandings in response to a variety of dance pieces and experiences;

**A3. Exploring Forms and Cultural Contexts:** demonstrate an understanding of a variety of dance forms and styles from the past and present, and their social and/or community contexts.

---

### FUNDAMENTAL CONCEPTS FOR GRADE 3

Students in Grade 3 will develop or extend understanding of the following concepts through participation in various dance experiences (e.g., exploring movement and pattern forms), with particular emphasis on time and energy.

ELEMENTS OF DANCE

- *body:* body actions, body shapes, locomotor movements (e.g., running, galloping, crawling), non-locomotor movements (e.g., lifting, pulling, marching, waving arms), body bases (e.g., seat as base), use of body zones (e.g., body areas of front and back)
- *space:* levels, pathways, directions, size of movement
- *time:* freeze, tempo (e.g., slow, sustained, fast)
- *energy:* force (e.g., lightness/strength), effort (e.g., pressing, gliding), quality (e.g., smoothly, cautiously, erratically, percussively)
- *relationship:* (e.g., interconnected shapes)

---

## SPECIFIC EXPECTATIONS

### A1. Creating and Presenting

By the end of Grade 3, students will:

**A1.1** imitate movements found in their natural environment in a variety of ways and incorporate them into a dance phrase (*e.g., modify the movements of animals, snow falling to the ground, ice melting, plants growing; connect a series of insect-like movements together to make a phrase*)

*Teacher prompt:* "How would the quality of your movements change if you were first moving like a bee and then moving like a butterfly [erratic, gliding]? Would your movements change to sharp and sudden, or smooth and slow? Would your path be direct and gliding or indirect and meandering?"

**A1.2** use dance as a language to represent ideas from diverse literature sources, with a focus on time and energy (*e.g., interpret stories, poems, and texts from other subject areas through dance; respond to a story about insects by depicting the sustained lifting and pulling actions of ants versus the sustained floating actions of butterflies*)

*Teacher prompts:* "When creating a dance phrase to represent the idea of this poem, consider the poem's punctuation. How would you express the dance equivalent of an exclamation mark for emphasis in the dance?" "Which combination of elements will you choose from the time and energy chart to portray the rest of the insect characters in the story?"

**A1.3** create dance phrases using a variety of pattern forms (*e.g., create dances with distinct, self-contained sections that share movement qualities using AB form, ABA form, or ABBA form; demonstrate a pattern physically by making "A" a soft and fluid section and "B" a fast and percussive section*)

*Teacher prompt:* "How would you show the water cycle using a pattern in dance? Which pattern form can you use to convey your idea?"

**A1.4** demonstrate how dance elements can be used to create and expand the movement vocabulary within different sections of a larger pattern (*e.g., A: varying the use of space while marching quickly; B: changing levels while waving arms slowly; A: varying locomotor and non-locomotor percussive movements while marching quickly*)

*Teacher prompt:* "In an ABA form, how can you vary your gestures and movements to make the A section distinctly different from the B section?"

## A2. Reflecting, Responding, and Analysing

By the end of Grade 3, students will:

**A2.1** demonstrate an understanding of how the elements of dance can be used in their own and others' dance phrases to illustrate or explore learning in other subject areas (*e.g., show and explain how the elements of body and relationship can be used to depict the science concept of magnetic attraction*)

*Teacher prompts:* "Kofie's choice to start his dance in a small shape was meant to show he was a seed. How did that information help us predict his ending shape?" "What similarities/differences can you see between the patterns we used in our dance and the patterns we used in math?"

**A2.2** identify, using dance vocabulary, the elements of dance used in their own and others' dance phrases and explain their purpose (*e.g., the use of body, space, time, and energy to create variety and interest; the use of levels, relationship, pathways, and shape to emphasize a mood; the use of canon, direction, grouping contrast, and repetition to explore pattern*)

*Teacher prompts:* "Which two patterns did we use? Why did we use different patterns?" "How did Antonio's actions help us know how he was feeling?"

**A2.3** identify and give examples of their strengths and areas for growth as dance creators and audience members (*e.g., share with a partner what they did well; write in a journal about what they need to improve*)

*Teacher prompt:* "What did you do well, or what would you change next time about your dance (or your use of the creative process)?"

## A3. Exploring Forms and Cultural Contexts

By the end of Grade 3, students will:

**A3.1** describe, with teacher guidance, a variety of dances from communities in Canada and around the world that they have seen in the media, at live performances and social gatherings, or in the classroom (*e.g., dance numbers in animated movie musicals such as* Happy Feet *and* Ice Age; *First Nation dances at a powwow; folk dances of the early settlers; the farandole of France*)

*Teacher prompts:* "When you viewed the sailor's hornpipe, did you see interesting dance movements or patterns that you would like to include in your own dance pieces? Can you describe or demonstrate some of them?" "Can you describe some of the ways in which STOMP uses garbage can lids, brooms, basketballs, and ladders as dance props?" "Can you describe how the dance you experienced with the visiting artist is similar to dance work we have done in class?"

**A3.2** identify and describe the role of dance in the community (*e.g., performances as entertainment; community dances as a way of socializing; traditional dances as a way of maintaining cultural connectedness; dance classes for learning and communicating*)

*Teacher prompt:* "Why do people in the community dance, even though they are not professionals?"

# B. DRAMA

## OVERALL EXPECTATIONS

By the end of Grade 3, students will:

**B1. Creating and Presenting:** apply the creative process (see pages 19–22) to dramatic play and process drama, using the elements and conventions of drama to communicate feelings, ideas, and stories;

**B2. Reflecting, Responding, and Analysing:** apply the critical analysis process (see pages 23–28) to communicate feelings, ideas, and understandings in response to a variety of drama works and experiences;

**B3. Exploring Forms and Cultural Contexts:** demonstrate an understanding of a variety of drama and theatre forms and styles from the past and present, and their social and/or community contexts.

---

### FUNDAMENTAL CONCEPTS FOR GRADE 3

Students in Grade 3 will develop or extend understanding of the following concepts through participation in various drama experiences.

ELEMENTS OF DRAMA

- *role/character:* adopting the attitude/point of view of a number of different fictional characters, dialogue
- *relationship:* listening and responding in role to other characters in role
- *time and place:* establishing a clear setting
- *tension:* identifying factors that contribute to mystery or tension in a drama
- *focus and emphasis:* identifying the central theme and/or problem in a drama

---

## SPECIFIC EXPECTATIONS

### B1. Creating and Presenting

By the end of Grade 3, students will:

**B1.1** engage in dramatic play and role play, with a focus on exploring themes, ideas, characters, and issues from imagination or in stories from diverse communities, times, and places (*e.g., act out moments from "a day in the life" of a main character from a story; improvise a short dialogue between two characters who are seeking a solution to a problem [as in Aboriginal teacher/trickster stories]*)

*Teacher prompts:* "What if you are the cook? What will you do?" "Which characters should try to solve the problem in this drama?" "What role will you adopt and what will you do to solve the problem in this drama?" "How will you make the audience believe you are the character in the story while in role?"

**B1.2** demonstrate an understanding of how the element of time and place can support the development of role (*e.g., present tableaux, with transitions and thought tracking, that show differences between urban and rural settings and/or lifestyles to convey information about the characters*)

*Teacher prompt:* "Make a clear picture of the setting I've described in your imagination. As we explore this imaginary place, using all of our senses and some simple actions, how can you show me what you are seeing, smelling, hearing, feeling, or doing?"

**B1.3** plan and shape the direction of a dramatic play or role play by building on their own and others' ideas, both in and out of role (*e.g.,* In role: *respond in role to extend the developing storyline in the drama [as townsfolk, plead with the mayor to save their town];* Out of role: *in partners or small groups, combine their ideas to create a plan for how the characters will solve the problem in the drama*)

*Teacher prompts: In role:* "How will we proceed? What are some possible courses of action?" *Out of role:* "What key questions should we ask (e.g., where? when? how?) to gain more information for when we go back into role?"

**B1.4** communicate feelings and ideas to a familiar audience *(e.g., classmates)* using audio, visual, and/or technological aids to support or enhance their drama work *(e.g., use items found in the classroom to create a feeling or a mood suggested by the teacher; use sound effects or music to create an element of surprise or tension)*

*Teacher prompt:* "What music can help to create an energetic mood for this drama? At what point in the drama will you change the music to create a different mood?"

## B2. Reflecting, Responding, and Analysing

By the end of Grade 3, students will:

**B2.1** express thoughts, feelings, and ideas about a variety of drama experiences and performances *(e.g., in a journal response, in a think-pair-share activity, in class discussion, by writing in role, in a four corners activity, in a small group improvisation or drawing)*

*Teacher prompts:* "Compared to all of the drama experiences we have had, in what ways was this experience unique?" "Describe a moment in the drama where you learned something new about the story or your role." "Which character's situation did you empathize with?"

**B2.2** describe, using drama terminology, how elements and conventions of drama are used to shape their own and others' work *(e.g., describe how different characters' actions help create suspense or tension; identify effective elements in a drama presentation; explain how setting highlights theme)*

*Teacher prompts:* "Describe a moment that stood out for you. What drama elements were involved?" "How did the setting help to tell the story of this scene?" "How did the actors communicate to the audience that they were friends (or not friends)?" "Were there any parts that were confusing? How could the meaning have been made clearer?"

**B2.3** identify and give examples of their strengths, interests, and areas for growth as drama participants and audience members *(e.g., describe how their understanding of role play is developing; identify a role they would like to play, and explain why)*

*Teacher prompt:* "Complete the following sentences: 'Two suggestions I made in role that helped build the drama were . . .'; 'Two suggestions I made out of role that helped build the drama were . . .'; 'One way I was being a supportive audience member was . . .'"

## B3. Exploring Forms and Cultural Contexts

By the end of Grade 3, students will:

**B3.1** identify some distinct stylistic features of a few drama and theatre forms they experience in their home, school, and community, and in the media *(e.g., puppet shows and mask plays use easily recognizable character types to tell a story; actors in live theatre productions use exaggerated gestures and reactions designed to project beyond the footlights; street festivals use amplified live and/or recorded music, costumes, emcees, and amplified announcements to celebrate special events; clown acts use mime featuring clumsy gestures and comical accidents)*

*Teacher prompts:* "In what ways are puppet shows and plays with actors similar and in what ways are they different?" "What does a clown do to be funny? Why are there different kinds of clowns?"

**B3.2** demonstrate an awareness of ideas and emotions expressed in drama works from communities around the world *(e.g., ideas about friendship or loyalty or power or perseverance in dramas based on fairy tales or myths from different countries; ethics and values found in Aboriginal plays)*

*Teacher prompts:* "Can you remember a character from another play who had the same problem or felt the same way as this character? How would you compare these two characters?" "Can you think of other plays, stories, TV shows, or movies with the same theme?"

# C. MUSIC

## OVERALL EXPECTATIONS

By the end of Grade 3, students will:

**C1. Creating and Performing:** apply the creative process (see pages 19–22) to create and perform music for a variety of purposes, using the elements and techniques of music;

**C2. Reflecting, Responding, and Analysing:** apply the critical analysis process (see pages 23–28) to communicate their feelings, ideas, and understandings in response to a variety of music and musical experiences;

**C3. Exploring Forms and Cultural Contexts:** demonstrate an understanding of a variety of musical genres and styles from the past and present, and their social and/or community contexts.

---

### FUNDAMENTAL CONCEPTS FOR GRADE 3

In Grade 3, students will build on their knowledge of the elements of music and related musical concepts that were introduced in Grades 1 and 2. Students will develop understanding of musical concepts through participation in various musical experiences (e.g., listening, singing, moving, simple instrumental playing, playing with musical manipulatives). They will also continue to use non-traditional forms of notation (e.g., simple rhythmic notation symbols, simple visual prompts).

ELEMENTS OF MUSIC

- *duration:* three beats per bar ($\frac{3}{4}$ metre), dotted half note, sixteenth-note patterns, sixteenth rest; very fast (*presto*), very slow (*largo*)

- *pitch:* low "so", low "la", higher and lower pitch, pitch contour

- *dynamics and other expressive controls:* standard symbols for soft (e.g., *piano – p*) and loud (e.g., *forte – f*); invented symbols for soft and loud; articulation and expression marks encountered in music listened to, sung, and played (e.g., *staccato*, *legato*, signs for *crescendo* and *decrescendo*)

- *timbre:* classification of instruments by means of sound production (e.g., sounds produced by strumming, striking, shaking, blowing)

- *texture/harmony:* simple two-part rounds, partner songs, canons

- *form:* section, ternary (ABA) form

---

## SPECIFIC EXPECTATIONS

### C1. Creating and Performing

By the end of Grade 3, students will:

**C1.1** sing, in tune, unison songs, partner songs, and rounds, and/or play accompaniments from a wide variety of cultures, styles, and historical periods (*e.g., sing or play an instrument accompanied by body percussion or found sounds; sing or play a rhythmic or melodic ostinato*)

*Teacher prompts:* "Which pitched or non-pitched percussion instrument could you use to accompany this song?" "This song is a round. At what point would the second group begin?"

**C1.2** apply the elements of music when singing, playing an instrument, and moving (*e.g., timbre: sort sound sources by the way their sound is produced and make choices about which instruments will play in specific sections; form: change direction in a circle to show A and B sections of a song in ABA form; duration: sing a song first very quickly then very slowly, and explain how the different tempi change their experience of the music*)

*Teacher prompts:* "How many different ways can you sort these instruments on the basis of how they are played or what sounds they make?" "Which instrument can you use to try to play this melody?"

**C1.3** create compositions for a specific purpose and a familiar audience (*e.g., create musical accompaniments for poems, stories, or dances they have created; create rhythmic ostinati based on significant words in a poem or words from a classroom topic or theme, then play them using instruments, body percussion, or found sounds; make changes to the rhythm and/or melody in a simple song that they know*)

*Teacher prompt:* "What kind of music should we create to introduce each character in our story?"

**C1.4** use the tools and techniques of musicianship in musical performances (*e.g., determine where breaths should be taken in a song; given the shape of a melody, suggest where a change in dynamics would be effective; use available technology such as software, electronic instruments, or recording devices*)

*Teacher prompts:* "What could we do to help the audience hear our words more clearly?" "How can we sing softly and stay in tune?"

**C1.5** demonstrate an understanding of standard and non-traditional musical notation (*e.g., design melody maps based on the direction of the melody; demonstrate various ways of representing sounds using devised symbols; perform melodic patterns based on the notes "do", "re", "mi", "so", and "la" by using solfège hand signs; create soundscapes illustrating dynamics and timbre*)

*Teacher prompts:* "Using your hand, how could you map the melody of this song in the air?" "How could we show others from another class how to sing 'Twinkle, Twinkle, Little Star' without singing it to them?"

## C2. Reflecting, Responding, and Analysing

By the end of Grade 3, students will:

**C2.1** express personal responses to musical performances in a variety of ways (*e.g., create a graphic or text response to a musical selection featuring a Latin American dance style*)

*Teacher prompts:* "What does this song remind you of?" "How can you use stick notation to write down the rhythm that I clap?"

**C2.2** describe ways in which the elements of music are used in the music they perform, listen to, and create (*e.g., use a Venn diagram to compare how the elements of two contrasting pieces create mood*)

*Teacher prompt:* "How do these two songs use dynamics differently to create uniquely expressive pieces? In what other ways do these two songs differ?"

**C2.3** identify and give examples of their strengths and areas for growth as musical performers, creators, interpreters, and audience members (*e.g., singing in tune, breathing at the end of phrases, watching the conductor or teacher while rehearsing and performing*)

*Teacher prompts:* "How has your interpretation of this song changed since we first heard it in class?" "What are some skills that are important for your musical development?"

## C3. Exploring Forms and Cultural Contexts

By the end of Grade 3, students will:

**C3.1** identify and describe ways in which music can be used in the community (*e.g., to celebrate events, to bring people together, to dance to, to communicate, to entertain, to help people remember product names or telephone numbers in advertising, to help people remember concepts*)

*Teacher prompts:* "When you see a parade, what types of music do you hear? Why is music part of every parade?" "How have songs or chants helped you remember things?" "Are there songs you like to sing only at home with your family?"

**C3.2** identify, through performing and/or listening, a variety of musical forms or pieces from different communities, times, and places (*e.g., songs, instrumental pieces, and dances in social activities or celebrations of early settlers and First Nation communities in Upper Canada*)

*Teacher prompts:* "For what purposes were fiddles used in early settlers' social occasions?" "For what purposes were drums used by First Nation peoples? What is the cultural meaning of the sound of the rattle?"

# D. VISUAL ARTS

## OVERALL EXPECTATIONS

By the end of Grade 3, students will:

**D1. Creating and Presenting:** apply the creative process (see pages 19–22) to produce a variety of two- and three-dimensional art works, using elements, principles, and techniques of visual arts to communicate feelings, ideas, and understandings;

**D2. Reflecting, Responding, and Analysing:** apply the critical analysis process (see pages 23–28) to communicate feelings, ideas, and understandings in response to a variety of art works and art experiences;

**D3. Exploring Forms and Cultural Contexts:** demonstrate an understanding of a variety of art forms, styles, and techniques from the past and present, and their social and/or community contexts.

---

### FUNDAMENTAL CONCEPTS FOR GRADE 3

In addition to the concepts introduced in Grades 1 and 2, students will develop understanding of the following concepts through participation in a variety of hands-on, open-ended visual arts experiences.

ELEMENTS OF DESIGN
Students will develop understanding of all elements of design.

- *line:* variety of line (e.g., thick, thin, dotted)
- *shape and form:* composite shapes; symmetrical and asymmetrical shapes and forms in both the human-made environment and the natural world (e.g., symmetrical: insects, flowers, skyscrapers; asymmetrical: windblown trees, some contemporary additions to buildings [asymmetrical façade in Daniel Libeskind's design for the Royal Ontario Museum])
- *space:* foreground, middle ground, and background to give illusion of depth
- *colour:* colour for expression (e.g., warm and cool colours); colour to indicate emotion; mixing of colours with white to make a range of warm and cool tints
- *texture:* real versus visual or illusory texture (e.g., smooth surface of a ceramic work versus drawing of rough tree bark); etching by scratching through surfaces (e.g., crayon etching on a scratchboard)
- *value:* mixing a range of light colours and dark colours

PRINCIPLES OF DESIGN
Students will develop understanding of all principles of design (that is, contrast, repetition and rhythm, variety, emphasis, proportion, balance, unity and harmony, and movement), but the focus in Grade 3 will be on variety.

- *variety:* slight variations on a major theme; strong contrasts (e.g., use of different lines, shapes, values, and colours to create interest [bright or light colour values, dark colour values])

## SPECIFIC EXPECTATIONS

### D1. Creating and Presenting

By the end of Grade 3, students will:

**D1.1** create two- and three-dimensional works of art that express personal feelings and ideas inspired by the environment or that have the community as their subject (*e.g., make a symmetrical sculpture of an insect or a flower, using natural materials such as wood, pebbles, dry seed pods, feathers; draw a picture depicting a solution to the problem of litter in their community; make a painting of nature, focusing on a feature of personal interest or meaning to themselves*)

*Teacher prompt:* "Let's look at how artist Andy Goldsworthy uses natural materials in his art. How can you use the textures and shapes of sticks, leaves, or stones to express your ideas about the natural environment?"

**D1.2** demonstrate an understanding of composition, using principles of design to create narrative art works or art works on a theme or topic (*e.g., use shapes of various sizes, in the foreground, middle ground, and background, to create an illusion of depth [perspective] in a painting about a make-believe world; create a mural to express a response to a community celebration, using a variety of lines and shapes; using a scratchboard that has a layer of various colours covered by india ink, make a high-contrast line drawing about a story by scratching the black surface to reveal the colours beneath the surface*)

*Teacher prompts:* "How can you vary the thickness of lines to make your characters stand out from the background?" "How can you use colours to show your feelings about the places in your mural?"

**D1.3** use elements of design in art works to communicate ideas, messages, and understandings (*e.g., use asymmetrical cut-paper composite shapes to depict a Canadian landscape, with a clear foreground, middle ground, and background; use colour values and shapes in a "What's inside me?" painting in the X-ray style of Norval Morrisseau to create contrast between the inside and the outside of the figure*)

*Teacher prompts:* "When creating a sense of space in your landscape, should you create the foreground, middle ground, or background first? Why?" "What colour choices did you make to create more or less contrast?" "Why do you think Tom Thomson chose to paint a windswept tree in *The Jack Pine* instead of a symmetrical tree? How can you use asymmetry in your own art work?"

**D1.4** use a variety of materials, tools, and techniques to respond to design challenges (*e.g.,*

- drawing: *use a variety of lines and shapes, drawn with pencil and marker, to show movement in a flipbook about weather*

- mixed media: *use wax crayons, oil pastels, paint resist, and materials of various textures [e.g. yarn, found objects] to depict a tree or plant above ground, and use the technique of elaboration to depict what is hidden below ground*

- painting: *create a watercolour or tempera painting of animals, using colour in a non-representational and expressive way*

- printmaking: *paint stencil prints in warm and cool colours, creating a simplified pattern inspired by a favourite fruit*

- sculpture: *use modelling clay to create organic forms that are inspired by nature, such as shells, seed pods, and water-worn stones, and that show some kind of metamorphosis or transformation into another form or figure*)

*Teacher prompts:* "How can you make the shapes move more smoothly in your flipbook? Would small or big changes in movement between one page and the next work better to create smoothness?" "What do the roots of a tree or plant look like below the ground? How could you draw a plant and show its roots?" "How does the emotional impact or mood of your print change when it is printed in warm instead of cool colours?"

### D2. Reflecting, Responding, and Analysing

By the end of Grade 3, students will:

**D2.1** express personal feelings and ideas about art experiences and images (*e.g., create a poster for an exhibition, using words of different sizes and colours to show their excitement about the event; express thoughts and ideas about an art work while in role as the artist in a peer artist interview*)

*Teacher prompts:* "What words will you choose to express your feelings about the exhibition in your poster?" "Using what you know about the artist, and looking carefully at the art work, what might the artist have said about his or her artistic choices?"

**D2.2** explain how elements and principles of design are used to communicate meaning or understanding in their own and others' art work (*e.g., colour value in Emily Carr's* Indian Church; *organic shapes to make the monsters look less frightening and more like stuffed animals in* Where the Wild Things Are *by Maurice Sendak*)

*Teacher prompts:* "What do you think this painting is about? What elements has the artist used to make the painting's message clear?" "What design elements has Sendak used on this book's cover? How have images, shapes, colours, and the letters of words been arranged on the cover to send a clear message?"

**D2.3** demonstrate an awareness of the meaning of signs and symbols encountered in their daily lives and in works of art (*e.g., fonts or logos that remind them of specific companies, messages, or moods; the meaning of animals such as the orca in Aboriginal clan symbols or the Inukshuk in Aboriginal art*)

*Teacher prompts:* "Where have you seen this symbol before? What makes it eye-catching?" "Why do companies create logos?" "How many examples can you think of where the same animal represents different ideas or emotions?" "How can you draw letters that suggest the mood or content of a story or movie?"

**D2.4** identify and document their strengths, their interests, and areas for improvement as creators of art (*e.g., keep an art journal to record what they think they have done well in their art works, or learned about in their art works, as they complete them; use the strategy of matching word and image to share their feelings about an art work or its creation*)

*Teacher prompts:* "What did you most enjoy doing when making your mask?" "What do you think is the most important thing in your painting?" "How can you explain to a partner why you chose to place that descriptive word or expressive emoticon on the art work?"

## D3. Exploring Forms and Cultural Contexts

By the end of Grade 3, students will:

**D3.1** identify and describe a variety of visual art forms they see in their home, at school, in the community, and in visual arts experiences (*e.g., original paintings at a community gallery, sculptures in a local park, art reproductions in offices, murals or sculptural monuments in the community, mixed media art works at arts festivals*)

*Teacher prompts:* "Where do you see art in our community? Where could you imagine there to be more? What are some of the different roles that the visual arts play in the community?" "What is the difference between original art works and reproductions?" "Where have you seen art exhibitions in our community? What did you find there? Why do people go to museums and art galleries?"

**D3.2** demonstrate an awareness of a variety of works of art and artistic traditions from diverse communities, times, and places (*e.g., a picture book that tells a story about people and the time and place in which they work, play, and build their community; George Littlechild's book* This Land Is My Land; *Daphne Odjig's historical mural* The Indian in Transition; *Jacob Lawrence's paintings of African-Americans working, playing, and interacting; classical Greek sculptures of sports figures, and contemporary sports sculptures, such as the fans in Michael Snow's* The Audience)

*Teacher prompts:* "Why do you think people create art work about their communities?" "What is the difference between telling a story in a painting and telling a story with words?" "What stands out for you in this art work?" "Which image do you relate to most? Why?" "What other art works are you reminded of?" "How would the image and message change if they were shown from a different point of view or in another style?"

# OVERVIEW OF GRADES 4 TO 6

The expectations for Grades 4 to 6 focus on the development of students' knowledge and skills in the arts and their ability to use the arts to understand, explore, and communicate feelings and ideas from and about their multicultural, multimedia environment.

Junior students' knowledge in the arts comes from their life experiences and prior knowledge and from the foundational arts knowledge and skills acquired in the primary school years. The expectations in the junior years build upon this foundation. Because the base of arts knowledge, experience, and skills varies from student to student, it is important for instruction to be differentiated to meet the needs of individuals and small groups of students.

Arts instruction in the junior years is designed to engage students in meaningful interactions with a wide variety of forms and disciplines in the arts. Junior students learn to identify and explore multiple perspectives, question the messages in works of dance, drama, music, and visual art, and consider the issues raised in them, including issues related to fairness, equity, and social justice. They analyse the structure and elements of a variety of art forms, explore a range of interpretations, and communicate their own ideas and opinions for a variety of purposes and audiences. Junior students develop their ability to monitor their own learning and select appropriate strategies to help them make sense of and create increasingly complex and/or challenging works for personally and socially relevant purposes. They reflect on and talk about the strategies that have helped them construct and communicate meaning and identify steps they can take to improve.

In all four disciplines, teachers should explicitly teach and model the use of the knowledge, skills, and strategies most relevant to the particular strand. Explicit teaching and modelling help students to identify the skills and strategies they need in order to become proficient creators and interpreters of dance, drama, music, and visual art works and move towards achievement of the expectations. Modelled, shared, and guided learning experiences provide the instructional support junior students need to communicate increasingly complex ideas and information using a greater variety of forms.

Appropriate instructional media are central to students' development of the knowledge, skills, and strategies embedded in the expectations across the arts strands. Subject matter that is designed to support and challenge students at their individual level of development in the arts will enhance the benefits of appropriately scaffolded instruction. It is important to ensure that students are able to choose from a wide range of topics and activities that are engaging and relevant to their personal experiences and interests. As well, all imagery, music, texts, and themes chosen for instruction should invite inquiry and promote antidiscrimination education. Junior students should have access to culturally diverse examples that allow them to explore more complex topics or issues and more subtle or abstract themes related to fairness, equity, and social justice. Oral forms such as dramatic presentations, oral reports, think-alouds, commentaries, speeches, monologues, and song lyrics; concrete forms such as artefacts, garments, and props; print forms such as posters, images, digital and print photographs, stories, biographies, graphic novels, poetry, myths, and legends; and media forms as movie trailers, graphic designs for various products, newspaper or magazine articles, video games, comic books, flyers, websites, and e-mails provide a variety of sources to motivate and engage diverse groups of students.

## Dance

In Grades 4 to 6, students further develop their movement vocabulary in response to a variety of stimuli, select appropriate forms, and manipulate dance elements such as relationship, time, and energy. They also experiment with various techniques to create different effects for different audiences and begin to use choreographic forms to guide and shape their choreography. Teacher- and student-led movement exercises such as body storming, mirroring, flocking, and verb chains may be used to build and shape movement vocabulary. In Grade 4, students begin to explore narrative form. In Grade 5, they focus on the use of the call-and-response form, while students in Grade 6 begin to use guided improvisation as a starting point for choreography. Junior students should be able to identify and analyse the effect of combining various elements of dance in their own and others' dance pieces.

## Drama

Students in Grades 4 to 6 continue to focus on role play as the foundational component of learning in drama. Process drama, small-group improvisations, partner role play, independent writing in role, and interpretation of simple scripts allow students to develop their ability to maintain focus and sustain belief while they are in role. Students also learn to enhance their roles and build belief in the fictional context of the drama by using the elements of relationship, time and place, tension, focus, and emphasis in their work. Opportunities to explore personally relevant themes, curricular topics, and current issues help to build interest for the junior learner. Students are encouraged to use the creative and critical analysis processes to make personal connections to the drama material they encounter, the performances they attend, and the drama experiences they share in the classroom setting. Teaching, modelling, and reinforcement of effective group skills continue to be important, as the students are expected to work collaboratively, both in and out of role. In groups, the students generate questions, pose and solve problems, inquire into meaning, and represent their understandings using a range of forms, techniques, and conventions.

Students continue to use the drama forms and conventions of the primary grades with growing understanding and greater competence. They also expand the range of forms and conventions to include more movement/dance connections, storytelling, prepared improvisation and short scenes, day in the life, inner/outer circle, and corridor of voices. In Grades 4 and 5, students select appropriate symbols, manipulate story elements, and experiment with various techniques to create different effects for different audiences. In Grade 6, they use research skills to expand their understanding of different kinds of problems and to help them find solutions. Their sense of audience continues to develop through their viewing of professional theatre productions, and through sharing their own work in classroom and/or more formal settings.

## Music

Students in Grades 4 to 6 focus on developing the ability to read music notation and on applying their knowledge of the elements of music through performing (singing, moving, playing instruments), creating, and listening. In Grade 4, students begin to read standard notation in the treble clef and sing or play music in two parts. They continue to create simple rhythms and melodies as accompaniments and to discover how music is organized. In Grade 5, students sing and/or play from standard music notation and other forms of notation, learn to use key signatures, and create compositions in a variety of forms using notational software. They explore the key influences affecting music in our past and present cultures. In Grade 6, students explore further aspects of standard notation, create and perform a variety of compositions, and continue to think critically about the music that they hear and perform. Students in Grades 4 to 6 are also expected to develop individual goals and to work in both large and small groups to solve musical problems. By the end of Grade 6 they should be able to provide constructive feedback regarding their own and others' efforts.

## Visual Arts

In Grades 4 to 6, students apply the elements of design to communicate for a variety of purposes and on a variety of themes. The focus of visual arts in these grades is to help students extend their exploration of relationships and personal experience in their own world. Students use a broader range of subject matter and media (tools, materials, processes, and techniques) to produce works of art. They grow more sophisticated in depicting movement, spatial relationships, and emotions. Students at this age display increased manual dexterity; however, their skills may not keep pace with their desire for increasingly elaborate work. This may lead to self-consciousness and insecurity about their artistic ability. The teacher's role at this stage is to provide a positive working environment, facilitate the growth of technical skills and observational skills, and help students recognize that mistakes can be turned into creative opportunities.

Students use their knowledge of the elements and principles of design to solve artistic problems and analyse works of art. They generate and develop visual ideas in response to a variety of motivations, using imagination, observation, and a study of artists' works, and incorporate into their art ideas gained from sources such as independent reading.

Students explore and describe how different media influence the communication and interpretation of ideas in their own and others' work. They look beyond the surface meaning of art works and observe not only what is present but what is missing, in order to analyse and evaluate an artist's intent. They also analyse and describe how art-making processes and procedures clarify meaning and intentions in their own and others' work and observe how artists tell stories and create mood in their work. Students use their growing analytical and evaluative skills to investigate the purpose(s) and significance of objects, images, and art works in past and present cultures and to examine the contexts in which they were or are made, viewed, and valued.

# GRADE **4**

# A. DANCE

## OVERALL EXPECTATIONS

By the end of Grade 4, students will:

**A1. Creating and Presenting:** apply the creative process (see pages 19–22) to the composition of movement sequences and short dance pieces, using the elements of dance to communicate feelings and ideas;

**A2. Reflecting, Responding, and Analysing:** apply the critical analysis process (see pages 23–28) to communicate their feelings, ideas, and understandings in response to a variety of dance pieces and experiences;

**A3. Exploring Forms and Cultural Contexts:** demonstrate an understanding of a variety of dance forms, traditions, and styles from the past and present, and their sociocultural and historical contexts.

---

### FUNDAMENTAL CONCEPTS FOR GRADE 4

Students in Grade 4 will develop or extend understanding of the following concepts through participation in various dance experiences (e.g., exploring movement sequences and narrative forms), with particular emphasis on time and energy.

ELEMENTS OF DANCE

- *body:* symmetry versus asymmetry, organic versus geometric shape, angular versus curved shape, gesture, body zones (e.g., cross-lateral [left arm and right leg])
- *space:* positive versus negative space, pathways (e.g., in air, on floor)
- *time:* tempo (e.g., increasing and decreasing speeds), rhythm (e.g., steady, irregular, erratic), pause, stillness, with music, without music, duration
- *energy:* effort, force, quality (e.g., punch, thrust, float, collapse, wiggle, explode, vibrate)
- *relationship:* meet/part, follow/lead, groupings

---

## SPECIFIC EXPECTATIONS

### A1. Creating and Presenting

By the end of Grade 4, students will:

**A1.1** translate into dance a variety of movement sequences observed in nature (*e.g., wind developing into a tornado; water freezing and melting on a landscape; rain transforming into a storm; a caterpillar evolving into a butterfly*)

*Teacher prompt:* "How could your sequence of movements demonstrate the transformation of rain into a flood or a hurricane?"

**A1.2** use dance as a language to explore and communicate ideas derived from a variety of literature sources (*e.g., develop dance movements based on actions or emotions depicted in myths, short stories, legends from different cultures, picture books, or poetry*)

*Teacher prompts:* "What action words from the legend give us clues about the kinds of movements that would help tell the story through dance?" "How could you and your partner use dance to communicate the dilemma in a book such as *The Great Kapok Tree*?" "How would your dance change if you recreated it to reflect the perspective of a different character from the story?"

**A1.3** use narrative form to create short dance pieces on a variety of themes *(e.g., a dance based on the theme of a quest or other type of journey; movements arranged [choreographed] to create a relationship [linking, parting] between some of the dancers)*

*Teacher prompts:* "How could your group create a dance piece inspired by one of the adventures of the Knights of the Round Table?" "How can you use choreography to give your dance an introduction, rising action, a climax, and resolution?"

**A1.4** use the elements of energy *(e.g., collapse, explode, float)* and time *(e.g., duration, suddenness)* in a dance piece to communicate an idea *(e.g., show the journey of a balloon as it floats, explodes suddenly, and then collapses back to the floor)*

*Teacher prompt:* "How would repeating the same dance phrase but changing its quality (e.g., firm, light, vibratory), tempo (e.g., decreasing speed), or rhythm (e.g., erratic) affect the message you are trying to communicate to the audience?"

## A2. Reflecting, Responding, and Analysing

By the end of Grade 4, students will:

**A2.1** demonstrate an understanding of how the language of dance can clarify and highlight ideas, images, and characters from familiar stories *(e.g., explain how gestures and actions reveal and express the mood or personality or social position of a character)*

*Teacher prompts:* "What kinds of movements did the jester use in the dance piece we just saw (quality, level, speed)? What did they tell you about his or her point of view?" "How did interpreting the story through dance help you understand the story better?"

**A2.2** identify, using dance vocabulary, the elements of dance used in their own and others' dance pieces and explain how each helps communicate ideas and feelings *(e.g., symmetry/asymmetry [body] can reflect themes of unity and separation;*

*sudden and sustained movements used sequentially can communicate the idea of a thunderstorm)*

*Teacher prompt:* "One example of relationship I noticed in this dance was that the dancers danced the first movement really close together, and then they repeated it but moved far apart. What did this variation communicate about the theme of togetherness?"

**A2.3** identify and give examples of their strengths and areas for growth as dance creators and audience members *(e.g., share with a small group what they did well, using dance terminology; explain what they need to practise to improve their ability to communicate through gesture and action)*

*Teacher prompt:* "What movement or phrase did you use in your dance that was effective in creating meaning, and why do you think it was effective?"

## A3. Exploring Forms and Cultural Contexts

By the end of Grade 4, students will:

**A3.1** describe, with teacher guidance, how forms and styles of dance reflect people's different social and political roles in various communities, times, and places *(e.g., court dances in different countries in the 1500s and 1600s reflect the customs of the upper class [kings, queens, and people of the court] while country dances reflect the customs of the common people; carnival dances in Toronto, Brazil, New Orleans, and Cuba reflect various cultural traditions; martial arts disguised as capoeira dance reflects a response to oppression)*

**A3.2** identify and describe the different roles of dance in their lives and in communities around the world *(e.g., to socialize; for entertainment; to communicate and tell stories; to enrich the school experience [through a dance club]; to celebrate a good harvest year; as part of religious ceremonies)*

*Teacher prompts:* "Based on the video we just saw, tell me one reason why dance is important to Aboriginal communities. Is this similar to why dance is important to you?" "Is it good for our school to have a lunchtime dance club? Why? How does it help us?"

# B. DRAMA

## OVERALL EXPECTATIONS

By the end of Grade 4, students will:

**B1. Creating and Presenting:** apply the creative process (see pages 19–22) to dramatic play and process drama, using the elements and conventions of drama to communicate feelings, ideas, and stories;

**B2. Reflecting, Responding, and Analysing:** apply the critical analysis process (see pages 23–28) to communicate feelings, ideas, and understandings in response to a variety of drama works and experiences;

**B3. Exploring Forms and Cultural Contexts:** demonstrate an understanding of a variety of drama and theatre forms, traditions, and styles from the past and present, and their sociocultural and historical contexts.

---

### FUNDAMENTAL CONCEPTS FOR GRADE 4

Students in Grade 4 will develop or extend understanding of the following concepts through participation in various drama experiences.

ELEMENTS OF DRAMA

- *role/character:* adopting a role and maintaining focus in role; communicating character traits and character choices through body language/movement and gestures; sustaining belief in character (e.g., using the first-person point of view while speaking); varying voice (e.g., diction, pace, volume, projection, enunciation)

- *relationship:* developing and analysing relationships between and among characters in a drama

- *time and place:* establishing a clear setting; sustaining belief in the setting

- *tension:* identifying factors that contribute to tension or mystery in a drama

- *focus and emphasis:* identifying the central theme and/or problem in a drama; drawing audience attention to specific aspects of the drama

---

## SPECIFIC EXPECTATIONS

### B1. Creating and Presenting

By the end of Grade 4, students will:

**B1.1** engage actively in drama exploration and role play, with a focus on exploring drama structures, key ideas, and pivotal moments in their own stories and stories from diverse communities, times, and places (*e.g., use role play to explore the hierarchical structure of medieval society; use "inner and outer circle" to examine moments of conflict and power imbalance in group improvisations on a common theme*)

*Teacher prompts:* "What do you know and what do you imagine about how people in medieval society behaved?" "How will you adjust your gestures and voice while in role to portray the status of a peasant in relation to a baron?"

**B1.2** demonstrate an understanding of the element of role by selectively using a few other elements of drama (*e.g., time and place; relationship; focus and emphasis*) to build belief in a role and establish its dramatic context

*Teacher prompts:* "Show me, in role, (1) what is most important to the character you are playing; or (2) your favourite place to be; or (3) a person you rely upon; or (4) something that you feel you must do." "What objects or props could you use to adapt the setting to emphasize your character's occupation as a scientist?"

**B1.3** plan and shape the direction of the drama or role play by posing questions and working with others to find solutions, both in and out of role (*e.g., In role: improvise possible solutions to a problem; Out of role: help select a drama form to represent the group's idea*)

*Teacher prompts:* "What words or phrases can we contribute to role on the wall to deepen understanding of and belief in this character?" "What action will your character take to solve the problems he/she is facing?"

**B1.4** communicate thoughts, feelings, and ideas to a specific audience, using audio, visual, and/or technological aids to enhance their drama work (*e.g., use dimmed lights, black lights, and music to suggest a mood; project images with an overhead/data projector; use a microphone to enhance or create sound effects or amplify narration [such as a spirit communication in an Aboriginal story])*

*Teacher prompts:* "How can you show the different meanings objects have in different contexts in everyday life (e.g., candles in ceremonies, birthdays, and festivals)?" "What objects could you use to symbolize who and what your character will miss on his/her journey?"

## B2. Reflecting, Responding, and Analysing

By the end of Grade 4, students will:

**B2.1** express personal responses and make connections to characters, themes, and issues presented in their own and others' drama works (*e.g., make a mural or map to explore the setting of the drama; interview a partner in and out of role to discover physical and personality traits of a character; write a diary entry describing the relationship between two fictitious characters*)

*Teacher prompts:* "What stands out for you in this drama/play?" "Which character do you most relate to? Why?" "What other stories or plays are you reminded of?"

**B2.2** explain, using drama terminology, how elements and drama conventions are used to produce specific effects and/or audience responses in their own and others' drama works (*e.g., characters' differing points of view can be used to create tension; comic characters and scenes can help relieve tension; thought tracking can give insight into a character*)

*Teacher prompts:* "Who is the intended audience for this drama? What drama elements were adapted specifically to interest that audience?" "Why do you think the audience responded with laughter at that moment in the drama?"

**B2.3** identify and give examples of their strengths, interests, and areas for growth as drama participants and audience members (*e.g., strength: using expressive gestures to communicate;* interest: *creative use of props and costumes;* area for growth: *maintaining focus in role*)

*Teacher prompts:* "With what conventions (e.g., tableaux, role playing) did you feel you did your best work?" "If you were to go back and redo any of your work in this drama, what do you feel you could do better, and why?" "Did you explore a variety of possible solutions to the problem?"

## B3. Exploring Forms and Cultural Contexts

By the end of Grade 4, students will:

**B3.1** identify and describe some similarities in the purposes of process drama and more formal, traditional theatre productions (*e.g., both forms use the elements of drama to tell stories, to allow the audience to imagine the possible outcomes and implications of human actions, and to engage the emotions of actors and audience*)

*Teacher prompt:* "When we are role-playing together, how is this similar to and different from being in a play?"

**B3.2** demonstrate an awareness of different kinds of drama and theatre from different times and places and of how they reflect their contexts (*e.g., popular contemporary forms such as films or television shows and public processions and spectacles; historical forms such as medieval tournaments; oral storytelling by troubadours in earlier times and in contemporary contexts; travelling plays or pageants*)

*Teacher prompts:* "How can drama help us to understand people, times, and places that we have never actually experienced in our own lives?" "What did you learn about medieval society by role-playing peasants, barons, and other community members?"

# C. MUSIC

## OVERALL EXPECTATIONS

By the end of Grade 4, students will:

**C1. Creating and Performing:** apply the creative process (see pages 19–22) to create and perform music for a variety of purposes, using the elements and techniques of music;

**C2. Reflecting, Responding, and Analysing:** apply the critical analysis process (see pages 23–28) to communicate their feelings, ideas, and understandings in response to a variety of music and musical experiences;

**C3. Exploring Forms and Cultural Contexts:** demonstrate an understanding of a variety of musical genres and styles from the past and present, and their sociocultural and historical contexts.

---

### FUNDAMENTAL CONCEPTS FOR GRADE 4

In Grade 4, students will build on their knowledge of the elements of music and related musical concepts that were introduced in Grades 1 to 3. Students will develop understanding of musical concepts through participation in musical experiences that involve listening, creating, and performing (e.g., singing, moving, playing instruments).

ELEMENTS OF MUSIC

- *duration:* syncopation using an eighth note followed by a quarter note and an eighth note (oral prompts: "ti-ta-ti" or "syn-co-pa"); sustaining a note or rest for longer than its value (pause or fermata)

- *pitch:* melody maps, five-line staff, absolute pitch names in treble clef (A, B, C, D, E, F, G), major and minor tonality, major scale (written with notes or numbers), intervals (unison, step, skip, leap), key signatures in the music they perform (e.g., no sharps or flats, one sharp, one flat), accidentals (sharp, flat, natural)

- *dynamics and other expressive controls:* changes in volume encountered in music listened to, sung, and played (e.g., *sforzando [sfz]*); articulation (e.g., phrase markings)

- *timbre:* homogeneous sound of ensemble instruments (e.g., individual instruments of the orchestra or other performing ensemble)

- *texture/harmony:* canon, simple two-part piece (simple polyphony)

- *form:* verse and chorus; piece with an introduction and/or a coda; simple repeats

---

## SPECIFIC EXPECTATIONS

### C1. Creating and Performing

By the end of Grade 4, students will:

**C1.1** sing and/or play, in tune, from musical notation, unison and two-part music with simple accompaniments from a wide variety of cultures, styles, and historical periods *(e.g., perform folk songs with syncopation and traditional songs with a simple harmony part)*

*Teacher prompts:* "What process can you use to sing or play an unfamiliar song from notation?" "What are the differences between the two parts?" "What is the rhythmic relationship between the melody and the accompaniment?"

**C1.2** apply the elements of music when singing and/or playing, composing, and arranging music to create a specific effect *(e.g., compose pieces using different expressive controls, such as staccato/legato or crescendo/decrescendo, to create contrasts and changes in mood; compose a pentatonic melody for recorder or voice with a bordun for an accompaniment)*

*Teacher prompts:* "What element could you change to further alter the effect?" "What family of instruments could you use for your arrangement? How would changing the instruments change the effect?" "What can you do to create a musical texture that is like the texture in a song from the Renaissance period?"

**C1.3** create musical compositions for specific purposes and audiences (*e.g., write a composition for recorder using musical notation on the five-line staff; compose a piece using non-traditional notation, such as a melody map or icons; compose a soundscape to represent the physical landscape of Canada; create a composition to accompany a dance piece*)

*Teacher prompt:* "Using your voice or an instrument, create a melodic contour that represents the contour of the boundary between Canada and the United States. How could you use your voice or an instrument to re-create this contour line?"

**C1.4** use the tools and techniques of musicianship in musical performances (*e.g., sing "O Canada" using controlled breathing technique and relaxed and straight posture while producing a clear and open head tone in their vocal range; play the xylophone using proper mallet technique*)

*Teacher prompts:* "How do you produce a sound that is clear and in tune when singing?" "How can you convey the meaning of the song to the listener?" "How can you use wrist action in playing a metallophone?"

**C1.5** demonstrate an understanding of musical signs and standard notation on the five-line staff, and use devised notation to record the sequence of sounds in a composition of their own (*e.g., create a soundscape with other students or a melody map using their own symbols; include fermata and sudden changes in dynamics in their compositions; use a system of syllables, numbers, or letters to represent simple pitch notation in a composition*)

*Teacher prompts:* "What is an easy way to help us remember the names of the notes on the five-line staff in the treble clef?" "How do note values relate to each other?" "Can you find a website to help us practise note names?"

## C2. Reflecting, Responding, and Analysing

By the end of Grade 4, students will:

**C2.1** express detailed personal responses to musical performances in a variety of ways (*e.g., respond by drawing, moving, using visual organizers, telling a story, making a collage; compare recordings of singers they think have a "good voice", and defend their preference*)

*Teacher prompts:* "How does this performance make you feel?" "What do you think is the purpose of this song?" "Why do you think the composer wrote this piece?"

**C2.2** identify the elements used in the music they perform, listen to, and create, and describe how they are used (*e.g., identify the mood of a piece and describe how the elements of music are used to create the mood*)

*Teacher prompts:* "Which elements do you think the composer was focusing on when writing this piece? Why?" "What mood do you think is created? How is it created?" "What different musical choices could you make to alter the mood of this piece?" "How did Benjamin Britten use the elements of music in the recording of *Young Person's Guide to the Orchestra*? How do you know?"

**C2.3** identify and give examples of their strengths and areas for growth as musical performers, creators, interpreters, and audience members (*e.g., identify two musical qualities that were effective in their group's performance and one area for improvement*)

*Teacher prompt:* "Which of the multiple intelligences did you use when learning to perform a piece of music on the recorder?"

## C3. Exploring Forms and Cultural Contexts

By the end of Grade 4, students will:

**C3.1** identify the role of music in a community today and compare it to its role in a community of the past (*e.g., music for gatherings now and in the Middle Ages; songs sung now and by the voyageurs*)

*Teacher prompts:* "What are the types of gatherings where music would be performed in the Middle Ages? And now?" "What kinds of music would be played or sung then and now?"

**C3.2** demonstrate an awareness, through listening, of the characteristics of musical forms and traditions of diverse times, places, and communities (*e.g., medieval musical genres performed by troubadours or minstrels, Indian classical music, music in Islamic cultures, music performed by female musical artists in North American culture, Aboriginal powwow music*)

*Teacher prompt:* "What kinds of songs did medieval troubadours perform? Where did they sing these songs?"

# D. VISUAL ARTS

## OVERALL EXPECTATIONS

By the end of Grade 4, students will:

**D1. Creating and Presenting:** apply the creative process (see pages 19–22) to produce a variety of two- and three-dimensional art works, using elements, principles, and techniques of visual arts to communicate feelings, ideas, and understandings;

**D2. Reflecting, Responding, and Analysing:** apply the critical analysis process (see pages 23–28) to communicate feelings, ideas, and understandings in response to a variety of art works and art experiences;

**D3. Exploring Forms and Cultural Contexts:** demonstrate an understanding of a variety of art forms, styles, and techniques from the past and present, and their sociocultural and historical contexts.

---

### FUNDAMENTAL CONCEPTS FOR GRADE 4

In addition to the concepts introduced in Grades 1 to 3, students will develop understanding of the following concepts through participation in a variety of hands-on, open-ended visual arts experiences.

ELEMENTS OF DESIGN

Students will develop understanding of all elements of design.

- *line:* lines to indicate emotion (e.g., smooth, horizontal lines can give a feeling of peace and harmony); contour lines (e.g., edges of objects); lines of various weights; repetition of lines to create visual rhythm

- *shape and form:* free-standing forms "in the round" (e.g., Henry Moore's figurative work) and "bas relief sculpture" (e.g., masks); shapes organized in a pattern showing radial symmetry and/or in a mosaic; changes in shapes, depending on the angle or point of view (e.g., view from the top, side, bottom); positive and negative shapes (e.g., closed curve with shape inside and outside); grouping of shapes; abstract shapes and forms

- *space:* positive and negative space in art work; diminishing perspective in various contexts (e.g., in vertical placement, in diminishing size, and/or in overlapping shapes); variation in size to create the illusion of depth

- *colour:* monochromatic colour scheme; colour emphasis through variations in intensity (e.g., subdued colours next to bright, intense colours); advancing colour

- *texture:* texture elaboration (e.g., embossing, piercing, pinching, pressing, scoring, scraping); texture quality (e.g., matte, sheen); low relief in collographs

- *value:* mixing of shades; variations in value to create emphasis (contrast in value)

PRINCIPLES OF DESIGN

Students will develop understanding of all principles of design (that is, contrast, repetition and rhythm, variety, emphasis, proportion, balance, unity and harmony, and movement), but the focus in Grade 4 will be on emphasis.

- *emphasis:* use of colour intensity, contrast in value, placement and size of shapes, and/or weight of line to create a particular focal point

# SPECIFIC EXPECTATIONS

## D1. Creating and Presenting

By the end of Grade 4, students will:

**D1.1** create two- and three-dimensional works of art that express feelings and ideas inspired by their interests and experiences (*e.g., a comic strip or a storyboard featuring a space voyage; an oil pastel drawing of peers in sports or dance poses; a painted still life of objects related to a hobby*)

*Teacher prompts:* "How can you make your classmates look as if they are participating in a sport? Can you 'freeze' them in a dynamic sports pose? How can you position them to show them in action, as in Ken Danby's goalie in *At the Crease*?" "How can you arrange and cluster the objects to create a focal point with the emphasis on the most important ones?"

**D1.2** demonstrate an understanding of composition, using selected principles of design to create narrative art works or art works on a theme or topic (*e.g., a collaborative mural depicting a historical or an imaginary landscape in which objects and figures placed in the foreground create areas of emphasis, and objects placed in the background show diminishing size; a relief print of a seascape in which shapes that are similar, but are different in size or colour, give the work both unity and variety*)

*Teacher prompts:* "How can you create emphasis in your art work by varying the value, width, and weight of your lines? In what other ways could you show emphasis?" "How can you repeat values of a colour in several places in your image to create unity?"

**D1.3** use elements of design in art works to communicate ideas, messages, and understandings (*e.g., create a poster using colour and cropping of space to propose a solution to climate change; use contour lines of various weights in a charcoal gesture drawing of a person to capture the impression of movement; create a paper sculpture portrait of a favourite comic character that explores positive and negative space, using techniques of folding, scoring, fringing, and crimping*)

*Teacher prompts:* "How can you use contrast, emphasis, or variety to capture students' attention and communicate your message?" "How would using recognizable symbols make your communication clearer or stronger?"

**D1.4** use a variety of materials, tools, and techniques to determine solutions to design challenges (*e.g.,*

- drawing: *make contour drawings of overlapping objects that are easily recognizable [e.g., a piece of fruit, a shoe, a glove, a pitcher], using soft graphite drawing pencils [e.g., primary printers] and depicting the objects from different points of view [e.g., from the front, the back, the side]*

- mixed media: *make a collage to depict a dream, using cut and torn paper, tissue paper, and found objects in contrasting shapes with a focus on positive and negative space*

- painting: *use tempera paint and a range of monochromatic colour values to represent the emotional state of a character at a critical moment in a story that they have written or read*

- printmaking: *use low-relief found objects [e.g., lace, textured leaves, and tin foil] to make a collograph in which texture and shape are used to create the composition, and embellish the final inked print with oil-pastel drawing*

- sculpture: *make a clay or papier mâché mask featuring exaggeration for dramatic effect and textures made by embossing, piercing, pinching, pressing, and/or scraping*)

*Teacher prompts:* "From which point of view was it most challenging to draw that object? Why?" "How have you used monochromatic colour to create a mood in your painting?" "How can you increase the number of different textures that you can apply to the mask to give the surface more variety?"

## D2. Reflecting, Responding, and Analysing

By the end of Grade 4, students will:

**D2.1** interpret a variety of art works, and identify the feelings, issues, themes, and social concerns that they convey (*e.g., express their response to student drawings on a classroom gallery walk; identify artistic techniques that are used to influence the viewer; in role as a famous artist, write a journal entry or letter identifying the artist's compositional choices and intentions*)

*Teacher prompts:* "If an artist such as David Blackwood changed the contrast and value in his prints, how might they suggest a different mood or feeling?" "How might different people experience and interpret the same object or image?"

**D2.2** analyse the use of elements and principles of design in a variety of art works, and explain how they are used to communicate meaning or understanding (*e.g., the use of texture and negative space in Henry Moore's abstract forms to suggest natural objects or figures; the use of tints and shades to explore vivid colour in Alma Thomas's aerial view paintings; the use of bright colours and rounded shapes in children's advertising to get their attention and convey a friendly feeling*)

*Teacher prompts:* "How important are negative shapes in an art work? Why?" "What message is the artist conveying by distorting and abstracting the subject?" "Who is the poster directed towards? How has the artist used different elements to appeal to his or her audience?"

**D2.3** demonstrate awareness of the meaning of signs, symbols, and styles in works of art (*e.g., symbols representing luck; fonts typically used in marketing; heraldic symbols; aboriginal totems around the world; Egyptian hieroglyphics*)

*Teacher prompts:* "How many good luck symbols can we list?" "What symbols are used in 'Good Luck' greeting cards?" "Why do some fonts attract your attention to products and messages more than other fonts?" "What does this Old English font make you think of?" "Why did knights put symbols on their shields?"

**D2.4** identify and document their strengths, their interests, and areas for improvement as creators and viewers of art (*e.g., review notes and sketches they have made during a visit to a public gallery, and summarize what tends to interest them when they look at art; after a classroom gallery walk, identify what they think are the most useful of the comments and suggestions that their classmates had written on sticky notes and placed on their art work*)

*Teacher prompts:* "Reflecting on what you have learned, what would you do differently if you were to use a similar medium, process, or theme?" "What do you notice first when you look at works of art? What do you consider when you give yourself time to think before deciding whether you like an art work?"

## D3. Exploring Forms and Cultural Contexts

By the end of Grade 4, students will:

**D3.1** describe how visual art forms and styles represent various messages and contexts in the past and present (*e.g., images that promote businesses, events, or festivals; paintings in art galleries that enrich, challenge, and engage viewers; picture books and graphic novels that inform and entertain; traditional and contemporary purposes of Aboriginal sculpture*)

*Teacher prompts:* "What is the role of visual arts in our community? How can this role be expanded?" "What is the difference between the role of the artist and the role of the viewer?" "Where in our community do people see works of art?"

**D3.2** demonstrate an awareness of a variety of art forms, styles, and traditions, and describe how they reflect the diverse cultures, times, and places in which they were made (*e.g., wax-resist batik as a national art form in Indonesia; masks used in the celebrations of various cultures; symbols, motifs, and designs on totem poles; radial symmetry in patterns in Islamic art; contemporary and historical oil paintings in an art gallery*)

*Teacher prompts:* "Where do they hold arts and crafts festivals in our community? What new art forms and art ideas did you see there that you'd never seen before?" "Why do people make masks? How were they used in the past and how are they used today?"

# GRADE **5**

# A. DANCE

## OVERALL EXPECTATIONS

By the end of Grade 5, students will

**A1. Creating and Presenting:** apply the creative process (see pages 19–22) to the composition of movement sequences and short dance pieces, using the elements of dance to communicate feelings and ideas;

**A2. Reflecting, Responding, and Analysing:** apply the critical analysis process (see pages 23–28) to communicate their feelings, ideas, and understandings in response to a variety of dance pieces and experiences;

**A3. Exploring Forms and Cultural Contexts:** demonstrate an understanding of a variety of dance forms, traditions, and styles from the past and present, and their sociocultural and historical contexts.

---

### FUNDAMENTAL CONCEPTS FOR GRADE 5

Students in Grade 5 will develop or extend understanding of the following concepts through participation in various dance experiences (e.g., communicating images and ideas through movement), with particular emphasis on relationship.

ELEMENTS OF DANCE

- *body:* body awareness, use of body parts, body shapes, locomotor and non-locomotor movements, body bases, symmetry versus asymmetry, geometric versus organic shape, angular versus curved shape

- *space:* levels, pathways, directions, pattern, positive versus negative space, various group formations, proximity of dancers to one another

- *time:* tempo, rhythm (e.g., regular, irregular), pause, stillness, with music, without music, duration

- *energy:* effort, force, quality (e.g., slash, press, shrink, open)

- *relationship:* meet/part, follow/lead, emotional connections between dancers, groupings

---

## SPECIFIC EXPECTATIONS

### A1. Creating and Presenting

By the end of Grade 5, students will:

**A1.1** translate into movement sequences a variety of images and ideas from other classroom subjects, including the arts (e.g., *portray the character of a young, boisterous child from a drama by using a variety of levels, quick movements, and indirect pathways in dance; develop movement phrases based on an image from a history textbook, a newspaper article, an Aboriginal story, or a painting in visual arts class*)

*Teacher prompt:* "With a partner or in a group, represent this piece of Henry Moore sculpture, first using only your body, then using a piece of cloth as a prop."

**A1.2** use dance as a language to explore, interpret, and communicate ideas derived from a variety of literature sources (e.g., *newspaper articles about sports, entertainment, or current events; stories, poems, picture books*)

*Teacher prompt:* "What movements, actions, or gestures can you use to clearly communicate the storyline?"

**A1.3** use movement in the choreographic form call and response in a variety of ways when creating dance pieces (e.g., *the teacher performs or calls a movement and the whole class responds; one student calls and the rest of the group responds; in partners, one student leads the movement and the other mirrors it*)

*Teacher prompts:* "How would you use call and response to suggest a friendly competition?" "How can you use your body to give instructions to your partner (who is responding)?"

**A1.4** use the element of relationship in short dance pieces to communicate an idea (*e.g., two dancers coming face to face to show either shared understanding or disagreement; a group of dancers holding hands to show unity*)

*Teacher prompt:* "How will you position yourself in relation to your partner? What movements and rhythms (e.g., regular, irregular) could you and your partner use to illustrate the benefits of teamwork?"

## A2. Reflecting, Responding, and Analysing

By the end of Grade 5, students will:

**A2.1** relate stories and characters in their own and others' dance pieces to personal knowledge and experience (*e.g., explain and demonstrate how dancers' postures and mannerisms reflect things they have observed in everyday life; describe how the dance informed, moved, or changed their own perspective on an issue*)

*Teacher prompts:* "Do the movements in this dance remind you of an experience in your own life?" "Are there similarities between the characters' perspectives in the dance and those of people you know in real life? What are some of them?" "Explain how the dance affected your thinking about the topic."

**A2.2** identify the elements of dance used in their own and others' dance pieces and explain how they help communicate a message (*e.g., describe their use of a high level, direct path, and strong movements to portray authority*)

*Teacher prompt:* "How did the change in speed affect the mood in the dance piece?"

**A2.3** identify and give examples of their strengths and areas for growth as dance creators and audience members (*e.g., identify two dance phrases that they believe were effective in their performance and explain their reasons for thinking so; assess whether they responded well to peer feedback about a performance and whether they implemented it*)

*Teacher prompt:* "When working with a group to generate a dance piece do you feel more comfortable generating ideas or implementing the plan of the group? How can you become better at a variety of group roles?"

## A3. Exploring Forms and Cultural Contexts

By the end of Grade 5, students will:

**A3.1** describe, with teacher guidance, dance forms and styles that reflect the beliefs and traditions of diverse communities, times, and places (*e.g., choral dance was used to honour the god Dionysus, who was revered in ancient Greece; ballet developed to entertain the aristocracy in European courts; group and partner dances – such as the swing and the salsa – reflect various types of social interaction; dance has a symbolic celebratory role in African-American wedding rituals*)

*Teacher prompt:* "What are some examples of dance that are associated with special events in your family? Do you know if they are connected to beliefs and traditions in your family or community? How could you find out?"

**A3.2** identify and describe some of the ways in which dance influences popular culture (*e.g., the influence of hip hop dance on people's mannerisms and behaviour, or on fashion, magazines, and music videos*)

*Teacher prompt:* "How has dance influenced the music in your favourite videos?"

# B. DRAMA

## OVERALL EXPECTATIONS

By the end of Grade 5, students will:

**B1. Creating and Presenting:** apply the creative process (see pages 19–22) to process drama and the development of drama works, using the elements and conventions of drama to communicate feelings, ideas, and stories;

**B2. Reflecting, Responding, and Analysing:** apply the critical analysis process (see pages 23–28) to communicate feelings, ideas, and understandings in response to a variety of drama works and experiences;

**B3. Exploring Forms and Cultural Contexts:** demonstrate an understanding of a variety of drama and theatre forms, traditions, and styles from the past and present, and their sociocultural and historical contexts.

### FUNDAMENTAL CONCEPTS FOR GRADE 5

Students in Grade 5 will develop or extend understanding of the following concepts through participation in various drama experiences.

ELEMENTS OF DRAMA

- *role/character:* adopting a variety of roles; considering both the inner and outer life in developing a character; sustaining familiar and unfamiliar roles; varying position (e.g., full front, quarter, profile, full back)
- *relationship:* developing and analysing a character in terms of his/her relationships with other characters
- *time and place:* establishing a clear setting (e.g., using simple objects and props to represent time and place)
- *tension:* using audio, visual, and/or technological aids and stage effects to heighten suspense and engage the audience
- *focus and emphasis:* using drama conventions to reveal/communicate key emotions and motivations to the audience and/or to draw audience attention to specific aspects of the drama

## SPECIFIC EXPECTATIONS

### B1. Creating and Presenting

By the end of Grade 5, students will:

**B1.1** engage actively in drama exploration and role play, with a focus on examining issues and themes in fiction and non-fiction sources from diverse communities, times, and places (*e.g., interview story characters who represent opposing views on an issue; use role play to explore social issues related to topics such as the environment, immigration, bullying, treaties, the rights and responsibilities of the child*)

*Teacher prompts:* "What strategies can you use in role to give a fair hearing to different sides on this issue?" "What drama strategy or convention can your group use to present solutions to the audience for your environmental issue?"

**B1.2** demonstrate an understanding of the element of role by selectively using some other elements of drama (*e.g., time and place, relationship*), to build belief in a role and establish its dramatic context (*e.g., select and use supporting artefacts or simple props; arrange furniture to establish setting; work with others to select or create objects to build a convincing setting, such as a character's room or the inside of a cave; use the drama convention of thought tracking to establish a relationship between two characters*)

*Teacher prompts:* "What conventions or strategies could you use to show your character's motivation to the audience? How can you show the audience the *reasons* for the character's problem?" "How can you focus the audience on the *relationship* between these two characters instead of emphasizing one character's dilemma?"

**B1.3** plan and shape the direction of the drama or role play by collaborating with others to develop ideas, both in and out of role (*e.g.,* In role: *improvise possible solutions to a dramatic conflict based on ideas from discussion and personal experience;* Out of role: *brainstorm in a group to generate ideas and make artistic choices*)

*Teacher prompts: In role:* "What do you think I can do, as a representative of the municipal government, to address your concerns?" *Out of role:* "What needs to be considered when you are getting ready to play the role of a government representative? What should be said? What feelings should be expressed?" "How can you plan the movements and placement of the characters in your performance to express their feelings in relation to the government official?"

**B1.4** communicate thoughts, feelings, and ideas to a specific audience, using audio, visual, and/or technological aids to achieve specific dramatic effects (*e.g., shine a spotlight on a performer who is making a key point; use a clash of cymbals to highlight a pivotal moment*)

*Teacher prompt:* "What can we do to create or enhance the intended mood?"

## B2. Reflecting, Responding, and Analysing

By the end of Grade 5, students will:

**B2.1** express personal responses and make connections to characters, themes, and issues presented in their own and others' drama works (*e.g., draw a picture or write poetry to show how they see a character at the beginning and end of the drama; use journal writing to convey a feeling of connection to a character in a drama*)

*Teacher prompts:* "How did this drama/play make you feel? What does it make you wonder about? If you could speak to the playwright or another character in the drama, what would you like to ask her or him?" "What character do you relate to and why?"

**B2.2** explain, using drama terminology, how different elements are used to communicate and reinforce the intended message in their own and others' drama works (*e.g., explain how*

specific scenes and/or relationships create tension and build up to the climax of the drama)

*Teacher prompts:* "What actions of the characters or performers helped them gain the empathy of the audience?" "What stage effects were used to help communicate a sense of danger?"

**B2.3** identify and give examples of their strengths, interests, and areas for improvement as drama creators, performers, and audience members (*e.g., use journals, charts, rubrics, and peer- and self-assessment charts to keep track of successful contributions, unproductive ideas or efforts, and evolving preferences in drama; describe how they used established criteria to evaluate their own and others' work; describe how they incorporated constructive feedback into their drama work; assess how well they differentiated between stereotypes and authentic characters when developing roles*)

*Teacher prompt:* "Complete the following sentences: 'One way I contributed to the drama was . . .'; 'One way to improve my work next time is . . .'; 'The part I enjoyed most was . . .'"

## B3. Exploring Forms and Cultural Contexts

By the end of Grade 5, students will:

**B3.1** describe forms of process drama, theatre, storytelling, and visual representation from diverse communities around the world, and explain how they may reflect some beliefs and traditions of their communities (*e.g., identify contexts in which the spoken word is a form of drama; describe historical and/or contemporary examples of forms from African, Asian, and/or Central or South American societies; identify examples of forms that reflect alternative viewpoints within communities*)

*Teacher prompts:* "What does this story (play, festival, visual representation) tell us about the family and community structures of its society of origin?" "What does our response to this drama tell us about ourselves?" "How does studying drama from around the world help us understand ourselves and others?" "How are life lessons communicated through these drama traditions?"

**B3.2** demonstrate an understanding of the broader world of drama and theatre by identifying and describing the roles and responsibilities of key theatre personnel (*e.g., describe what a producer, director, actor, stage manager, set or costume designer, and/or lighting or sound technician does in a typical day and what each needs in order to complete his or her work*)

# C. MUSIC

## OVERALL EXPECTATIONS

By the end of Grade 5, students will:

**C1. Creating and Performing:** apply the creative process (see pages 19–22) to create and perform music for a variety of purposes, using the elements and techniques of music;

**C2. Reflecting, Responding, and Analysing:** apply the critical analysis process (see pages 23–28) to communicate their feelings, ideas, and understandings in response to a variety of music and musical experiences;

**C3. Exploring Forms and Cultural Contexts:** demonstrate an understanding of a variety of musical genres and styles from the past and present, and their sociocultural and historical contexts.

---

### FUNDAMENTAL CONCEPTS FOR GRADE 5

In Grade 5, students will build on their knowledge of the elements of music and related musical concepts that were introduced in Grades 1 to 4. Students will develop understanding of musical concepts through participation in musical experiences that involve listening, creating, and performing (e.g., singing, moving, playing instruments).

ELEMENTS OF MUSIC
- *duration:* dotted quarter note followed by an eighth note (oral prompt: "tam-ti"); dotted eighth note and sixteenth note (oral prompt: "tim-ka"); rhythms, including those with eighth notes ("ti-ti") and sixteenth notes ("tika-tika"), in various combinations (e.g., "tika-ti, ti-tika, ti-ti, ta"), $\frac{6}{8}$ metre (oral count, with primary emphasis on "one" and secondary emphasis on "two": "*one*-and-a-*two*-and-a")
- *pitch:* key signatures in the music they perform (e.g., D major, G minor), clefs used for any instruments they play
- *dynamics and other expressive controls:* dynamics and articulation encountered in music listened to, sung, and played, and their signs
- *timbre:* tone colour for particular purposes (e.g., use of trumpets for a fanfare, flutes for depicting birds, various instruments for creating specific moods)
- *texture/harmony:* part singing (homophonic or polyphonic), chord progressions using I and V
- *form:* compositions in four or more sections (e.g., AABA, ABAC [alternation between a chorus, A, and improvisations, B and C], rondo [e.g., ABACADA])

---

## SPECIFIC EXPECTATIONS

### C1. Creating and Performing

By the end of Grade 5, students will:

**C1.1** sing and/or play, in tune, from musical notation, unison and two-part music with accompaniments, from a wide variety of cultures, styles, and historical periods (*e.g., perform a recorder duet that has a variety of rhythmic and melodic patterns*)

*Teacher prompts:* "What are some of the challenges when playing in two parts? Brainstorm some strategies to meet these challenges."

"What similarities and differences are there between the melodies and rhythms of the two parts you are going to perform?"

**C1.2** apply the elements of music when singing and/or playing, composing, and arranging music to create a specific effect (*e.g., form, timbre: create a rondo [ABACADA form] using a familiar song as the repeating A section, and compose short rhythmic or melodic materials for the B, C, and D sections using pitched or non-pitched percussion* instruments, found sounds, recorders, or body percussion)

*Teacher prompts: pitch:* "While singing the French-Canadian song 'Bonhomme, Bonhomme,' what patterns do you notice in the melody? [repetition, sequences]"; *timbre, form:* "What sounds will you use in the C section of your rondo and how long will this section be?"; "How will you give special attention to the elements of music that you focused on?"

**C1.3** create musical compositions for specific purposes and audiences (*e.g., compose an accompaniment for a story, poem, or drama presentation to address an environmental issue such as water conservation, recycling, or planting trees; create a piece that uses a rhythmic ostinato in $\frac{4}{4}$ time and that includes both eighth and six-teenth notes; use body percussion, found sounds, voice, and non-pitched percussion instruments to vary the timbres in their work*)

*Teacher prompts:* "What dynamic level and tempo would support the mood of this piece?" "How does your accompaniment reflect the story or poem?"

**C1.4** use the tools and techniques of musicianship in musical performances (*e.g., play recorder using proper hand position and posture; sing and/or play pitches and rhythms accurately; observe markings for dynamics and articulation; interpret accidentals and key signatures through playing and/or singing; sing and/or play songs in major and minor keys*)

*Teacher prompts:* "What strategies can you use to match your pitch to that of others in your class?" "How might you describe music sung or played without changes in dynamics?" "What happens when we perform some pitches without taking the key signature into consideration?"

**C1.5** demonstrate an understanding of standard and other types of musical notation through performance and composition (*e.g., notation of rhythms of skipping songs in $\frac{6}{8}$ metre; dynamic markings, clefs, key signatures; notational soft-ware for scoring their own compositions; guitar tablature*)

*Teacher prompts:* "How does standard notation compare with guitar tablature?" "Why do we use musical signs and symbols to communicate in the 'language' of music? What other symbol systems do use to communicate with? [e.g., maps with legends, sign language, road signs, math symbols, computer language]"

## C2. Reflecting, Responding, and Analysing

By the end of Grade 5, students will:

**C2.1** express detailed personal responses to musical performances in a variety of ways (*e.g., describe the sounds of a steel band, using musical terminology; analyse a movement from Vivaldi's* Four Seasons *in a think-pair-share listening activity, and describe their feelings and personal impressions; compare the mood of a piece from today and a piece from the baroque period, using Venn diagrams*)

*Teacher prompts:* "How do you feel when you hear the music of a steel band?" "What in the 'Spring' movement of Vivaldi's *Four Seasons* makes you think of spring?"

**C2.2** identify the elements of music in the music they perform, listen to, and create, and describe how they are used (*e.g., timbre: describe how brass instruments are used in a marching band; duration: clap dotted rhythm patterns in a fanfare, describe how a slow tempo contributes to the mood of a funeral march, describe the use of syncopation in rhythms in Latin American music; form and texture: graphically portray the layering of melodies in a round; dynamics: relate the soft or loud sounds in a ballad to the meaning of the text*)

*Teacher prompts:* "Why do you think the composer chose specific instruments for this work?" "Are short or long notes being used primarily? How does the rhythm affect the overall energy of the piece?" "What is the range of dynamics being used?" "How might we describe the mood of this piece? Why?"

**C2.3** identify and give examples of their strengths and areas for growth as musical performers, creators, interpreters, and audience members (*e.g., balancing the volume of their own singing part in relation to the volume of another singing part; using expressive controls while playing recorder; providing peer feedback in preparation for a musical performance; writing a reflection on a live or recorded musical performance*)

*Teacher prompts:* "If you are singing a round, what do you need to do when the second group comes in?" "How do you know if you are blending with the other singers/players in your performing group?" "How are the ways we respond to a performance at a symphony concert different from the ways we respond to a rock concert or sporting event?"

## C3. Exploring Forms and Cultural Contexts

By the end of Grade 5, students will:

**C3.1** identify and describe some of the key influences of music within contemporary culture (*e.g., describe the use of music in film and advertising; identify effects of musical trends on young people's musical tastes; describe examples of fusion in different musical styles and genres*)

*Teacher prompt:* "I'm going to play a musical excerpt from a movie or television show. While it is playing, imagine what kind of action would take place, what the setting is, who the characters are, and what dialogue would occur while this music is played in the background."

**C3.2** demonstrate an awareness of the use of music and musical instruments in various traditions, from early times to today (*e.g., describe the use of the drum in various cultures, including Aboriginal cultures, and at various times around the world in ceremonial and celebratory music*)

*Teacher prompts:* "How was the drum used in early civilizations? Was its use similar to or different from its usage now?" "Why is the drum used in so many cultures?" "How is the drum used now in various African countries?"

# D. VISUAL ARTS

## OVERALL EXPECTATIONS

By the end of Grade 5, students will:

**D1. Creating and Presenting:** apply the creative process (see pages 19–22) to produce a variety of two- and three-dimensional art works, using elements, principles, and techniques of visual arts to communicate feelings, ideas, and understandings;

**D2. Reflecting, Responding, and Analysing:** apply the critical analysis process (see pages 23–28) to communicate feelings, ideas, and understandings in response to a variety of art works and art experiences;

**D3. Exploring Forms and Cultural Contexts:** demonstrate an understanding of a variety of art forms, styles, and techniques from the past and present, and their sociocultural and historical contexts.

---

### FUNDAMENTAL CONCEPTS FOR GRADE 5

In addition to the concepts introduced in Grades 1 to 4, students in Grade 5 will develop understanding of the following concepts through participation in a variety of hands-on, open-ended visual arts experiences.

ELEMENTS OF DESIGN

Students will develop understanding of all elements of design.

- *line:* linear and curved hatching and cross-hatching that add a sense of depth to shape and form; gesture drawings; chenile stick sculptures of figures in action; implied lines for movement and depth

- *shape and form:* symmetrical and asymmetrical shapes and forms in font and image; positive and negative shapes that occur in the environment; convex, concave, non-objective shapes

- *space:* shading and cast shadows that create the illusion of depth; atmospheric perspective; microscopic and telescopic views

- *colour:* complementary colours, hue, intensity (e.g., dulling, or neutralizing, colour intensity by mixing the colour with a small amount of its complementary hue)

- *texture:* textures created with a variety of tools, materials, and techniques; patterning

- *value:* gradations of value to create illusion of depth, shading

PRINCIPLES OF DESIGN

Students will develop understanding of all principles of design (that is, contrast, repetition and rhythm, variety, emphasis, proportion, balance, unity and harmony, and movement), but the focus in Grade 5 will be on proportion.

- *proportion:* the relationship of the size and shape of the parts of a figure to the whole figure; the scale of one object compared to its surroundings, with indications of how close and how large the object is (e.g., figures with childlike proportions that are approximately "five heads high" and adult figures that are approximately "seven or eight heads high"; caricature; use of improbable scale for imaginary settings and creatures)

# SPECIFIC EXPECTATIONS

## D1. Creating and Presenting

By the end of Grade 5, students will:

**D1.1** create two- and three-dimensional art works that express feelings and ideas inspired by their own and others' points of view *(e.g., a painting based on a photo montage about children's rights and responsibilities; a coloured line drawing of an underwater setting or the view from an airplane that addresses environmental awareness by showing the interconnectedness of ecosystems; a painting of someone in a particular situation in which empathy for him or her is created through characterization)*

*Teacher prompts:* "How can you use size and shape in your painting to express your feelings or point of view about the importance of the different images in your montage?" "How does our impression of the world change when we look at it from a bird's-eye view rather than a worm's-eye view? How can you use a particular point of view in your painting (not necessarily these) to create a particular impression?"

**D1.2** demonstrate an understanding of composition, using selected principles of design to create narrative art works or art works on a theme or topic *(e.g., create an abstract painting using different proportions of complementary colours; create a simple sculpture of a human form that depicts an emotional response and shows awareness of proportion and negative space [in the style of Barbara Hepworth]; create an impression of depth and space by neutralizing colour intensity and brightness in a landscape painting [atmospheric perspective])*

*Teacher prompts:* "How have you used colour to create a point of emphasis and a sense of space?" "How will you use your in-class sketches of student poses to help you decide on the emotion to express with the position of the figure?" "How did you dull the colours to show things that are in the distance?"

**D1.3** use elements of design in art works to communicate ideas, messages, and understandings *(e.g., a series of three relief prints that use a glue-line relief print process to illustrate the beginning, middle, and end of a story; a poster that presents solutions to stereotyping, bias, or bullying, using angle of view; a graffiti-style mural that addresses a community issue, using convex shapes that lead the eye with implied lines)*

*Teacher prompts:* "How did you use asymmetrical geometric shapes to simplify the text and image? How did the use of proportion and

scale change your message when your poster had faces that were larger than life?" "Which elements and principles of design did you use to focus and simplify the text and image in the mural? How did you use gradations of value to create the illusion of depth in your designs?"

**D1.4** use a variety of materials, tools, and techniques to determine solutions to design challenges *(e.g.,*

- drawing: *coloured pencils to create a caricature of a celebrity that exaggerates facial features and uses linear shading and cast shadows*

- mixed media: *a composite image that uses photographs, photocopies, transfers, images, and selected opaque and transparent materials to reflect their self-identity*

- painting: *tempera paint or watercolour pencils using unusual colours or perspectives to suggest a fantasy world*

- printmaking: *a relief print transferred from a textured surface, made with glue lines, craft foam, cardboard, paper, or string glued to board, using shapes to create a graphic design that explores pattern in a non-objective op art style*

- sculpture: *a human figure or an imaginary creature made from clay, using basic hand-building methods such as making the piece with coils or slabs of clay or by pinching and pulling the clay)*

*Teacher prompts:* "How could you make the lines in your caricature more fluid and the shapes more expressive?" "How are the images you used in your art work and their placement and composition symbolic of how you see yourself?"

## D2. Reflecting, Responding, and Analysing

By the end of Grade 5, students will:

**D2.1** interpret a variety of art works and identify the feelings, issues, themes, and social concerns that they convey *(e.g., use an image round-table technique to compare interpretations of emotions suggested by abstract forms or figures in art work; sort and classify a variety of art images, such as Nigerian, Egyptian, Mayan, and Chinese sculptures, to determine common subjects or themes)*

*Teacher prompts:* "When you look at how Constantin Brancusi makes the human form abstract in his sculptures, what do the shapes remind you of?" "What different emotions does the pose of this art work suggest to you? If the figure in the art work could come to life, what would it say to you?" "How is proportion used to convey importance?"

**D2.2** explain how the elements and principles of design are used in their own and others' art work to communicate meaning or understanding (*e.g., packaging designs [cereal boxes, drink packaging] that use complementary colours create an impression different from that created by packages that use other colour schemes; Alexander Calder's mobiles and Piet Mondrian's paintings use colour, line, and geometric shape to create an impression of movement; colour, line, and pattern are used to convey a story in the illuminated manuscript of the Ramayana*)

*Teacher prompts:* "How does the use of colour engage the viewer and help sell the product? Which colour scheme do you think is most effective in persuading the buyer, and why?" "How does Mondrian's *Broadway Boogie Woogie* use colour, line, and shape to create an impression of movement?" "How have artists arranged shapes, lines, patterns, and colours to create a sense of order and rhythm?" "How do the details on the characters help the viewer focus on and understand the story?"

**D2.3** demonstrate an understanding of how to read and interpret signs, symbols, and style in art works (*e.g., Carl Ray's paintings use symbols in the Woodland style of Aboriginal art to tell a story; Picasso's cubist portraits use stylistic features from African masks; a tiger is used in Asian art to signify bravery*)

*Teacher prompts:* "Why are creatures such as the thunderbird or eagle associated with the idea of power and privilege in some art works?" "In what ways are some of Picasso's art works inspired by African masks?" "How do Group of Seven paintings show the influence of a variety of modernist styles (Impressionism, post-Impressionism, and art nouveau)?"

**D2.4** identify and explain their strengths, their interests, and areas for improvement as creators, interpreters, and viewers of art (*e.g., use of appropriate terminology in talking about their own art work; discussion of others' ideas with sensitivity and respect; provision of reasons for their artistic choices in a diary entry in their art journal or sketchbook*)

*Teacher prompts:* "Why is the medium you have picked the best choice for your narrative line drawing?" "How does the choice of media

and tools change how the same subject matter is perceived?" "Do you think good art needs to take a long time to make? Why or why not?" "What did you find when you compared your work with the ways in which different artists have expressed ideas about themselves in self-portraits (e.g., self-portraits by Vincent Van Gogh, Frida Kahlo, Andy Warhol)?"

## D3. Exploring Forms and Cultural Contexts

By the end of Grade 5, students will:

**D3.1** describe how forms and styles of visual and media arts represent various messages and contexts in the past and present (*e.g., sculptural monuments to honour people in the past such as war veterans; promotion of ideas or products on film, television, and the Internet in everyday life*)

*Teacher prompts:* "What is the relationship between form and purpose in this sculpture?" "How do you know that an advertisement is intended for you and your friends? What elements of design are being used to attract your attention to a product and make that product desirable?"

**D3.2** demonstrate an awareness of ways in which visual arts reflect the beliefs and traditions of a variety of peoples and of people in different times and places (*e.g., the use of contemporary Aboriginal art to support cultural revitalization; the use of images on ancient Greek vases to reflect narratives of daily life, legends, and war; the relationship between public art and its location; exhibitions of the art of local artists in local festivals; displays and exhibitions of art works in galleries and museums*)

*Teacher prompts:* "How does the work of Baffin Island printmakers reflect ways in which Inuit life has changed over time and how they preserve stories?" "How is art a reflection of personal, local, or cultural identity?" "Whose voices or beliefs are not represented in this exhibition?" "How can community groups advocate for the arts?"

# GRADE **6**

# A. DANCE

## OVERALL EXPECTATIONS

By the end of Grade 6, students will:

**A1. Creating and Presenting:** apply the creative process (see pages 19–22) to the composition of short dance pieces, using the elements of dance to communicate feelings and ideas;

**A2. Reflecting, Responding, and Analysing:** apply the critical analysis process (see pages 23–28) to communicate their feelings, ideas, and understandings in response to a variety of dance pieces and experiences;

**A3. Exploring Forms and Cultural Contexts:** demonstrate an understanding of a variety of dance forms, traditions, and styles from the past and present, and their sociocultural and historical contexts.

---

### FUNDAMENTAL CONCEPTS FOR GRADE 6

Students in Grade 6 will develop or extend understanding of the following concepts through participation in various dance experiences (e.g., communicating a variety of ideas through combined elements), with particular emphasis on body, space, time, energy, and relationship.

ELEMENTS OF DANCE

- *body:* body awareness, use of body parts, body shapes, locomotor and non-locomotor movements, body bases, symmetry versus asymmetry, geometric versus organic shape, curved versus angular shape

- *space:* pathways, directions, positive versus negative space, proximity of dancers to one another, various group formations

- *time:* tempo, rhythm, pause, stillness, with music, without music, duration (e.g., short, long), acceleration/deceleration

- *energy:* effort, force, quality (e.g., flick, fold, stab, poke, flow freely)

- *relationship:* dancers to props/objects (e.g., in front of, inside, over, around), meet/part, follow/lead, emotional connections between dancers, groupings

---

## SPECIFIC EXPECTATIONS

### A1. Creating and Presenting

By the end of Grade 6, students will:

**A1.1** incorporate the use of props and materials *(e.g., fabric, chairs, hats, hula hoops, balls, sticks)* into dance pieces they create *(e.g., use fabric as a shawl or an extension of an arm gesture or the movement of a ship's sail; use a stretchy fabric body bag to create abstract shapes; use an artefact like a garbage can to explore rhythm and body movement)*

*Teacher prompts:* "When creating a dance, how could you use chairs to explore relationship (e.g., over, in front of, behind), shape, and levels?" "How can you use the prop (e.g., streamer, fabric) as an extension of your body to make shapes, pathways, and lines to emphasize or extend movement?"

**A1.2** use dance as a language to interpret and depict central themes in literature *(e.g., develop a movement vocabulary that reinterprets themes such as good versus evil or humans versus nature; construct a dance that explores bravery in a legend or peace in a poem)*

*Teacher prompts:* "What types of shapes or pathways would you use to communicate frustration?" "How could you use level to depict feelings of freedom or authority?"

**A1.3** use guided improvisation in a variety of ways as a starting point for choreography *(e.g., use exercises such as mirroring, flocking, and body storming to create movement material for choreography)*

*Teacher prompt:* "How can a guided improvisation like flocking expand your movement vocabulary?"

**A1.4** combine the elements of dance in different ways to communicate a variety of ideas *(e.g., combine a low level and a wavy pathway to show evasion; use the sudden, quick, and indirect movements of a dynamic orchestra conductor and translate them into a whole body expression of the music)*

*Teacher prompts:* "What elements could you combine to show that you are on a dangerous mission?" "What elements could you combine to show that you are excited? Or bored?"

## A2. Reflecting, Responding, and Analysing

By the end of Grade 6, students will:

**A2.1** construct personal interpretations of dance pieces that depict stories, issues, and themes, and explain their interpretations, using dance terminology *(e.g., write an opinion paragraph on a recorded or live community dance performance [Red Sky]; write a response journal entry on a dance piece performed by peers about a social issue [emotional or physical bullying, friendship, safety, fairness, family, inclusion, equity])*

*Teacher prompts:* "How do we know this dance is about bullying? What elements helped make the theme clear?" "What did this dance mean to you? What themes or stories did you see in it?"

**A2.2** analyse, using dance vocabulary, how the elements of dance are used in their own and others' dance pieces and explain how they help communicate messages and ideas *(e.g., pairing free-flowing movements with slow music suggests a dreamy mood; using low levels and quick, short movements suggests busyness; using symmetry and asymmetry conveys the idea of change or transformation)*

*Teacher prompt:* "What elements did the dancers use to communicate joy/surprise? Were the ideas clearly communicated through movement? What does the dancing suggest that couldn't have been expressed in another way?"

**A2.3** identify and give examples of their strengths and areas for growth as choreographers and audience members *(e.g., determine how their preparations for a performance improved the performance and what they might do differently to strengthen future performances)*

*Teacher prompts:* "What skills do you need to be a choreographer? How can you hone these skills?" "How could you use a movement web to generate more ideas for your next dance?"

## A3. Exploring Forms and Cultural Contexts

By the end of Grade 6, students will:

**A3.1** describe, with teacher guidance, types of dances used among Aboriginal peoples in the past and the present that express aspects of their cultural identity *(e.g., war dances to express prayers for victory and/or gratitude for success; initiation dances to mark rites of passage; shamans' dances to assist in physical or spiritual healing; contemporary powwow dances for cultural affirmation and/or revitalization)*

*Teacher prompt:* "How would you describe the regalia and dance styles of powwow dances? How do these features help express the cultural identity and heritage of the dancers?"

**A3.2** identify and describe ways in which pop culture and the media influence our awareness, understanding, and appreciation of dance *(e.g., by making us aware of different kinds of dance and diverse uses of dance in society; by providing male role models in dance and helping us view dance as a way to have a healthy, active lifestyle)*

*Teacher prompts:* "Do you watch popular TV shows about dance? What influence do these dance shows have on you?" "What are some of the barriers and issues around popular competitive dance shows?"

GRADE 6

DANCE

123

# B. DRAMA

## OVERALL EXPECTATIONS

By the end of Grade 6, students will:

**B1.** **Creating and Presenting:** apply the creative process (see pages 19–22) to process drama and the development of drama works, using the elements and conventions of drama to communicate feelings, ideas, and multiple perspectives;

**B2.** **Reflecting, Responding, and Analysing:** apply the critical analysis process (see pages 23–28) to communicate feelings, ideas, and understandings in response to a variety of drama works and experiences;

**B3.** **Exploring Forms and Cultural Contexts:** demonstrate an understanding of a variety of drama and theatre forms, traditions, and styles from the past and present, and their sociocultural and historical contexts.

---

### FUNDAMENTAL CONCEPTS FOR GRADE 6

Students in Grade 6 will develop or extend understanding of the following concepts through participation in various drama experiences.

ELEMENTS OF DRAMA
- *role/character:* considering in depth the inner and outer life in developing a character; differentiating between authentic characters and stereotypes; using gestures and movement to convey character
- *relationship:* analysing and portraying how relationships influence character development/change
- *time and place:* establishing a clear setting; sustaining belief in the fictional setting
- *tension:* using sound, light, technology, and stage effects to heighten tension/suspense
- *focus and emphasis:* using drama conventions to reveal or communicate key emotions, motivations, perspectives, and ideas to the audience

---

## SPECIFIC EXPECTATIONS

### B1. Creating and Presenting

By the end of Grade 6, students will:

**B1.1** engage actively in drama exploration and role play, with a focus on identifying and examining a range of issues, themes, and ideas from a variety of fiction and non-fiction sources and diverse communities, times, and places *(e.g., adapt roles and develop improvised scenes based on human rights issues and/or environmental issues such as species extinction; dramatize opinions about cultural appropriation; role-play historical characters; prepare a presentation about peace for Remembrance Day; use choral speaking and role playing to interpret poetry)*

*Teacher prompts:* "What do you hope to learn about this character through role playing?" "What is the theme of our drama?" "How could you use the drama conventions of hot seating or voices in the head or thought tracking to develop a deeper understanding of a character's intentions and motivations?"

**B1.2** demonstrate an understanding of the element of role by selectively using other elements *(e.g., time and place; relationship; tension)* to build belief in a role and establish its dramatic context *(e.g., develop a character in the context of a courtroom drama: judge, lawyer, witness, juror, the accused)*

*Teacher prompts:* "What elements are critically important to build belief in the drama?" "What will the jury be doing when the accused person enters?" "How will we know where and when the action is taking place?" "How can tension be created in this scene?" "What different points of view will be represented by the different roles?"

**B1.3** plan and shape the direction of the drama or role play by introducing new perspectives and ideas, both in and out of role (*e.g., In role: conduct a "hot seat" interview with the protagonist or antagonist; Out of role: make suggestions and introduce new ideas when planning a drama presentation*)

*Teacher prompts: Out of role:* "What questions might you ask when you go back into role to help us understand the emotions and motivations the character has at this key moment?" *In role:* "Why do you feel this way? What do you really want to see happen?"

**B1.4** communicate feelings, thoughts, and ideas to a specific audience, using audio, visual, and/or technological aids to strengthen the impact on the viewer (*e.g., use a data projector to project evocative imagery; use filters and gels to create unusual effects with lighting; use music to suggest a mood; use masks to highlight specific character traits*)

*Teacher prompts:* "What features of your mask have you exaggerated to allow the audience to see the character from a distance (e.g., heavy brows, large nose, large eyes, jutting chin)?" "How can you use a photograph or everyday object from another historical period to communicate an aspect of that person/time/place?" "What visual effect would emphasize what this character is feeling on the inside?"

## B2. Reflecting, Responding, and Analysing

By the end of Grade 6, students will:

**B2.1** express personal responses and preferences and make connections to themes and issues presented in their own and others' drama works (*e.g., describe their response to the attitudes and beliefs of specific characters in a drama*)

*Teacher prompts:* "How did this drama/play make you feel? Of what does it remind you?" "What did you like/dislike about this play? Why?" "Select one moment that you would like to revisit to change. How would you change it?" "Identify a moment in your drama when you felt fully in role."

**B2.2** identify a favourite scene and give reasons for their preference, using correct drama terminology to describe how the elements of drama contribute to its effectiveness (*e.g., explain what elements made the final confrontation between the hero and the villain exciting to perform or watch*)

*Teacher prompts:* "How was symbolism used in this scene? How effectively did it help create a particular mood?" "Why was it important for the actor to stop in mid-sentence while speaking?"

**B2.3** identify and give examples of their strengths, interests, and areas for improvement as drama creators, performers, and audience members (*e.g., write a journal entry about a new strategy they have learned; write a letter to a new student about how to cope with stage fright; respond to interview questions about their growth and development; explain to the teacher how they collaborated and contributed to the group work of developing, planning, and designing a drama*)

*Teacher prompts:* "What advice about (topic X) would you give a student who is new to drama?" "What are some important skills people need to work in drama?" "Describe your own strengths in drama." "How did you give/receive constructive feedback on ways in which space, gesture, and voice are used to communicate within a drama work? Was the feedback used to refine the drama work?" "What ideas did you submit to individual and collective decisions to develop the drama?" "How did you show a commitment to maintaining your role?"

## B3. Exploring Forms and Cultural Contexts

By the end of Grade 6, students will:

**B3.1** demonstrate an understanding of some drama and theatre themes and traditions from a variety of times, communities, and places (*e.g., Aboriginal communities: storytelling forms – the Seven Grandfather teachings, Haida tales, Medicine Wheel stories; theatre forms – Red Sky Performance Theatre, De-ba-jeh-mu-jig Theatre*)

*Teacher prompt:* "Different communities have different versions of this shared story. What elements are the same in many versions? What elements are different? How might we explain some of the similarities and differences?"

**B3.2** identify and describe key contributions drama and theatre make to the community (*e.g., provide opportunities for self-expression and creativity to both amateurs and professionals; provide employment for a wide variety of workers; encourage tourism; promote strengthening and healing in Aboriginal communities*)

*Teacher prompts:* "What careers related to theatre do not involve acting?" "In what ways can drama and theatre help build community?"

# C. MUSIC

## OVERALL EXPECTATIONS

By the end of Grade 6, students will:

**C1. Creating and Performing:** apply the creative process (see pages 19–22) to create and perform music for a variety of purposes, using the elements and techniques of music;

**C2. Reflecting, Responding, and Analysing:** apply the critical analysis process (see pages 23–28) to communicate their feelings, ideas, and understandings in response to a variety of music and musical experiences;

**C3. Exploring Forms and Cultural Contexts:** demonstrate an understanding of a variety of musical genres and styles from the past and present, and their sociocultural and historical contexts.

---

### FUNDAMENTAL CONCEPTS FOR GRADE 6

In Grade 6, students will build on their knowledge of the elements of music and related musical concepts that were introduced in Grades 1 to 5. Students will develop understanding of musical concepts through participation in musical experiences that involve listening, moving, creating, and performing (vocal and/or instrumental music).

ELEMENTS OF MUSIC

- *duration:* $\frac{9}{8}$ metre (oral count, with primary emphasis on "one" and secondary emphasis on "two" and "three": "*one*-and-a-*two*-and-a-*three*-and-a") and other compound metres (e.g., $\frac{6}{4}$); $\frac{5}{4}$ metre; pick-up note(s) (anacrusis); triplets; common Italian tempo marks (e.g., *allegro, adagio*) and others encountered in the repertoire performed

- *pitch:* ledger lines above or below the staff; major, minor, and perfect intervals (e.g. major third, perfect fifth)

- *dynamics and other expressive controls:* those encountered in repertoire (e.g., very soft [*pianissimo – pp*], very loud [*fortissimo – ff*], slurs)

- *timbre:* electronic sounds; Orff ensemble (xylophone, recorder, pitched and non-pitched percussion); other ensemble sonorities (drum line, choir, guitar, marching band)

- *texture/harmony:* layering of electronic sounds, chord progressions using I, IV, and V

- *form:* theme and variations; repeats (e.g., first and second endings)

---

## SPECIFIC EXPECTATIONS

### C1. Creating and Performing

By the end of Grade 6, students will:

**C1.1** sing and/or play, in tune, from musical notation, unison music and music in two or more parts from a wide variety of cultures, styles, and historical periods (*e.g., perform three- and four-part rounds by Canadian choral composers; perform pieces for Orff ensemble using recorder and pitched and non-pitched percussion; perform pieces, using technology to provide the accompaniment*)

*Teacher prompts:* "What are some ways we can use body percussion to create a four-part round?" "What would be an effective ostinato to support your melody?"

**C1.2** apply the elements of music when singing and/or playing, composing, and arranging music to create a specific effect (*e.g., compose a piece in the theme and variations form, using a well-known song for the theme to engage the listener; change the metre of a familiar eight-bar melody and describe the effect of the change; remove tone bars on a xylophone to create a pentatonic tonality, and then improvise a pentatonic response on the xylophone to a call played on a recorder*)

*Teacher prompts:* "How will you change your theme to create a set of variations?" "What effect will changing the metre of 'Frère Jacques' have on the music?" "Explain why your composition should (or should not) include an introduction or coda."

**C1.3** create musical compositions for specific purposes and audiences (*e.g., write a melodic composition reflecting a piece of art of their own or by another, such as Norval Morrisseau or Emily Carr; create a rhythmic composition using non-pitched percussion to accompany a First Nation legend, story, or poem; with a partner, compose a song to promote Canada to the rest of the world*)

*Teacher prompts:* "What do the lines in the painting tell you about the direction the pitches should move in?" "How could the rhythm of the syllables in your name be used as the rhythmic base for your composition?" "What is the purpose of selecting specific timbres in your accompaniment of a First Nation legend?"

**C1.4** use the tools and techniques of musicianship in musical performances (*e.g., conduct pieces in duple and triple metres, listen for balance and blend when singing and/or playing, interpret musical markings and Italian terms during performance*)

*Teacher prompt:* "What are the musical characteristics that you intend to demonstrate in your performance? How will you demonstrate them?"

**C1.5** demonstrate an understanding of standard and other types of musical notation through performance and composition (*e.g., perform music that includes ledger lines, triplets, simple and compound metres; use original graphic or symbolic systems to represent vocal and instrumental sounds and musical ideas*)

*Teacher prompts:* "What are the steps you need to follow in order to read and interpret this music?" "What are the similarities and differences between this devised notation system and standard notation?"

## C2. Reflecting, Responding, and Analysing

By the end of Grade 6, students will:

**C2.1** express detailed personal responses to musical performances in a variety of ways (*e.g., write a critical review of a live or recorded performance; write analyses of works they have listened to in a log or journal; create a drawing or graphic representation of their initial reaction to a song*)

*Teacher prompts:* "What do you think is the mood of this piece and how is it created?"

"Using musical terms, how would you describe the overall form and effect of the music?"

**C2.2** identify the elements of music in the repertoire they perform, listen to, and create, and describe how they are used (*e.g., describe the way in which dotted rhythms, the sound quality of brass instruments, higher pitches, loud dynamics, and accented articulation combine to suggest music that introduces royalty*)

*Teacher prompts:* "How would you describe the rhythm?" "What are the primary instruments used by the composer?" "How is the music organized?"

**C2.3** identify and give examples of their strengths and areas for improvement as composers, musical performers, interpreters, and audience members (*e.g., reflect on their first draft of an original composition and incorporate suggestions from their peers into their final piece*)

*Teacher prompts:* "What type of behaviour would you expect from your audience if you were playing a solo for the class?" "How can you improve your performance next time?"

## C3. Exploring Forms and Cultural Contexts

By the end of Grade 6, students will:

**C3.1** identify and describe ways in which awareness or appreciation of music is affected by culture and the media (*e.g., people attend concerts of music that they know and like or have found out about through the media; people can be influenced to buy products that are advertised with music that they relate to*)

*Teacher prompts:* "What style of music – for example orchestral, jazz, pop, rock, funk, rap, or hip hop – would you use to advertise a new video game? Why?" "Explain the appeal of using rap music to address issues of oppression and identity among Aboriginal youth."

**C3.2** compare some aspects of the music of one culture and/or historical period with aspects of the music of another culture and/or historical period (*e.g., compare selected characteristics of music from the baroque and classical periods, using a Venn diagram; write a review of music from another society, comparing the music of that society with the music with which they are familiar*)

*Teacher prompts:* "In what ways is popular music from other cultures different from or similar to North American popular music?" "Which elements of music seem to be common in all cultures?"

# D. VISUAL ARTS

## OVERALL EXPECTATIONS

By the end of Grade 6, students will:

**D1. Creating and Presenting:** apply the creative process (see pages 19–22) to produce art works in a variety of traditional two- and three-dimensional forms, as well as multimedia art works, that communicate feelings, ideas, and understandings, using elements, principles, and techniques of visual arts as well as current media technologies;

**D2. Reflecting, Responding, and Analysing:** apply the critical analysis process (see pages 23–28) to communicate feelings, ideas, and understandings in response to a variety of art works and art experiences;

**D3. Exploring Forms and Cultural Contexts:** demonstrate an understanding of a variety of art forms, styles, and techniques from the past and present, and their sociocultural and historical contexts.

---

### FUNDAMENTAL CONCEPTS FOR GRADE 6

In addition to the concepts introduced in Grades 1 to 5, students in Grade 6 will develop understanding of the following concepts through participation in a variety of hands-on, open-ended visual arts experiences.

ELEMENTS OF DESIGN
Students will develop understanding of all elements of design.

* *line:* lines that direct the viewer's attention; lines that create the illusion of force or movement (e.g., wavy and wiggly lines used in op art); contour drawings of objects that are not easily recognizable (e.g., crumpled paper)

* *shape and form:* exaggerated proportions, motifs, fonts; geometric (e.g., conical, pyramidal) shapes and forms

* *space:* centre of interest (focal point) and one-point perspective; basic facial proportions; horizontal and vertical symmetry

* *colour:* the colour wheel; tertiary colours; colour for expressive purposes; colour for creating naturalistic images

* *texture:* textures created with a variety of tools, materials, and techniques (e.g., gouged marks in a softoleum print)

* *value:* shading that suggests volume; gradation

PRINCIPLES OF DESIGN
Students will develop understanding of all principles of design (that is, contrast, repetition and rhythm, variety, emphasis, proportion, balance, unity and harmony, and movement), but the focus in Grade 6 will be on balance.

* *balance:* arrangement of the elements of design to create the impression of equality in weight or importance (e.g., a formal or symmetrical arrangement produced through distribution of shapes; an informal or asymmetrical arrangement produced through use of colour); colour concepts to be used in creating balance (e.g., light or neutral colours appear lighter in "weight" than dark or brilliant colours; warm colours seem to expand, cool colours seem to contract; transparent areas seem to "weigh" less than opaque areas)

# SPECIFIC EXPECTATIONS

## D1. Creating and Presenting

By the end of Grade 6, students will:

**D1.1** create two-dimensional, three-dimensional, and multimedia art works that explore feelings, ideas, and issues from a variety of points of view (*e.g., art work inspired by the motifs in other art forms [dance, music] or by hopes and dreams; a mixed-media piece or one-minute video "short" about adaptation and survival; a still-life painting that offers a social commentary on fast-food packaging*)

*Teacher prompts:* "How does the music make you feel? Now, close your eyes and try to see the music. How does what you hear, feel, and see (e.g., an abstract painting by Wassily Kandinsky) influence what you create?" "How will you convey the movement of the dancer in your sculpture?" "How will you edit the text and images in your art work to capture the viewer's attention and convey your ideas?" "How can you compose your image to represent a particular point of view?"

**D1.2** demonstrate an understanding of composition, using selected principles of design to create narrative art works or art works on a theme or topic (*e.g., use a larger area of a lighter tint and a smaller area of a darker tone of one colour in an asymmetrically balanced painting; use repetition, simplification, and exaggeration of proportion and shape to create a sense of rhythm in a graphite-and-pastel drawing of musical instruments and their shadows*)

*Teacher prompts:* "How have you used line and the repetition of shape and colour to create a sense of rhythm and the illusion of movement? What else could you repeat to create rhythm?" "How can you use small areas of brilliant, warm colour to visually balance large areas of either neutral or cool colours?"

**D1.3** use elements of design in art works to communicate ideas, messages, and understandings (*e.g., a design of a letter of the alphabet using shapes, symbols, colour, and font style to represent a selected animal and its habitat; a DVD cover design or movie poster that uses line, shape, space, colour, and value to communicate information about the content*)

*Teacher prompts:* "How can colour be used in your letter design to separate your letter shape from the background?" "What images will you select and will they symbolize something in your design?" "How would you change the images and colours in your poster to appeal to younger students?" "What is the message of your work, and how has it been conveyed to the audience?"

**D1.4** use a variety of materials, tools, techniques, and technologies to determine solutions to design challenges (*e.g.,*

- drawing: *use charcoal to create a shaded drawing of the exaggerated details of a face, a figure, or natural objects [e.g., shells, pods] on earth-toned papers [e.g., tan construction paper]*

- mixed media: *create a collage that uses a limited colour palette by cutting, pasting, and layering to combine images, symbols, textured papers, and text about consumerism or cultural pride*

- painting: *use a variety of paint techniques [e.g., blending, scumbling, glazing] in a mural of a landscape or cityscape incorporating stylistic elements from contemporary pop culture*

- printmaking: *cut and gouge a variety of lines and marks to enhance the background and negative spaces in a softoleum, linoleum, or block print that depicts an endangered animal species*

- sculpture: *create an assemblage on a topic or theme, using found objects that are painted or otherwise unified through colour, in the style of a sculpture by Louise Nevelson*

- technology: *create a digital photo montage that represents aspects of environmentalism*)

*Teacher prompts:* "How can you arrange photographs to create balance and harmony in your collage or montage?" "How can you manipulate the relationship of shape or form in your collage by gluing some paper flat and some in relief?"

## D2. Reflecting, Responding, and Analysing

By the end of Grade 6, students will:

**D2.1** interpret a variety of art works and identify the feelings, issues, themes, and social concerns that they convey (*e.g., describe Ted Harrison's use of line, colour, brushstrokes, and rhythm to create a feeling of movement and excitement; compare the themes and the emotions conveyed in selected Western animations and in Japanese animations such as those by Hayao Miyazaki*)

*Teacher prompts:* "How does the artist convey a particular emotion through this art work?" "How does each comic style use facial expression, body language, and colour to express emotion? How have current media technologies influenced the expression of ideas in animations and comics?"

**D2.2** explain how the elements and principles of design are used in their own and others' art work to communicate meaning or understanding (*e.g., identify the point of view or gaze of the main subject, and explain how it is used to influence an intended audience of an art work or a media work; explain how Kenojuak Ashevak's use of formal balance (symmetry) in* The World Around Me *conveys a sense of harmony in nature; explain how a rough texture can be used to represent strength, anger, or something unpleasant*)

*Teacher prompts:* "How could you show the same message in another art form, such as a sculpture, a digital medium, or a painting?" "How does Bill Reid's *The Raven and the First Men* depict the relationship of form to its surroundings through the use of positive and negative space?"

**D2.3** demonstrate an understanding of how to read and interpret signs, symbols, and style in art works (*e.g., symbolism for sending messages and telling stories in Egyptian hieroglyphs, Agawa rock paintings, or graffiti art; symbols on currency or in advertisements that have specific national or other connotations; meanings associated with colour in different cultures [white dresses symbolize purity in Western culture but mourning and death in some Asian cultures]*)

*Teacher prompts:* "What are some of the feelings and ideas associated with Canadian symbols (e.g., maple leaf, beaver), and what are some of the things that they say about us as a nation?" "What assumptions do you make about a product when its advertisement shows a man and woman holding hands? How can designers change the image to manipulate those assumptions?"

**D2.4** identify and explain their strengths, their interests, and areas for improvement as creators, interpreters, and viewers of art (*e.g., reflect on challenges and successes in the form of an artist's statement; maintain a sketchbook or collection of ideas and images for art works; do peer reviews of each other's art works, using a checklist of criteria created by the class to help them identify areas that need revision, and provide suggestions*)

*Teacher prompts:* "How did you adapt these new ideas, situations, media, materials, processes, or technologies to help you convey your ideas?" "How did you use imagination, observation, and the study of other art works to help you develop your ideas?" "How did

you negotiate designs with other members of the group and agree on the techniques, ideas, and composition you used?" "How did you approach the challenges you faced in making sure your sculpture was interesting to look at from more than one side? What would you do differently next time?"

## D3. Exploring Forms and Cultural Contexts

By the end of Grade 6, students will:

**D3.1** identify and describe some of the ways in which art forms and styles reflect the beliefs and traditions of a variety of communities, times, and places (*e.g., art can represent ways in which people view their personal identity; contemporary Aboriginal artists use their artistic traditions to comment on identity, society, and the world; art can be a record of human experience; differences in style among different artists can be associated with a specific reason, intent, or motivation*)

*Teacher prompts:* "How do contemporary artists use the influences of various global and/or historical art forms to explore ideas and themes that have personal relevance?" "How does Jane Ash Poitras' combining of autobiographical elements, traditional Cree iconography, text, photographs, newspaper clippings, and painted elements address ideas about identity and acculturation?" "Describe some of the differences and similarities between the depictions of men and the depictions of women in historical and contemporary art works."

**D3.2** demonstrate an understanding of key contributions and functions of visual and media arts in various contexts at both the local and the national levels (*e.g., community art schools or programs provide opportunities for creative expression and instruction by and for both amateurs and professionals; a wide variety of workers are employed by arts industries such as advertising, design, movie making, and broadcast media; artists contribute to Canada's economy by providing both goods and services*)

*Teacher prompts:* "In what ways do the visual arts contribute to the economies of urban and rural communities?" "In what ways are the visual arts involved in international trade?" "What are the various professions or careers that have a basis in visual arts, and what education is required? How can we find out more about these careers?"

# OVERVIEW OF GRADES 7 AND 8

The expectations for Grades 7 and 8 focus on the consolidation of students' knowledge, skills, and strategies in the arts and their ability to use the arts independently and effectively to enhance their learning in school and to communicate feelings and ideas about their multicultural, multimedia world. It continues to be important at this level to differentiate instruction to address students' individual needs.

During the primary and junior years, students have acquired essential knowledge about forms and conventions in the various arts. They have also developed the ability to reflect on, monitor, and take steps to improve their arts knowledge and skills in all strands. The expectations for Grades 7 and 8 build upon this foundation. Intermediate students consolidate and apply their arts knowledge, skills, and strategies across the curriculum in order to learn in all subject areas as the content becomes increasingly challenging.

Teachers in the intermediate division should explicitly teach and model the use of arts knowledge, skills, and strategies across all subject areas. Explicit teaching and modelling help students to identify the skills and strategies they need in order to become proficient creators, viewers, and interpreters of art works in a variety of contexts and to move towards achievement of the expectations. Students require multiple, diverse opportunities to practise independently and demonstrate their achievement of the learning expectations.

The expectations encourage students to explore issues related to personal identity and community concerns as they interact with increasingly complex and/or challenging media; to critically analyse and evaluate perspectives in works of dance, drama, music, and visual art; to use inquiry and research skills to extend their interpretive and creative abilities; and to use the arts to explore and comment on topics of relevance that matter in their daily lives. Issues of social justice are often highly engaging for students at this age. Exploration and communication of multiple perspectives and points of view should be emphasized.

The arts curriculum for Grades 7 and 8 is designed to engage students in tasks that they see as meaningful and motivate them to learn about and create art works out of interest as well as to meet curriculum expectations. In addition to the materials provided for instruction, students should have access to a wide range of themes, materials, and activities that are relevant to their personal experiences and interests as creators, artists, and critically literate viewers. All topics and activities chosen for instruction should invite interaction, inquiry, creative exploration, and critical analysis, and should promote antidiscrimination education. All students, especially young adolescents, need to see themselves in the material they encounter. They need to be able to choose independently to interact with content that has personal relevance in their day-to-day lives, including material that deals with issues related to fairness, equity, and social justice.

## Dance

In Grades 7 and 8, students refine their kinesthetic awareness and use all of the elements of dance (body, space, time, energy, relationship) to create dance works that express a point of view about a variety of issues, concepts, and themes. Students at the intermediate level should be able to select a form of choreography appropriate to their theme and combine all the elements of dance effectively to communicate meaning. They should also be able to use technology and/or props to enhance the message of their dance pieces. Students apply their knowledge of dance; reflect on their strengths and next steps as dancers, choreographers, and audience members; and think critically about the role of dance in the media and in their lives. Students also demonstrate an increased understanding of the role of dance in various cultures, societies, and historical periods and refine their ability to evaluate the quality of performances by writing critiques of their own and others' work and reviewing dance performances.

## Drama

Students in Grades 7 and 8 continue to focus on role play and the development of believable characters as foundational components of both process drama and theatre performance. In addition to role/character, they incorporate the elements of relationship, time and place, tension, focus, and emphasis in drama works they create, and apply their knowledge of the elements in analysing drama works. At this level, an issues-based focus encourages students to deepen their capacity for empathy and for critical analysis of issues. Because drama is a highly social art form, teaching, modelling, and guidance in the development of effective group skills are essential.

In partners, small groups, and whole-class formats, students create drama using a variety of forms, techniques, and conventions. Students continue to use the drama forms and conventions learned in the primary and junior grades to explore more complex material, while also broadening their knowledge of forms and conventions to include improvisation, devised scenes, collaborative play building, interpreting and performing scripts, reader's theatre, and docudrama. Students should also have opportunities to create, reflect, and analyse independently in a variety of ways (e.g., through writing in role, monologue writing and performance, journal reflections, visual representation). Through frequent, well-structured opportunities to discuss, speculate about, reflect on, critique, and comment on their own and others' drama work, they broaden and deepen their understanding and appreciation of drama as an art form. They strengthen their understanding of the function of drama in society and the roles and responsibilities of different theatre professionals. They also refine their ability to evaluate the quality of performances by writing critiques of their own and others' work and reviewing theatrical performances.

## Music

The acquisition of musical knowledge and skills is cumulative and sequential, based on the learning from earlier grades. In Grades 7 and 8, students consolidate their prior music learning through a variety of opportunities for listening, performing, and creating. In Grade 7, students apply their knowledge of music, reflect on their strengths, and determine next steps when creating and interpreting music. They analyse the role of music in their lives and the ways in which music has changed in response to a variety of historical, cultural, and other influences. In Grade 8, students perform in a variety of ensembles and use musical knowledge, musicianship, and creative abilities to create musical works for specific purposes. They develop their own learning profile and apply this knowledge to their work in the music classroom. Students in both grades should have opportunities to solve musical problems in groups and individually, and should demonstrate the ability to use logical arguments to support analyses and judgements of their own and others' musical efforts, while showing respect for the opinions and efforts of others.

## Visual Arts

In Grades 7 and 8, students' own art making becomes infused with a variety of images and approaches. They are very aware of elements from popular culture and eager to incorporate them into their art. Students continue to make compositional decisions and to use a variety of materials and techniques to generate and produce two- and three-dimensional works of art, as well as multimedia forms. Through creative activities, students continue their process of exploration, discovery, and learning in the visual arts and broaden their knowledge and appreciation of the field. The transition to Grade 8 brings an increased emphasis on students' development of technical competence and a distinctive personal style.

The study of art in its historical and cultural contexts gives students insight into the visual arts both as a record of human achievement and as inspiration for their own creation of art. It is important to encourage students to view and respond to works from both the past and present and to support their growing understanding that artists are concerned with issues that are relevant to their own lives and societies. Students in both grades should have opportunities to investigate art works that represent a variety of historical periods, cultures, and styles. As they consider a variety of art works in historical perspective, students ask more refined and probing questions and gain a clearer understanding of what they themselves value. Recognizing artistic practices that resonate with their own personal and creative concerns can motivate students to think more deeply about their own art-making process. As students examine, analyse, and discuss art works, they become more confident and skilled in expressing informed opinions about and preferences for specific works. They also become aware that others' preferences may differ from their own and that multiple artistic solutions and interpretations are possible and acceptable.

# GRADE 7

# A. DANCE

## OVERALL EXPECTATIONS

By the end of Grade 7, students will:

**A1. Creating and Presenting:** apply the creative process (see pages 19–22) to the composition of a variety of dance pieces, using the elements of dance to communicate feelings and ideas;

**A2. Reflecting, Responding, and Analysing:** apply the critical analysis process (see pages 23–28) to communicate their feelings, ideas, and understandings in response to a variety of dance pieces and experiences;

**A3. Exploring Forms and Cultural Contexts:** demonstrate an understanding of a variety of dance forms, traditions, and styles from the past and present, and their sociocultural and historical contexts.

---

### FUNDAMENTAL CONCEPTS FOR GRADE 7

Students in Grade 7 will develop or extend understanding of the following concepts through participation in various dance experiences (e.g., using elements and choreographic forms to communicate themes and moods).

ELEMENTS OF DANCE
- *body:* body awareness, use of body parts, body shapes, locomotor and non-locomotor movements, body bases, symmetry versus asymmetry, geometric versus organic shape, angular versus curved shape, isolation of body parts (e.g., moving just the shoulder when the rest of the body is still), weight transfer (e.g., lunge, leap, roll)
- *space:* levels, pathways, directions, positive versus negative space, proximity of dancers to one another, various group formations, performance space (e.g., confined, large)
- *time:* pause, freeze, with music, without music, duration, rhythm, tempo, acceleration/deceleration
- *energy:* effort, force, quality, inaction versus action, percussion, fluidity (e.g., wring, dab, mould, flow, bind)
- *relationship:* dancers to objects, opposition, groupings (e.g., large and small groups), meet/part, follow/lead, emotional connections between dancers, groupings

---

## SPECIFIC EXPECTATIONS

### A1. Creating and Presenting

By the end of Grade 7, students will:

**A1.1** create dance pieces to represent or respond to specific rhythms and pieces of music (*e.g., use the body, body parts, and the floor [stamping, stepping, body slapping] to replicate the rhythms in the music; transform a music imaging exercise into a dance interpretation*)

*Teacher prompt:* "While listening to this piece of music, record on paper words, pictures, and shapes that come to mind and think of how you can translate these abstract images into movement."

**A1.2** use dance as a language to communicate ideas from their own writing or media works (*e.g., create a dance piece inspired by a student-authored poem about relationships with the natural world or by a student media work about divorce or loss*)

*Teacher prompts:* "What are some images from your poem that you could represent in dance? How would you do so?" "What elements of dance (e.g., movements, levels, pathways) would best communicate the different perspectives presented in your writing or media presentation?"

**A1.3** use theme and variations in a variety of ways when creating dance pieces (*e.g., create a simple movement phrase [theme] and then repeat it in modified form [variation] using choreographic manipulations [retrograding the original phrase, facing another dancer, adding more dancers]*)

*Teacher prompts:* "What new manipulation that we haven't explored yet could you use to create another variation on the original phrase (theme)?" "Can we use the same set of movements to show bullying from the perspective of a variety of people? How will the movements have to change to show the different perspectives? Show me."

**A1.4** use the elements of dance and choreographic forms (*e.g., pattern forms, narrative forms*) to communicate a variety of themes or moods (*e.g., use entrances or exits to communicate beginnings or endings; use a recurring sequence of movements to signal a particular mood or character; use canon form for emphasis*)

*Teacher prompt:* "What message could be conveyed by a repeated pattern? What message might be conveyed when you *interrupt* a repeated pattern?"

## A2. Reflecting, Responding, and Analysing

By the end of Grade 7, students will:

**A2.1** construct personal interpretations of the messages in their own and others' dance pieces, including messages about issues relevant to their community and/or the world (*e.g., dance pieces on topics such as urban sprawl, land claims, poverty, homophobia, homelessness*), and communicate their responses in a variety of ways (*e.g., through writing, class discussion, oral reports, song, drama, visual art*)

*Teacher prompt:* "What statement did the dance we just watched make about global warming? Do you agree or disagree with the message the dance conveyed? Why? Was the message effectively conveyed?"

**A2.2** analyse, using dance vocabulary, their own and others' dance pieces to identify the elements of dance and the choreographic forms used in them and explain how they help communicate meaning (*e.g., use of crouching shapes low to the ground and bound energy communicates the idea of confined space; use of site-specific locations [outdoor playground] to structure a dance communicates the idea of connection to the environment*)

*Teacher prompts:* "How did the use of the canon form emphasize the message of the dance piece?" "How did the fact that the dancers performed in theatre in the round help reinforce their message of confinement?"

**A2.3** identify and give examples of their strengths and areas for growth as dance creators, interpreters, and audience members (*e.g., share with a partner what they did well during a performance, using dance vocabulary; use a concept map to explain their choice of dance movements*)

*Teacher prompts:* "When creating dance pieces, do you prefer to translate literature into dance or to use themes and ideas of your own? Why?" "As an audience member, what do you look for to help you understand what is being said? The dancers' body actions, perhaps? What other elements? Do you think your interpretations are usually accurate? Can you give an example when you showed particularly good understanding of the dancers' message?"

## A3. Exploring Forms and Cultural Contexts

By the end of Grade 7, students will:

**A3.1** describe the evolution of dance and performance as different groups of people have responded to external factors such as migration, a new environment, and/or contact with other groups or cultures (*e.g., the evolution of Maritime Acadian folk dances into Louisiana Cajun dances such as fais do do and the Mardi Gras dance Krewes; the origins and development of French and Scottish jigs; the evolution of the Métis jig out of imitations of wildlife movements [prairie wild birds] and the intricate footwork of Native dancing and European jigs*)

*Teacher prompt:* "How did the dances of the Acadians evolve when they were forced to immigrate to Louisiana? What factors influenced this evolution?"

**A3.2** identify ways in which dance and its depictions in the media may influence a person's character development and sense of identity (*e.g., by influencing young people's sense of themselves and their bodies; by providing dance role models who represent or promote particular lifestyles, values, and attitudes*)

*Teacher prompts:* "How has the way the media depict dance influenced the way you feel about your own dancing?" "How has dance in the media influenced your body image?" "Are the traditional dances of your community shown in the media? Do the media depictions give an accurate idea of the dances of your community as you experience them?"

# B. DRAMA

## OVERALL EXPECTATIONS

By the end of Grade 7, students will:

**B1. Creating and Presenting:** apply the creative process (see pages 19–22) to process drama and the development of drama works, using the elements and conventions of drama to communicate feelings, ideas, and multiple perspectives;

**B2. Reflecting, Responding, and Analysing:** apply the critical analysis process (see pages 23–28) to communicate feelings, ideas, and understandings in response to a variety of drama works and experiences;

**B3. Exploring Forms and Cultural Contexts:** demonstrate an understanding of a variety of drama and theatre forms, traditions, and styles from the past and present, and their sociocultural and historical contexts.

### FUNDAMENTAL CONCEPTS FOR GRADE 7

Students in Grade 7 will develop or extend understanding of the following concepts through participation in various drama experiences.

ELEMENTS OF DRAMA
- *role/character:* considering motivations of historical and fictional characters; considering various facets of multidimensional characters; revealing character through the use of props and movement/blocking; maintaining commitment to role
- *relationship:* developing and analysing multidimensional relationships in the drama
- *time and place:* improvising with/adapting available materials to establish setting; using blocking (e.g., when and where to move) and stage areas (e.g., upstage right, downstage centre) in planning and performance
- *tension:* using sound, lighting, technology, and stage effects to heighten tension; using foreshadowing to create suspense
- *focus and emphasis:* using a range of devices and effects to highlight specific aspects of the performance for the audience

## SPECIFIC EXPECTATIONS

### B1. Creating and Presenting

By the end of Grade 7, students will:

**B1.1** engage actively in drama exploration and role play, with a focus on examining multiple perspectives related to current issues, themes, and relationships from a wide variety of sources and diverse communities (*e.g., identify significant perspectives related to an issue such as peer pressure, treaty rights, or cultural identity, and assume roles to express the different perspectives; use prepared improvisation to communicate insights about life events and relationships; use thought tracking and symbolic artefacts to present a persona associated with a past historical event*)

*Teacher prompt:* "What drama conventions (e.g., mime, overheard conversation, a day in the life) could you use to inform the audience about the events leading up to the issue? What roles should be adopted to represent the range of perspectives related to the key themes of our drama (e.g., differing world views of Europeans and Aboriginal people at the time of contact)?"

**B1.2** demonstrate an understanding of the elements of drama by selecting and combining several elements and conventions to create dramatic effects (*e.g., develop a drama presentation incorporating a series of tableaux, a group soundscape, a movement piece, and a rap/song*)

*Teacher prompts:* "Which convention will you use to begin the piece? End the piece?" "What roles could be introduced to explore the relationships in more detail?"

**B1.3** plan and shape the direction of the drama by working with others, both in and out of role, to generate ideas and explore multiple perspectives *(e.g., In role: use thought tracking or writing in role to explore the feelings and motivations of a character; introduce a new perspective during role play to foster a sense of empathy with the character; Out of role: use a place mat activity to select ideas that group members agree upon; use invented notation to explain the movement of the character)*

*Teacher prompts:* "How could you use the conventions of flashback and flash forward to examine turning points and major decisions in your drama piece?" "How might you physically represent the different emotions experienced by different characters in the drama?"

**B1.4** communicate feelings, thoughts, and abstract ideas through drama works, using audio, visual, and/or technological aids to heighten the dramatic experience *(e.g., use music to create mood; use video and drums/noisemakers to signal the climax; use a digital slide presentation to create a backdrop of words or images; use costumes, props, fabric to establish character and/or setting)*

*Teacher prompts:* "What is different when we develop a drama for a recording studio versus the classroom, a street or mall performance, or an arts night performance?" "How could you use sound technology to help listeners visualize the action of a radio drama?" "How could you use lighting and projection technology to enhance the setting for your stage production?" "What images could you project that would provide a clarifying contrast to the action on the stage?"

## B2. Reflecting, Responding, and Analysing

By the end of Grade 7, students will:

**B2.1** construct personal interpretations of drama works, connecting drama issues and themes to their own and others' ideas, feelings, and experiences *(e.g., use a series of tableaux or freeze-frame images of key moments in a drama to show which moments had the greatest impact on them; write in role about an environmental issue,*

*first from the point of view of an audience member and then from the point of view of an animal whose habitat is threatened)*

*Teacher prompt:* "This drama presented one side of an environmental issue. Whose perspective is missing? Why do you think it has been left out? How do you feel about that? What words might you give to this voice?"

**B2.2** analyse and describe, using drama terminology, how drama elements are used to communicate meaning in a variety of drama works and shared drama experiences *(e.g., compare and contrast how the director of a play and the director of a film might use body positioning and sound to communicate a character's feelings to the audience)*

*Teacher prompts:* "How do the elements work together to convey a message?" "Do you think the central character's intentions are clearly communicated? What evidence can you give to support your point of view?" "In what ways did (drama convention X) help establish the context of the drama?"

**B2.3** identify and give examples of their strengths, interests, and areas for improvement as drama creators, performers, and audience members *(e.g., create a chart listing strengths and areas for improvement; highlight an area to work on in their next drama production; write a report on their learning in drama for a school newsletter)*

*Teacher prompts:* "What aspects of drama do you enjoy most?" "What skills are you most proud of?" "Can you identify one skill that you feel you need to practise?" "In what ways did you contribute to the group's collaborative drama?"

## B3. Exploring Forms and Cultural Contexts

By the end of Grade 7, students will:

**B3.1** compare and contrast how social values are communicated in several different drama forms and/or styles of live theatre from different times and places *(e.g., how views of colonist-Aboriginal relationships differ in plays from earlier times versus contemporary plays; how themes of loyalty to family and/or country are treated in comic forms versus serious drama forms)*

*Teacher prompt:* "How have some theatre productions changed as they are reinterpreted by performers in different times and places? What do you think the changes tell us about the societies that produced them?"

**B3.2** identify and describe several ways in which drama and theatre (*e.g., street festivals, film festivals, theatre festivals, local theatre groups*) contribute to contemporary social, economic, and cultural life (*e.g., attract tourists; provide jobs; provide entertainment; promote cultural understanding; raise people's awareness of social issues*)

*Teacher prompts:* "Why is it beneficial to have local theatre groups in our community?" "What theatre jobs require performance skills?" "If you interviewed people involved in drama or theatre in the community (e.g., actors, directors, theatre group members, playwrights, designers), what could you ask them about the value they place on theatre as part of their own lives and the life of the community?" "What value do you think your work in drama has in your own life? In the life of the community?"

# C. MUSIC

## OVERALL EXPECTATIONS

By the end of Grade 7, students will:

**C1. Creating and Performing:** apply the creative process (see pages 19–22) to create and perform music for a variety of purposes, using the elements and techniques of music;

**C2. Reflecting, Responding, and Analysing:** apply the critical analysis process (see pages 23–28) to communicate their feelings, ideas, and understandings in response to a variety of music and musical experiences;

**C3. Exploring Forms and Cultural Contexts:** demonstrate an understanding of a variety of musical genres and styles from the past and present, and their sociocultural and historical contexts.

---

### FUNDAMENTAL CONCEPTS FOR GRADE 7

In Grade 7, students will build on their knowledge of the elements of music and related musical concepts that were introduced in Grades 1 to 6. Students will develop understanding of musical concepts through participation in musical experiences that involve listening, moving, creating, and performing (vocal and/or instrumental music).

**ELEMENTS OF MUSIC**

* *duration:* tempo markings (e.g., *allegro, vivace, largo*), rhythms in the repertoire they play and/or sing
* *pitch:* blues scale, grand staff, keys encountered in the repertoire they perform
* *dynamics and other expressive controls:* articulation and expression marks encountered in the repertoire they perform (e.g., *marcato, maestoso*)
* *timbre:* tone colour of complex ensembles (e.g., jazz, gamelan, choral, orchestral)
* *texture/harmony:* major and minor triads
* *form:* 12-bar blues

---

## SPECIFIC EXPECTATIONS

### C1. Creating and Performing

By the end of Grade 7, students will:

**C1.1** sing and/or play, in tune, from musical notation, unison music and music in two or more parts from diverse cultures, styles, and historical periods (*e.g., perform selections from a method book, student compositions, instrumental scores, ensemble repertoire, African drum rhythms, choral repertoire, jazz charts, spirituals, steel band music*)

*Teacher prompt:* "How long are the phrases in this example? What will you need to do to bring out the phrasing?"

**C1.2** apply the elements of music when singing and/or playing, composing, and arranging music, using them for specific effects and clear purposes (*e.g., create a class chant or song to build community spirit; manipulate the rhythm or dynamics in a familiar piece to create an accompaniment for a media presentation*)

*Teacher prompts:* "In your chant, how did you communicate your message through the elements of music you focused on?" "How will changing the tempo affect the mood of the piece?"

**C1.3** create musical compositions in a variety of forms for specific purposes and audiences (*e.g., use available instruments to create a composition in response to an object, a visual image, or a silent film; add rhythmic, melodic, or chordal accompaniment to a familiar song; improvise rhythmic or melodic phrases over a variety of ostinati; create compositions using found sounds or recycled materials*)

*Teacher prompt:* "Which instrumental sounds might you use to represent the colours in the painting? Why?"

**C1.4** use the tools and techniques of musicianship in musical performances (*e.g., apply markings for dynamics, tempo, phrasing, and articulation when performing; use proper breath control throughout their singing range*)

*Teacher prompt:* "What do we know about the conventions for performing a march that can help us determine how best to play this piece?"

**C1.5** demonstrate an understanding of standard and other musical notation through performance and composition (*e.g., read and respond to accidentals, repeat signs, various tempo markings; notate and perform a variety of scales, including the blues scale; explain how some contemporary music, children's songs, or Aboriginal singing, drumming, and dancing are transmitted through oral tradition*)

*Teacher prompts:* "Why is it important to know how the major scale is constructed when reading and writing music?" "How are contemporary Canadian Aboriginal musicians ensuring that their oral traditions are being preserved?"

## C2. Reflecting, Responding, and Analysing

By the end of Grade 7, students will:

**C2.1** express analytical, personal responses to musical performances in a variety of ways (*e.g., represent musical scenes in* Pictures at an Exhibition *through art work or dramatization; record detailed analyses of music they have listened to in a log or reflection journal to explain why they enjoy it and how the elements of music are used*)

*Teacher prompt:* "Art works by visual artist Viktor Hartmann inspired Modest Mussorgsky to compose *Pictures at an Exhibition*. Having listened to this piece, how would your musical interpretation of the art works be different from Mussorgsky's? What inspires your creation of music?"

**C2.2** analyse, using musical terminology, ways in which the elements are used in the music that they perform, listen to, and create (*e.g., compare the use of drums in different social and cultural contexts, such as Asian, Aboriginal, and African communities; listen to a Brazilian folk song or a current popular song, and describe how the use of the various elements affects their response to the music*)

*Teacher prompt:* "How does the addition of rhythm and melody affect the nature of the lyrics in popular music?"

**C2.3** identify and give examples of their strengths and areas for improvement as composers, musical performers, interpreters, and audience members (*e.g., set a goal to improve their performance skills, reflect on how successful they were in attaining their goal, keep a practice journal, record and analyse their performances throughout the term*)

*Teacher prompt:* "Write a résumé highlighting your achievements as a musician. What careers related to music would best suit your interests and areas of strength?"

## C3. Exploring Forms and Cultural Contexts

By the end of Grade 7, students will:

**C3.1** analyse the influences of music and the media on the development of personal and cultural identity (*e.g., describe how their personal musical preferences have been formed from listening to music readily available in the media; explain how cultural identity, including a sense of Aboriginal pride for Aboriginal students, can be reinforced by listening to music of their own culture*)

*Teacher prompts:* "What is the influence or role of music in your family life, your school life, and your social life?" "What do you admire about the musical artists who are key influences in your life?" "How does music connect us, divide us, or call us to action?" "What is the most important role of music in your life?"

**C3.2** analyse some historical, cultural, and technological influences on style, genre, and innovation in music (*e.g., the impact of the invention of the piano or the electric guitar*)

*Teacher prompt:* "How did the development of the piano and other musical instruments affect composers, performers, and audiences?"

# D. VISUAL ARTS

## OVERALL EXPECTATIONS

By the end of Grade 7, students will:

**D1. Creating and Presenting:** apply the creative process (see pages 19–22) to produce art works in a variety of traditional two- and three-dimensional forms, as well as multimedia art works, that communicate feelings, ideas, and understandings, using elements, principles, and techniques of visual arts as well as current media technologies;

**D2. Reflecting, Responding, and Analysing:** apply the critical analysis process (see pages 23–28) to communicate feelings, ideas, and understandings in response to a variety of art works and art experiences;

**D3. Exploring Forms and Cultural Contexts:** demonstrate an understanding of a variety of art forms, styles, and techniques from the past and present, and their sociocultural and historical contexts.

### FUNDAMENTAL CONCEPTS FOR GRADE 7

In addition to the concepts introduced in Grades 1 to 6, students in Grade 7 will develop understanding of the following concepts through participation in a variety of hands-on, open-ended visual arts experiences.

ELEMENTS OF DESIGN
Students will develop understanding of all elements of design.

- *line:* lines for expressive purposes; diagonal and converging lines to create depth of space; repetition of lines to create visual rhythm
- *shape and form:* various shapes and forms, symbols, icons, logos, radial balance
- *space:* use of blue or complementary colours in shadows and shading to create depth; one- and two-point perspective; open-form sculpture versus closed-form sculpture; installations
- *colour:* analogous colours; transparent colour created with watercolour or tissue paper decoupage
  **Note:** In creating multimedia art works, students may need some understanding of different colour models, such as RGB and CMY(K), and websafe colours.
- *texture:* textures created with a variety of tools, materials, and techniques (e.g., use of texture in a landscape work)
- *value:* shading (e.g., modulation, scumbling, stippling)

PRINCIPLES OF DESIGN
Students will develop understanding of all principles of design (that is, contrast, repetition and rhythm, variety, emphasis, proportion, balance, unity and harmony, and movement), but the focus in Grade 7 will be on unity and harmony.

- *unity and harmony:* radial balance (e.g., a mandala); similarity (e.g., consistency and completeness through repetition of colours, shapes, values, textures, or lines); continuity (e.g., treatment of different elements in a similar manner); alignment (e.g., arrangement of shapes to follow an implied axis); proximity (e.g., grouping of related items together)

# SPECIFIC EXPECTATIONS

## D1. Creating and Presenting

By the end of Grade 7, students will:

**D1.1** create art works, using a variety of traditional forms and current media technologies, that express feelings, ideas, and issues, including opposing points of view (*e.g., an acrylic painting that uses symbols to represent conflict and resolution; performance art or an installation that portrays both sides of the struggle between humankind and nature; a mixed-media or digital composition of a personal mandala that shows both unity and opposing forces*)

*Teacher prompts:* "How will your art work convey opposing perspectives on an issue that you have chosen to explore (e.g., consumerism versus sustainability, land development versus conservation, global warming, poverty)?" "With the symbols you have chosen, how can you show resolution as clearly as you have shown conflict?" "How does your installation communicate the benefits and challenges of environmental stewardship?"

**D1.2** demonstrate an understanding of composition, using multiple principles of design and the "rule of thirds" to create narrative art works or art works on a theme or topic (*e.g., use colour [analogous, monochromatic] to unify a montage of newspaper and magazine images and text on a social issue; use smooth, horizontal lines to give a feeling of harmony in a drawing; create a landscape that shows unity, using repetition of shapes, values, textures, and/or lines, a particular area of focus, and the rule of thirds*)

*Teacher prompts:* "How will you use colour to unify your art work and convey your message?" "How can you create unity and harmony in your landscape painting by repeating shapes and selected analogous colours?" "How can you lead the eye through the painting using implied directional lines along a diagonal axis?"

**D1.3** use elements of design in art works to communicate ideas, messages, and understandings for a specific audience and purpose (*e.g., create balance in positive and negative space in a personal logo design, using drawing or paper cut-outs of black-and-white shapes on a grey background; selectively manipulate the colour, values, and text in a digital composition to change the message of a print advertisement*)

*Teacher prompts:* "How could you elaborate on the visual metaphor in your logo? How could you simplify the design of the logo and still retain a balance between positive and negative shapes?" "How could you change the colours, values, and symbols used in a print advertisement for a popular soft drink to convey an objection to consumerism?"

**D1.4** use a variety of materials, tools, techniques, and technologies to determine solutions to increasingly complex design challenges (*e.g.,*

- drawing: *make a cubist still life of objects with reflective or textured surfaces, using both wet [e.g., ink, watercolour pencils] and dry [e.g., conté, chalk] materials to simulate highlights and transparency*

- mixed media: *make a hand-made or altered book, using various materials and techniques to represent ideas about selected elements in dance, drama, music, and/or the visual arts*

- painting: *make a cityscape that will serve as a background in an animated short movie, using experimental watercolour techniques such as wet on wet or salt resist*

- printmaking: *make a collograph or chine collé that communicates a personal experience through the use of shape and analogous colour*

- sculpture: *make clay or papier mâché gargoyles or "crossed creatures" that have exaggerated features, using open and closed forms*

- technology: *make a high-contrast self-portrait or caricature with software, using techniques such as blurring, cloning, cropping, distortion, layering, rotation, and selection*)

*Teacher prompts:* "What aspects of your subject's personality will you emphasize or exaggerate in your gargoyle or portrait?" "How do different printmaking techniques limit or change your choices of design and subject matter?"

## D2. Reflecting, Responding, and Analysing

By the end of Grade 7, students will:

**D2.1** interpret a variety of art works and identify the feelings, issues, themes, and social concerns that they convey (*e.g., compare the mood of two different works by two peers, such as* Above the Gravel Pit *by Emily Carr and* Reflections, Bishop's Pond *by David Milne; categorize a variety of art works on the basis of the themes and issues that are explored by the artists*)

*Teacher prompts:* "What mood do you think is created by the artist in each painting?" "What do you think is the relationship between artistic intent and the expressive work?" "How might others understand this image differently because of differences in age, life experience, culture, or beliefs?" "Why is it important for people to be able to evaluate visual images as a part of daily life?" "How do individual and societal values affect our response to art?"

**D2.2** explain how the elements and principles of design are used in their own and others' art work to communicate meaning or understanding *(e.g., the use of complementary colours for shadow detail in a still life by Cézanne; the use of contrast to emphasize the features in a portrait; Brian Jungen's use of positive and negative space and the colours in traditional First Nation art works to convey ideas about consumerism and culture in masks that he created out of brand-name running shoes)*

*Teacher prompts:* "Notice how many different colours Cézanne used to paint the pear. Which colour relationship (complementary or analogous) has he used to show the shadow on the pear as blue-green while the highlights are bright yellow?" "How are artistic layout considerations of image and text used in this art work to convey its message?"

**D2.3** demonstrate an understanding of how to read and interpret signs, symbols, and style in art works *(e.g., visual metaphors, such as a single tree, used to evoke loneliness in paintings by Group of Seven artists; objects used as symbols in* Sadako and the Thousand Paper Cranes *by Eleanor Coerr; messages conveyed by the use of traditional symbols in contemporary art; an artist's manipulation of the intended message of an advertisement by modifying symbols and elements of design in the imagery that is appropriated, or "borrowed", from the original ad)*

*Teacher prompts:* "What symbols can you identify in this art work?" "How can art be seen as a visual metaphor?" "How can an object represent an idea, a concept, or an abstraction?" "What do you think are examples of universal symbols?" "What images do the media use to target youth?"

**D2.4** identify and explain their strengths, their interests, and areas for improvement as creators, interpreters, and viewers of art *(e.g., explain their preferences for selected works of art, using appropriate visual arts vocabulary; provide constructive feedback in a critique of their own work and the work of others; identify the strategies they used in planning, producing, and critiquing their own and others' works of art)*

*Teacher prompts:* "When you planned your mixed media art work, what sources did you use? What strategies did you use to plan your design? What was the message of your art work? What would you do differently next time?" "How does your art work show originality and imagination in the way it expresses your thoughts, experiences, and feelings?" "What feelings were you trying to convey by using bold colours in your self-portrait?" "Are there other possible solutions to the design problem?"

## D3. Exploring Forms and Cultural Contexts

By the end of Grade 7, students will:

**D3.1** identify and describe some of the ways in which visual art forms and styles reflect the beliefs and traditions of a variety of cultures and civilizations *(e.g., art works created within a tradition for functional and aesthetic purposes; beliefs reflected in art works by artists working within an artistic movement in the past or present; the purposes of architecture, objects, and images in past and present cultures and the contexts in which they were made, viewed, and valued; art works that challenge, sustain, and reflect society's beliefs and traditions)*

*Teacher prompts:* "How are the content and medium chosen by an avant-garde artist affected by the time, place, and society in which the work is created?" "Compare the ways in which Impressionist artists and contemporary Cree artists depict nature. How are they different?" "How are the designs of Frank Gehry (a contemporary architect) similar to and different from those of Antoni Gaudí (an art nouveau architect who worked in Spain)?" "How do the arts allow a culture to define its identity and communicate it to others? What cultural influences can you point to in your own art work?"

**D3.2** demonstrate an understanding of the function of visual and media arts in various contexts today and in the past, and of their influence on the development of personal and cultural identity *(e.g., the function of traditional and contemporary styles of Aboriginal art in the development of cultural identity and revitalization; the contributions of people in various arts careers to community events, festivals, businesses, galleries, and museums; the significance of the art work of individuals and the arts of cultural groups in local and global contexts)*

*Teacher prompts:* "How does Carl Beam use juxtaposition of traditional Aboriginal symbols and pop culture images to connect personal memory to larger world issues?" "Describe the roles of visual arts in communities around the world. What is our role in supporting visual arts in our community?" "What role does art have in lifelong learning?" "How do the visual arts and media influence the individual and society?"

# GRADE **8**

# A. DANCE

## OVERALL EXPECTATIONS

By the end of Grade 8, students will:

**A1. Creating and Presenting:** apply the creative process (see pages 19–22) to the composition of a variety of dance pieces, using the elements of dance to communicate feelings and ideas;

**A2. Reflecting, Responding, and Analysing:** apply the critical analysis process (see pages 23–28) to communicate their feelings, ideas, and understandings in response to a variety of dance pieces and experiences;

**A3. Exploring Forms and Cultural Contexts:** demonstrate an understanding of a variety of dance forms, traditions, and styles from the past and present, and their sociocultural and historical contexts.

---

**FUNDAMENTAL CONCEPTS FOR GRADE 8**

Students in Grade 8 will develop or extend understanding of the following concepts through participation in various dance experiences (e.g., using elements and choreographic forms to communicate ideas and issues).

ELEMENTS OF DANCE

- *body:* body awareness, use of body parts (e.g., hips, shoulders), body shapes (e.g., angular, stretched, twisted), locomotor movements (e.g., leap, dart), non-locomotor movements (e.g., twist, rock), body bases, symmetry versus asymmetry, geometric versus organic shape, curved versus angular shape, isolation of body parts, weight transfer

- *space:* levels, pathways, directions, positive versus negative space, proximity of dancers to one another, various group formations, use of performance space

- *time:* stillness, rhythm, tempo, pause, freeze, with music, without music, duration, acceleration/deceleration

- *energy:* quality, inaction versus action, percussion, fluidity (e.g., glide, sink, fall, shiver)

- *relationship:* dancers to objects, opposition, groupings (e.g., large and small groups), meet/part, follow/lead, emotional connections between dancers

---

## SPECIFIC EXPECTATIONS

### A1. Creating and Presenting

By the end of Grade 8, students will:

**A1.1** create dance pieces to respond to issues that are personally meaningful to them (*e.g., young people's relationship to authority, global warming [glacial melting, extreme weather events], recycling, land claims, bike lanes*)

*Teacher prompts:* "How would you structure a dance to convey the impact of a tsunami (the calm before the storm, storm escalating, chaos) on the environment and humans?" "What kinds of movements would help you convey your ideas about peace?"

**A1.2** use dance as a language to communicate messages about themes of social justice and/or environmental health (*e.g., possible solutions to bullying, poverty, racism, pollution, land claims, homelessness, war, deforestation, oppression, colonization*)

*Teacher prompt:* "What formations could you use to show racism (e.g., one dancer separates from the group)? What type of movements would help you communicate your message clearly? How do you change the movements to convey togetherness and acceptance?"

**A1.3** determine the appropriate choreographic form and create dance pieces for a specific audience or venue (*e.g., use a narrative dance structure for a primary class; use features of a site-specific outdoor space to structure a dance on an environmental theme*)

*Teacher prompt:* "How can you use theme and variation to convey a message of peace at a Remembrance Day assembly? If you are performing alone, what are some ways that the movements can be varied using different elements?"

**A1.4** use technology, including multimedia, to enhance the message communicated by the choreography in a dance piece (*e.g., use lights and costumes to create a mood; project images on the dancers or a backdrop to illustrate a theme*)

*Teacher prompt:* "How could you use light and/or sound technology to enhance the message of your dance piece about the majesty of forests?"

## A2. Reflecting, Responding, and Analysing

By the end of Grade 8, students will:

**A2.1** construct personal and/or group interpretations of the themes in their own and others' dance pieces (*e.g., the role of greed in deforestation, war, global warming, poverty*) and communicate their responses in a variety of ways (*e.g., through writing, discussion, oral report, song, drama, visual art, dance*)

*Teacher prompts:* "How do the projected images (e.g., of deforestation, war, global warming, poverty) in this dance piece reinforce the choreographer's intent?" "What choices did you make in your dance about how to convey your opinion on homelessness?"

**A2.2** analyse, using dance vocabulary, their own and others' dance pieces to identify the elements of dance and the choreographic forms used in them (*e.g.,* body: *geometric shapes, stretched shapes*; space: *levels*; time: *duration*; energy: *percussion*; relationship: *opposition*; choreographic form: *theme and variation*) and explain how they help communicate meaning (*e.g., percussion and opposition are used to suggest conflict; theme and variation are used to explore a relationship between continuity and change*)

*Teacher prompts:* "How did this group's manipulation of the element of energy change the message of the main theme?" "What

feeling did the abrupt movements in the dance create?"

**A2.3** identify and give examples of their strengths and areas for growth as dance creators, interpreters, and audience members (*e.g., describe a suggestion they made to a peer about how to improve the first draft of a dance work, and evaluate their personal contribution to the success of the final performance*)

*Teacher prompt:* "How did you make constructive suggestions without appearing to comment negatively on someone else's work? What was good about your approach? What might you change next time? How could you use invented dance notation to visually represent the suggestions for improvement?"

## A3. Exploring Forms and Cultural Contexts

By the end of Grade 8, students will:

**A3.1** describe how social, political, and economic factors influenced the emergence and development of a dance form or genre of their choice (*e.g.,* factors: *funding to artists, the commercialization of dance, support for dance programs in schools;* genres/forms: *modern dance in the early twentieth century, the waltz in nineteenth-century Europe*)

*Teacher prompts:* "What social factors led to the emergence of this dance (e.g., hip hop, Celtic dance, the waltz)?" "Why do you think swing developed during the Depression in the 1930s (e.g., escapism)?"

**A3.2** identify a variety of types of dances and relate them to their different roles in society (*e.g., contemporary Aboriginal dance/folk dance contributes to ceremony/ritual; dance numbers in stage plays and movies provide entertainment; classical ballet offers scope for artistic expression and provides elite entertainment; disco dancing and solo performance allow creative self-expression; dances at parties or social events contribute to social bonding; jazz and hip hop make a social and/or cultural statement*)

*Teacher prompt:* "How did the street dance 'Cool' in the musical *West Side Story* depict the culture of American gangs in the 1950s? What impressions do you have of the dance? How do you think this dance might have affected audiences when the film was released in 1961?"

# B. DRAMA

## OVERALL EXPECTATIONS

By the end of Grade 8, students will:

**B1. Creating and Presenting:** apply the creative process (see pages 19–22) to process drama and the development of drama works, using the elements and conventions of drama to communicate feelings, ideas, and multiple perspectives;

**B2. Reflecting, Responding, and Analysing:** apply the critical analysis process (see pages 23–28) to communicate feelings, ideas, and understandings in response to a variety of drama works and experiences;

**B3. Exploring Forms and Cultural Contexts:** demonstrate an understanding of a variety of drama and theatre forms, traditions and styles from the past and present, and their sociocultural and historical contexts.

---

**FUNDAMENTAL CONCEPTS FOR GRADE 8**

Students in Grade 8 will develop or extend understanding of the following concepts through participation in various drama experiences.

ELEMENTS OF DRAMA

- *role/character:* analysing the background, motivation, speech, and actions of characters to build roles; using voice, stance, gesture, and facial expression to portray character
- *relationship:* analysing relationships to develop the interplay between characters
- *time and place:* using props, costumes, and furniture to establish setting; modifying production elements to suit different audiences
- *tension:* using various stage effects to produce specific audience reactions
- *focus and emphasis:* using a wide range of devices to highlight the central theme for the audience; making deliberate artistic choices to sharpen focus

---

## SPECIFIC EXPECTATIONS

### B1. Creating and Presenting

By the end of Grade 8, students will:

**B1.1** engage actively in drama exploration and role play, with a focus on examining multiple perspectives and possible outcomes related to complex issues, themes, and relationships from a wide variety of sources and diverse communities (*e.g., identify significant perspectives related to an issue and assume roles to give voice to the different perspectives; use improvisation to communicate insights about life events and relationships; develop and present anthology dramas, short scripts, or multi-role plays for a single actor*)

*Teacher prompt:* "How could you use drama conventions such as conversations, mapping, or role on the wall to dramatize two opposing views on a community issue (e.g., consumerism, landfills, bike lanes)?"

**B1.2** demonstrate an understanding of the elements of drama by selecting and manipulating multiple elements and conventions to create and enhance a variety of drama works and shared drama experiences (*e.g., use "a day in the life" to compare farming, fishing, or hunting practices at the beginning of the twentieth century to those of today; create sets to depict the physical setting of a drama using available materials; use knowledge of movement and blocking to achieve well-paced action and create visual interest*)

*Teacher prompts:* "How can corridor of voices help you to understand your role more deeply and also to experience other perspectives on what the character might think and feel?" "In your prepared improvisation, how can your physical movements in relation to one another be used to highlight the nature of your emotional relationship?"

**B1.3** plan and shape the direction of the drama by negotiating ideas and perspectives with others, both in and out of role (*e.g., In role: use group improvisation to work out a time line of events in a drama story; Out of role: use the talking stick in group discussion about the best way to resolve the drama's central conflict*)

*Teacher prompt:* "In your group, discuss one aspect of your presentation that communicates your meaning clearly. Identify one thing that could be changed to strengthen your presentation."

**B1.4** communicate feelings, thoughts, and abstract ideas through drama works, using audio, visual, and/or technological aids for specific purposes and audiences (*e.g., music/soundtracks to intensify audience reaction; video as counterpoint to action or to add details; costumes, props, fabric to establish character and setting; an audio recording of a soundscape to accompany and reinforce ideas and feelings in a mimed sequence*)

*Teacher prompts:* "What are some ways you can use objects or technology to represent the moods of these different characters? Masks? A 'signature tune'?" "How could you use technology to signal to the audience when an actor's speech represents the character's private, inner thoughts? A spotlight? Another kind of lighting change?"

## B2. Reflecting, Responding, and Analysing

By the end of Grade 8, students will:

**B2.1** construct personal interpretations of drama works, connecting drama issues and themes to social concerns at both the local and global level (*e.g., create a web with the main idea of the drama in the centre and words describing personal and global connections leading out from the centre; explain in discussion or a journal entry why they disagree or empathize with the motivations of a character*)

*Teacher prompts:* "What are the key messages of this drama/play? How does its message relate to your own life experiences and opinions?" "Can you sum up what this play was about for you in a paragraph? A sentence? A word?" "Is this an important play for others to see? Why?" "How does the play's theme or point of view connect to another drama experience that we've shared?"

**B2.2** evaluate, using drama terminology, how effectively drama works and shared drama experiences use the elements of drama to engage the audience and communicate a theme or message (*e.g., determine whether the use of contrasting comic and serious scenes strengthened the impact of the theme or weakened it; determine whether using a historical setting enhanced the presentation of a contemporary theme*)

*Teacher prompts:* "Imagine that you are a theatre critic. How many stars (on a scale of one to five) does this drama deserve? What key elements were used in the drama? In your opinion did they help make it stronger or weaker? Why?" "How successful were the actors in using movement, voice, and gesture to create interest?"

**B2.3** identify and give examples of their strengths, interests, and areas for improvement as drama creators, performers, and audience members (*e.g., write a journal entry outlining the process they used to solve a given problem, what worked, and what they would do differently next time; develop and use rubrics and/or assessment charts to evaluate their contribution to group work*)

*Teacher prompts:* "About what area of drama do you feel most confident? What areas do you want to pursue in the future?" "What drama conventions did you use most successfully to express your thoughts, feelings, and ideas?"

## B3. Exploring Forms and Cultural Contexts

By the end of Grade 8, students will:

**B3.1** analyse the influence of the media on a wide variety of drama forms and/or styles of live theatre (*e.g., introduction of digital storytelling, multimedia presentations, and dance-drama into drama forms; incorporation of technologies from different media to enhance sets, backdrops, and special effects; use of virtual role play to explore options for avatar characters*)

*Teacher prompts:* "What are some similarities and differences in how drama expresses ideas and emotions compared to other art forms (e.g., dance, film, music, art)?" "In what ways can the use of technology enhance or detract from the message or meaning in a drama presentation?"

**B3.2** identify and describe a wide variety of ways in which drama and theatre make or have made contributions to social, cultural, and economic life in a variety of times and places (*e.g., by providing opportunities for personal enjoyment, celebration, and entertainment; by providing jobs; by attracting tourists; by communicating and teaching about a range of topics; by enhancing participants' life skills of communication and collaboration; by raising awareness of political, environmental, medical, and other social/global issues*)

*Teacher prompts:* "Why do we provide opportunities to participate in drama in school and in the community?" "Why might theatrical performances have been important in times when very few people could read and write?" "How do theatre performances help the economy?"

# C. MUSIC

## OVERALL EXPECTATIONS

By the end of Grade 8, students will:

**C1. Creating and Performing:** apply the creative process (see pages 19–22) to create and perform music for a variety of purposes, using the elements and techniques of music;

**C2. Reflecting, Responding, and Analysing:** apply the critical analysis process (see pages 23–28) to communicate their feelings, ideas, and understandings in response to a variety of music and musical experiences;

**C3. Exploring Forms and Cultural Contexts:** demonstrate an understanding of a variety of musical genres and styles from the past and present, and their sociocultural and historical contexts.

---

### FUNDAMENTAL CONCEPTS FOR GRADE 8

In Grade 8, students will build on their knowledge of the elements of music and related musical concepts that were introduced in Grades 1 to 7. Students will develop understanding of musical concepts through participation in musical experiences that involve listening, moving, creating, and performing (vocal and/or instrumental music).

ELEMENTS OF MUSIC

- *duration:* tempo markings and rhythms encountered in the repertoire
- *pitch:* major and minor tonality; keys encountered in the repertoire
- *dynamics and other expressive controls:* all intensity levels; changes in levels
- *timbre:* tone colours of world music ensembles and instruments (e.g., gamelan, shakuhachi, doumbek, sitar, djembe, ocarina)
- *texture/harmony:* monophonic, homophonic, and polyphonic music
- *form:* forms encountered in performance repertoire (e.g., minuet)

---

## SPECIFIC EXPECTATIONS

### C1. Creating and Performing

By the end of Grade 8, students will:

**C1.1** sing and/or play, in tune, music in unison and in two or more parts from a variety of cultures, styles, and historical periods (*e.g., perform in large and small ensembles, prepare a solo, improvise in a drum circle*)

*Teacher prompts:* "How can you interpret the expressive markings in music when you perform?" "When composing, how can you indicate with musical symbols how the performer is to perform your composition?"

**C1.2** apply the elements of music through performing, composing, and arranging music for a specific effect or clear purpose (*e.g., create a jingle to advertise a product; improvise a simple* melody over a 12-bar blues progression; arrange a piece of their choice from their method book for a quartet of mixed instruments)

*Teacher prompts:* "How did the elements that you chose for your jingle help sell the product?" "What did you need to take into consideration when arranging the piece for your quartet?"

**C1.3** create musical compositions in a variety of forms for specific purposes and audiences (*e.g., write lyrics and a melody for a protest song based upon a current social issue; compose a melodic theme for a computer game*)

*Teacher prompts:* "Explain how the rhythm and melody of your song communicate your intended message." "What does a composer have to consider when writing music for computer games?"

**C1.4** use the tools and techniques of musicianship in musical performances (*e.g., apply blend, articulation, phrasing, conducting patterns; maintain straight and relaxed posture when singing or playing; keep instrument, hand, arm, and/or mouth in playing position; use proper breath, bow, or stick control*)

*Teacher prompts:* "What are the functions of your right and left hands when conducting?" "How can you communicate dynamics, articulation, phrasing, and tempo through your conducting gestures?"

**C1.5** demonstrate an understanding of standard and other musical notation through performance and composition (*e.g., interpret repeat signs such as D. C. al coda, d. s. al coda, d. s. al fine; interpret Italian terms and abbreviations for dynamics and tempo; use the notes of the chromatic scale; arrange a piece for a duet using notation software*)

*Teacher prompts:* "How many bars of music will you actually sing or play in this piece if you follow the repeats indicated by the composer?" "What are all of the different dynamic and tempo markings in this piece?" "What will you need to do in your singing or playing to effectively follow these markings?"

## C2. Reflecting, Responding, and Analysing

By the end of Grade 8, students will:

**C2.1** express analytical, personal responses to musical performances in a variety of ways (*e.g., use graphic organizers, journals, or reflection logs to record their responses; conduct or respond in an interview in which they describe a musical experience; analyse a performance in the way that a musical commentator on the radio might do it; depict scenes from* Love Songs for a Small Planet *by Alexina Louie or* The Moldau *by Smetana using visual arts*)

**C2.2** analyse, using musical terminology, ways in which the elements of music are used in various styles and genres they perform, listen to, and create (*e.g., use of form and dynamics in absolute music, such as the Symphony no. 40 in G minor by Mozart, and in program music, such as* The Firebird *by Stravinsky*)

*Teacher prompts:* "What are the differences between absolute and program music? How did the composer use such musical elements as timbre, form, and dynamics to suggest certain images?" "Which musical elements made the images in *The Firebird* the clearest for you? Why?" "How do the lyrics in a song affect

your interpretation of the music? What happens when we change the lyrics? How is the song's overall effect different? Why?"

**C2.3** identify and give examples of their strengths and areas for improvement as composers, musical performers, interpreters, and audience members (*e.g., set a goal to improve their performance skills, reflect on how successfully they attained their goal, keep a practice journal, record and analyse their own performances throughout the term*)

*Teacher prompts:* "Having followed your music as you listen to your performance, what are your strengths and next steps as a performer?" "About what area of music do you feel most confident? What area do you want to pursue in the future?"

## C3. Exploring Forms and Cultural Contexts

By the end of Grade 8, students will:

**C3.1** analyse some of the social, political, and economic factors that affect the creation of music (*e.g., historical events that inspired the composition of nationalistic music; the development of jazz, rap, and heavy metal, and their effect on culture; the social and/or cultural origins of folk songs, love songs, national anthems, and dance music; the economic purposes for commercial music played in stores; purposes and effects of Aboriginal activism through song*)

*Teacher prompts:* "What factors might influence someone to compose this type of music?" "Do composers have a target audience in mind when composing music?" "How does nationalistic music influence the listener?" "How might the style of the music affect your interpretation of the lyrics?"

**C3.2** compare and contrast music from the past and present (*e.g., differences and similarities between music from various cultures and contemporary fusion forms; similarities and differences between traditional Aboriginal music and music sung and played by contemporary Aboriginal musicians; differences and similarities between dance music from the seventeenth century, Chopin waltzes, hip hop, and mariachi*)

*Teacher prompts:* "What are the key characteristics that distinguish folk music from popular commercial music? Are there any similarities?" "How has the role of music in our lives changed?"

# D. VISUAL ARTS

## OVERALL EXPECTATIONS

By the end of Grade 8, students will:

**D1. Creating and Presenting:** apply the creative process (see pages 19–22) to produce art works in a variety of traditional two- and three-dimensional forms, as well as multimedia art works, that communicate feelings, ideas, and understandings, using elements, principles, and techniques of visual arts as well as current media technologies;

**D2. Reflecting, Responding, and Analysing:** apply the critical analysis process (see pages 23–28) to communicate feelings, ideas, and understandings in response to a variety of art works and art experiences;

**D3. Exploring Forms and Cultural Contexts:** demonstrate an understanding of a variety of art forms, styles, and techniques from the past and present, and their sociocultural and historical contexts.

### FUNDAMENTAL CONCEPTS FOR GRADE 8

In addition to the concepts introduced in Grades 1 to 7, students in Grade 8 will develop understanding of the following concepts through participation in a variety of hands-on, open-ended visual arts experiences.

ELEMENTS OF DESIGN
Students will develop understanding of all elements of design.

- *line:* directional lines; one- and two-point perspective to create depth; contour drawings of figures
- *shape and form:* various visual "weights" of forms (e.g., large, light-coloured forms can seem to have less weight than smaller, dark forms); complex three-dimensional constructions and motifs; gradation in size
- *space:* one- and two-point perspective or foreshortening to create illusory space; informal converging lines in an image creating the illusion of space; adult human figures that are seven to eight heads in height; alternative systems for representing space (e.g., layered images in medieval art; disproportion-ately small images of people within a vast landscape in Chinese art to show the smallness of humans in relation to nature; images seen from several points of view simultaneously in Egyptian and cubist paintings)
- *colour:* tertiary colours; contrast of colour; absence of colour
  *Note:* In creating multimedia art works, students may need some understanding of different colour models, such as RGB and CMY(K), and websafe colours.
- *texture:* real and illusory textures that appear in the environment
- *value:* cross-hatching to suggest volume and shadows; variation and increased range of gradation in value

PRINCIPLES OF DESIGN
Students will develop understanding of all principles of design (that is, contrast, repetition and rhythm, variety, emphasis, proportion, balance, unity and harmony, and movement), but the focus in Grade 8 will be on movement.

- *movement:* actual lines to lead the viewer's eye (e.g., solid lines, dotted lines); subtle or implied "paths" using shape, value, and/or colour (e.g., an invisible path created by leading the eye from large shapes to small shapes, from shapes in dark colours to shapes in lighter colours, from familiar shapes to unfamiliar shapes, from colour to no colour); actual action (e.g., kinetic sculpture, animation); implied action (e.g., an invisible path created by an arrow, a gaze, or a pointing finger; the "freeze frame" effect of an object in motion, such as a bouncing ball suspended in mid-air or a runner about to take the next step)

# SPECIFIC EXPECTATIONS

## D1. Creating and Presenting

By the end of Grade 8, students will:

**D1.1** create art works, using a variety of traditional forms and current media technologies, that express feelings, ideas, and issues and that demonstrate an awareness of multiple points of view *(e.g., create a collage that shows contrast between two points of view or a cause-and-effect relationship; create an art work on a current event or issue, using the conventions of sequential art or comics, or using found images and text to express a point of view in the style of a contemporary artist such as Martin Firrel, Jenny Holzer, or Barbara Kruger)*

*Teacher prompts:* "How can you juxtapose text and images to create a message that challenges what the text is saying?" "In your monochromatic comic layout, how will you use angle of view, images, and text to show two sides of the story?" "How can stereotypes be reinforced or challenged in art works?"

**D1.2** demonstrate an understanding of composition, using multiple principles of design and other layout considerations such as compositional triangles to create narrative art works or art works on a theme or topic *(e.g., a figure drawing of a historically influential person that makes use of the whole paper or space to create a sense of unity and balance, with a single word or motif in the background; an abstract painting in which movement is created by using line, value, colour, and/or shape; a stop-motion animation that tells a simple story and that demonstrates the principle of movement through sequential images in which the character or object moves in relation to the frame)*

*Teacher prompts:* "How would your image be different if your figure took up only one side of the paper?" "How can you use colour and variation in value, like Mary Pratt, to capture light in a still-life composition that leads the viewer's eye throughout the art work?" "How can you use implied action through a technique such as automotion or through the gaze or gestures of the figures?"

**D1.3** use elements of design in art works to communicate ideas, messages, and understandings for a specific audience and purpose *(e.g., an illustration for a children's book that uses colour and rhythm to appeal to its audience; a short movie*

or animation that uses space, time, and framing to highlight a contemporary issue; a portrait of a person made from junk-food or brand packaging to communicate an opinion, in the style of Giuseppe Arcimboldo's series of allegorical portraits made from fruit, vegetables, and other unlikely objects such as pots and books)*

*Teacher prompts:* "How would manipulating the colour change the meaning of the image? How would your illustration differ if you used colours from the opposite side of the colour wheel?" "How will you use a variety of camera angles and shots (e.g., wide, medium, close-up) to include different perspectives and enhance your message?"

**D1.4** use a variety of materials, tools, techniques, and technologies to determine solutions to increasingly complex design challenges *(e.g.,*

- drawing: *create a pastel composition or flipbook that combines or contrasts styles of two artists or styles from two cultures*

- mixed media: *make a series of small artist trading cards [ATCs] in a variety of media, illustrating a contemporary issue or topic*

- painting: *make an acrylic painting of a magnified section of a sketch or an image that is seen through a viewfinder or frame, then make changes to the painted surface with oil pastels to create a personal interpretation of the image*

- printmaking: *make a series of two-colour softoleum, linoleum, or block prints that are variations on a social theme and that are printed on papers of different colours and textures [magazine paper, coloured bond paper, newsprint, tissue paper, handmade paper]*

- sculpture: *make a sculptural portrait of a hero or favourite person out of papier mâché or plaster bandage that captures what the person means to them*

- technology: *create a short movie from an animated image sequence or video, using editing software to create suspense, a feeling of speed, or a sense of the passage of time)*

*Teacher prompts:* "How would the feeling and message of the print change if you printed it on a magazine advertisement rather than on coloured paper? Which one serves your purpose better?" "How can you use storyboards to plan a variety of shots and camera angles?"

## D2. Reflecting, Responding, and Analysing

By the end of Grade 8, students will:

**D2.1** interpret a variety of art works and identify the feelings, issues, themes, and social concerns that they convey (*e.g., hold a mock debate between artists on a topic such as the emotional impact of realist versus expressionist styles of art; compare art works in different artistic media that express a common theme, such as wartime suffering in the art work of Käthe Kollwitz and Francisco Goya; interpret images of social issues that are explored in historical art works, contemporary art works, and media arts*)

*Teacher prompts:* "How can a landscape image express ideas or concepts, such as the power of nature in works by printmaker Hokusai or photographer Ansel Adams?" "How have you been influenced by art work from other cultures or historical periods?" "What makes one image a stereotyped illustration and another image an authentic expression?"

**D2.2** analyse ways in which elements and principles of design are used in a variety of art works to communicate a theme or message, and evaluate the effectiveness of their use on the basis of criteria generated by the class (*e.g., the use of colour and exaggeration in Balinese masks to evoke feelings of fear; the use of line, colour, and shape in the work of Daphne Odjig and Norval Morrisseau to represent spiritual ideas; Molly Bang's use of colour, size, and asymmetrical balance in* Picture This *to reinforce a mood or narrative; substitution of fur for a ceramic textural surface in* Beyond the Teacup *by Meret Oppenheim*)

*Teacher prompts:* "What message do you think Bang wants to convey in her image?" "How effective are the elements of design as the 'words' of a visual language?" "How do the elements of design allow you to identify the intended audience for a book after you've looked at its cover?" "How does the representation of an image from two or three points of view at once in Egyptian or cubist art show you another way to represent perception?"

**D2.3** demonstrate an understanding of how to read and interpret signs, symbols, and style in art works (*e.g.,* Horse and Train *by Alex Colville as an allegory of the impact of the industrial age; the style of an artist or director of a film who is using compositional framing, point of view, and selective focus to guide the attention of the viewer*

*or audience; the purposes of logos, icons, and images in advertisements; symbolic reuse and transformation of popular images or iconography as a form of commentary ["culture jamming"]; use of traditional Aboriginal symbols in contemporary art*)

*Teacher prompts:* "How are the symbol systems in a variety of cultures similar or different?" "How has the artist implied meanings in his or her image? Explain why you think this art work is or is not an allegory."

**D2.4** identify and explain their strengths, their interests, and areas for improvement as creators, interpreters, and viewers of art (*e.g., organize and participate in a non-competitive art show that documents the stages of the artistic process from artists' statements, concept drawings, and photos of works in progress to the final art works; select, critique, and organize a display of personally meaningful images from their own portfolios; use feedback to evaluate the effectiveness of their own art works*)

*Teacher prompts:* "How does your art work reflect a sense of personal or social responsibility?" "How have you taken the venue or audience into consideration in your display or portfolio of work?" "How did you demonstrate imagination, flexibility, initiative, or judgement as you explored ideas to make, interpret, or present art works?" "What strategies did you use to resolve problems when planning your art work?"

## D3. Exploring Forms and Cultural Contexts

By the end of Grade 8, students will:

**D3.1** identify and explain some of the ways in which artistic traditions in a variety of times and places have been maintained, adapted, or appropriated (*e.g., art works support or challenge personal and societal beliefs or practices; migration or contact with other cultures has an influence on the forms and styles of art and architecture; art styles of other times and places have sometimes been appropriated by artists to create hybrid art works that explore, represent, or challenge ideas*)

*Teacher prompts:* "What are some contemporary clothing designs that show influences from other cultures and designers from around the world?" "How are Inuit artists using traditional elements and forms to create art that is relevant today?" "How can artists incorporate the work of other artists or cultural traditions to make original art work while also showing respect for others' cultural or intellectual property?" "How do exhibitions or research organized by theme or topic, instead of time period or culture, change the way art works are perceived?"

**D3.2** identify and analyse some of the social, political, and economic factors that affect the creation of visual and media arts and the visual and media arts community (*e.g., the influence of love, loss, anger, or war on creative expression; collaboration within production teams or artistic communities; effects on artists of changes in government, changes in the amount of government funding, the creation of arts festivals, and the availability of exhibition opportunities; influence of location, era, and changes in technology on art and architecture*)

*Teacher prompts:* "How does the social and political context change the ways in which universal themes or ideas (e.g., love, war, family, ritual) are represented in art works?" "Which lifestyles, values, or points of view are represented in this image? Which are omitted?" "How are collaboration and group work used to produce, edit, and promote a movie?" "What external factors have led to the creation of a new art movement?" "How is visual culture shaped by the beliefs, technologies, arts funding, and values of society?"

# GLOSSARY

The following definitions of terms are intended to help teachers and parents use this document. Terms that apply throughout the document are listed first, then terms connected with Dance, Drama, Music, and Visual Arts.

*Aboriginal person.* A person who is a descendant of the original inhabitants of North America. The Canadian Constitution (1982) recognizes three primary groups as Aboriginal peoples: Indians, Inuit, and Métis.

*achievement levels.* Brief descriptions of four different degrees of student achievement of the provincial curriculum expectations for any given grade. Level 3, which is the "provincial standard", identifies a high level of achievement of the provincial expectations. Parents of students achieving at level 3 in a particular grade can be confident that their children will be prepared for work at the next grade level. Level 1 identifies achievement that falls much below the provincial standard. Level 2 identifies achievement that approaches the standard. Level 4 identifies achievement that surpasses the standard.

*expectations.* The knowledge and skills that students are expected to develop and to demonstrate in their class work, on tests, and in various other activities on which their achievement is assessed. Overall expectations describe in general terms the knowledge and skills that students are expected to demonstrate by the end of each grade. Specific expectations describe the expected knowledge and skills in greater detail.

*strands.* The four major areas of knowledge and skills into which the curriculum for the arts is organized. The strands for the arts are: Dance, Drama, Music, and Visual Arts.

## DANCE

*AB.* A two-part choreographic pattern form with an A theme and a B theme. The form consists of two distinct, self-contained dance sequences or sections.

*ABA.* A three-part choreographic pattern form with an A theme and a B theme in which the second section contrasts with the first section and the third section restates the first section in a condensed, abbreviated, or extended form.

*accent.* A strong movement or gesture used for emphasis.

*asymmetry.* (1) A difference in size, shape, or position between parts on opposite sides of a dividing line (e.g., different arm and leg positions on the right and left sides of the body). (2) A difference in the placement of dancers in a space on opposite sides of a dividing line.

*audience etiquette.* Acceptable audience behaviour for a dance performance.

*balance.* Maintenance of a controlled position of the body, whether the body is in movement or still; *also*, a state of equilibrium in the spatial arrangement of bodies (e.g., in performance space).

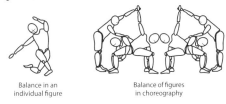

Balance in an individual figure        Balance of figures in choreography

*body. See* **elements of dance**.

*body base.* The part of the body that is supporting the rest of the body. When someone is kneeling, for example, the knees are the body base.

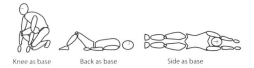

Knee as base        Back as base        Side as base

*body storming.* A strategy, analogous to brainstorming, that uses the body as a means of trying out movement possibilities linked to themes, issues, and ideas that students may be exploring. Students work together in a whole group, in small groups, or individually to generate
movement ideas before shaping their work. The teacher suggests different elements of movement to encourage students to try out a range of variations.

*body zones.* Regions of the body, including front, back, left side, right side, upper half, and lower half.

*bound movement.* A highly controlled movement that can be stopped at any moment. It is often associated with *energy*.

*call and response.* A choreographic form in which one soloist or group performs, followed by a second soloist or group whose performance responds to the first.

*canon.* A choreographic form in which a dance phrase is performed by more than one soloist or group and begins at different times so that the phrases overlap (analogous to a *round* in music).

*choreographer.* A person who plans and creates dance pieces.

*choreographic form.* A structure that organizes movements. Compositional forms may be defined as *narrative* or *patterned* (e.g., canon, call and response, retrograde, ABA, rondo). *See also* **compositional form; dance form**.

*choreography.* The creation and composition of dances by planning or inventing steps, movements, and patterns of movements and arranging them into a meaningful whole to communicate a feeling, idea or theme. This includes dance as a solo, in duets, trios and small ensembles.

*collage.* In dance, a choreographic form consisting of a series of phrases that are often unrelated but have been brought together to create a single dance with a beginning, middle, and end.

*compositional form.* A dance sequence that is created with a specific intent to communicate a feeling, idea, or theme using movement; used in solo dance, as well as duets, trios, and small ensembles. *See also* **choreographic form; dance form**.

*contact improvisation.* Spontaneously created movement in response to body contact with another dancer. This is usually done in a duet. The partners are often moving in and out of physical contact while mutually supporting and following each other's movements. It is often a starting point for choreography.

*contrast.* The pairing of unlike movements. In dance, two contrasting movements might differ in energy, space (e.g., size, direction, level), shape (e.g., symmetrical/asymmetrical, open/closed), or timing (fast/slow, even/uneven). Contrast is often used to emphasize differences.

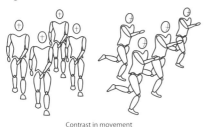

Contrast in movement

Contrast in level and shape

*dance form.* The overall structural organization of a dance piece (e.g., AB, ABA, call and response, theme and variation, canon). *See also* **choreographic form; compositional form.**

*dance piece.* A series of connected phrases.

*dance sequence.* Part of a larger dance piece. Dancers connect choreographed or personal movements (movement vocabulary) to form a sequence. A dance sequence is longer than a phrase but shorter than a section. It may be performed in isolation or be part of a larger dance piece. It conveys a sense of rhythmic completion and contains a beginning, middle, and end.

*dance style.* A way of performing dance that is characteristic of a particular period, setting, choreographer, performer, group, culture, or other category. *See* **genre.**

*direct action.* A movement that takes the shortest path to its destination (e.g., walking in a straight line or pointing out straight in front of your body).

*duration.* The length of time needed to complete a movement. Dancers often think of duration in conjunction with space.

*elements of dance.* Fundamental components of dance, which include the following:

– *body.* The instrument of dance. The term *body* may also refer to the body's position or shape (e.g., curved, straight, angular, twisted, symmetrical, asymmetrical); *also,* how the body is moving (e.g., using locomotor or non-locomotor movements).

– *energy.* The force with which the body moves (e.g., light, strong, sustained, sudden).

– *relationship.* The way in which two or more things are connected to or associated with one another (e.g., dancer to dancer, dancer to object, right arm to left arm).

– *space.* The physical area in which the body moves; also, the area surrounding the body.

– *time.* An element of dance involving rhythm, tempo, accent, and duration. Time can be based on measured beats, as in music, or on body rhythms, such as breath, emotions, and heartbeat.

*energy. See* **elements of dance.**

*ensemble.* A group of performers.

*entrance* and *exit.* The physical location of entry and exit; *also,* the way in which a dancer enters and exits the performance space.

*flocking.* A type of improvisation in which students move in groups, with no set pattern or in a diamond formation, following a leader and all doing the same movements simultaneously. This is an extended version of mirroring for three or more people. Participants do not necessarily need to be able to watch each other, as long as they can see the leader.

*fluid movement.* Movement that is easily changing, smooth, or unconstrained.

*force.* The degree of muscular tension and use of energy in movements. *See* **elements of dance: energy.**

*free-flow movement.* A movement that is unrestrained. Often associated with energy.

*freeze.* A stop; an absence of movement.

*general space.* The larger space that encompasses the overall dance area. The term is usually used in contrast to *personal space.*

*genre.* A category or style of dance characterized by particular movements or ways of moving (e.g., ballet, jazz, belly dancing, hip hop, Highland, African).

*geometric.* Resembling a shape or pattern from geometry (e.g., triangle, straight line).

*gesture.* A movement of a body part or parts used to communicate feelings and ideas, with emphasis on the expressive aspects of the movement (e.g., tapping the foot to show boredom; raising the shoulders in a shrug to show not knowing or caring).

*guided improvisation.* In dance, a movement or series of movements created spontaneously by a dancer, with teacher guidance. *See* **improvisation**.

*improvisation.* In dance, a movement or series of movements created spontaneously by a dancer, either independently or in a group.

*indirect action.* A locomotor or gestural movement characterized by a detour en route (e.g., walking in a zigzag line).

*initiation.* In dance, the origin of movement (e.g., the elbow may lead the arm motion; the toes may lead the leg motion).

*level.* The height of the dancer's movements in relation to the floor, usually measured as high, medium, and low.

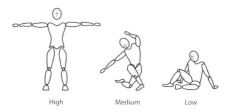

High          Medium          Low

*locomotor movement.* A movement that involves travelling from one place to another across a space (e.g., walking, galloping, rolling).

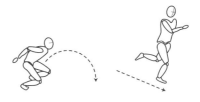

*manipulations.* Slight alterations made to a performance or dance phrase. It is not always performed.

*mirroring.* A type of improvisation. Two students face each other. Student A initiates the movement, while student B follows, maintaining eye contact as appropriate; students switch roles after a set time.

*modes of expression/modes of communication.* Ways in which thoughts and ideas can be expressed (e.g., through discussion, drawing, writing in a journal – as well as through movement and dance).

*motif.* A distinctive recurring gesture, movement, sequence, or image that can be elaborated upon in a variety of ways. A motif may be used to provide a theme or unifying idea for a dance piece.

*movement vocabulary.* A repertoire of steps, movements, and sequences that might be used in creating a dance piece. They can be particular to a dance form (e.g., traditional dance) or personal (e.g., creative dance).

*narrative form.* A choreographic form that follows a storyline, often conveys a specific message, and usually includes an introduction, rising action, a climax, and a resolution (e.g., the ballet *The Nutcracker*).

*negative space.* The unoccupied space surrounding a body, in the opening created by body shapes, or between bodies. *See also* **positive space**.

*non-locomotor movement.* A non-travelling movement, where the body is anchored in one place; also called *axial movement* (e.g., moving the arms and/or twisting the body while staying in one spot).

*notation (invented dance notation).* A written system of symbols, shapes, and lines that represent body position and movement. These are invented visuals used to plan, map, or record movement, as opposed to formal forms of dance notation. The following are some examples.

– *movement notation:*

– *pathway notation:*

– *position notation:*

*organic movement.* Movement of the body, often based on the motion of natural objects, in a shape or form that is non-geometric or free flowing (e.g., bodies moving like water flowing). Organic movement can also be movement that comes from a deeper place in the body, often from an internal stimulus, possibly fuelled by an emotion or memory that triggers a physical manifestation, response, or movement impulse.

*pathway.* The route or movement taken from point A to point B; *or* a pattern or design created on the floor or in the air by movements of the body (e.g., the arm moving in a circular motion creates a circular air pathway; galloping across the general space in a zigzag motion creates a ground pathway). The following are some examples.

– *air pathway:*

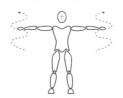

*– ground pathways:*

*pattern.* An arrangement or sequence of elements in which one or more of the elements is repeated in a planned way.

*pattern form.* A choreographic form used to communicate an abstract idea or message (as opposed to a narrative). Examples of pattern forms include AB, ABA, call and response, canon, collage, motif, pattern, retrograde, rondo, theme and variation.

*pedestrian movement.* Movements that imitate everyday gestures or actions (e.g., walking, bouncing a basketball, sitting, opening a door). In the context of choreography, pedestrian movement can be exaggerated, shaped, or stylized for theatrical, aesthetic, choreographic, or conceptual purposes.

*percussive movement.* Sharp, explosive movement (with or without sound) in which the impetus is quickly checked.

*personal space.* The space around the body, with the outer edges determined by how far the body and body parts can reach. It includes all levels, places, and directions extending out from the body's centre.

*phrase.* A small group of movements that stand together as a unit (analogous to a phrase in language arts).

*positive space.* The space that a body uses or occupies. *See also* **negative space**.

*posture.* The way a person carries his or her body.

*prop.* A portable object used in dance to support or enhance a performance. A prop may be used in dance as a creative stimulus or as an extension of the body and/or movement.

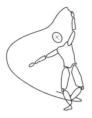

*quality.* The manner in which a movement is performed (e.g., jerkily, smoothly, cautiously; in a gliding, slashing, or dabbing manner), usually in order to communicate information about the physical and/or emotional state the performer is attempting to portray.

*relationship. See* **elements of dance**.

*repetition.* The repeated use of movement phrases or parts of phrases for emphasis or to create some other effect. Repetition can help relate sections of dance to each other.

*retrograde.* A choreographic form in which a dance or movement sequence is performed in reverse order (e.g., a dance phrase performed from back to front).

*rhythmic movement.* Movement characterized by the regular recurrence of heavy and light accents.

*rondo.* A choreographic form which expands on ABA form to ABACADA (lengthened indefinitely), in which the A theme is repeated or varied.

*shape.* The position the body takes in space (e.g., angled, curved, straight). It can refer to body zones, the whole body, body parts, and levels.

*site specific.* Created for a specific location (e.g., a dance that can be danced only in a particular location because the physical environment is part of the dance).

*space. See* **elements of dance**.

*static.* Unmoving; used to describe a movement that is paused.

*stimulus.* An inspiration for creating a dance phrase or piece (e.g., a story, theme, idea, or object).

*style.* The distinguishing way in which a dance is created and performed; style is often associated with a particular performer, performance group, choreographer, or time period.

*sustained movement.* A movement that is prolonged and controlled rather than sudden or sharp.

*symmetry.* (1) An exact match in size, shape, and position between the parts on opposite sides of a dividing line (e.g., identical arm and leg positions on the right and left sides of the body). (2) An exact match in the positioning of dancers in relation to other dancers on opposite sides of a dividing line.

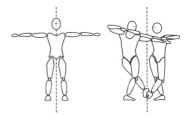

*technique.* The physical skills of a dancer that enable him or her to execute the steps and movements of dance. *Technique* also refers to a set of movements that are characteristic of a particular form or genre of dance (e.g., ballet, modern dance).

*tempo.* The speed at which a dance is performed or music is played.

*theatre in the round.* A performance in which the audience surrounds the performers.

*theme and variation.* A choreographic form that starts with an original movement idea that is repeated with various modifications (e.g., performed faster or slower, with lighter or stronger movements, in a new place) while still maintaining its structure and sequence, resulting in an A-A1-A2-A3 pattern. The theme may be repeated between the variations.

*time. See* **elements of dance**.

*transitions.* The links between dance movements and phrases.

*unison movement.* A movement or action performed in exactly the same way by two or more people at the same time.

# DRAMA

*a day in the life.* A convention in which students explore the experience of a person by working backwards from a significant moment or turning point in a character's life to build the story that accounts for the event. Students work in groups, using tableau, improvisation, and/or role play to depict key moments that may have occurred in the last twenty-four hours of the character's life. The scenes are then run in chronological sequence to depict the events leading up to the dramatically significant moment.

*Anansi stories/tales.* Anansi stories originated in West Africa, where the tradition of story-telling has thrived for generations. The Ashanti people in Ghana in the west of Africa still tell stories of Kweku Anansi, the spider, a trickster figure in African folktales, who both entertains and teaches life lessons. Many of the Anansi tales, or adapted versions of them with different heroes, now exist in North America, South America, the West Indies, and the Caribbean.

*antagonist.* The character who is the principal opponent of the main character in a play.

*artefacts.* Props, posters, maps, letters, or media materials that can be used to establish a character, enhance a setting, and/or advance a story.

*atmosphere.* The mood established for a drama, or for a scene within a drama. Music, lighting, sets, and costumes may all be used to help create a particular mood or atmosphere.

*audience.* (1) In a formal or traditional play, the audience is typically seated in front of or around the action of the play. (2) In a shared drama experience or role play in the classroom, the students typically are both actors and spectators in the experience. At times, the students are all in role together; at other times, some are out of role viewing a group presentation as audience members. They may also be audience members viewing a scene or presentation while they are in role (e.g., in role as the king's assistant, viewing a presentation by local villagers).

*blocking.* A technique used in the staging of a theatrical production to prescribe the positions and patterns of movement of actors on the stage.

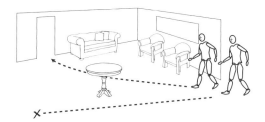

*body position.* A general term used to refer to an actor's position in relation to the audience. The range of positions includes:

– *full front* (i.e., the actor faces the audience directly)

– *profile right* or *left* (i.e., the actor's right or left side is facing the audience)

– *one-quarter right* or *left* (i.e., the actor faces about halfway between full front and profile)

– *full back* (i.e., the actor's back is to the audience)

– *three-quarters right* or *left* (i.e., the actor faces about halfway between full back and profile)

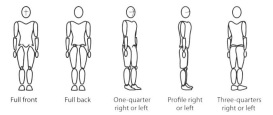

Full front    Full back    One-quarter right or left    Profile right or left    Three-quarters right or left

*caption making.* A convention in which students work in groups to devise slogans, titles, newspaper headlines, or chapter headings that convey in words the intended message of tableaux or pictures. The captions may be shared orally by the groups, read out by a narrator, or written on placards to be read by the class.

*ceremony/ritual.* A set of actions prescribed by the beliefs or traditions of a community or culture and thought to have symbolic value.

*choral speaking, chanting.* The reading or reciting of a text by a group. Preparation for a performance may involve interpretation of the text; experimentation with language, rhythm, volume, pace, and different numbers of voices; and rehearsal.

**chorus.** A convention in which individuals or groups provide spoken explanation or commentary on the main action of a drama.

**collective conscience.** A convention in which students act together in a group to give the main character advice.

**collective creation.** A widely used genre in which students collaborate in a group to agree on a shared vision that represents a place or person in a drama. The idea can then be used as a reference for discussing ideas about the place or person. *See also* **collective understanding**.

**collective drawing.** A convention that focuses on building a context. An image is created by the class or small groups to represent a place or people in the drama. The image can then be used as a reference for discussing ideas about the place or person.

**collective understanding.** An interpretation of a character and what he or she is experiencing that is agreed on by all members of a group. *See also* **collective creation**.

**conventions of drama.** Practices and forms of representation that are widely accepted for use in drama instruction as ways to help students explore meaning and deepen understanding. Hot seating, voices in the head, and freeze-frame images are a few examples, among many.

**corridor of voices.** A convention used to explore the inner life of a character in drama. The character moves along the "corridor" between two lines of students who voice feelings, thoughts, or moral concerns the character might be likely to have. The convention can also be used to explore the thoughts of a character who is facing a difficult task or decision. In this case, the voices would give advice and warnings. *See also* **voices in the head**.

**creating an environment.** The use of available materials and furniture to represent the setting for a drama (e.g., a courtroom, a bedroom). Sometimes a visual arts extension may be introduced to build belief in the drama (e.g., sheets of fabric painted to look like the walls of a cave).

**crossing-stage procedure.** Customary practice when two or more actors cross the stage. The actor closest to the audience (the downstage actor) slightly trails the other actor, so as not to block that actor, as shown below.

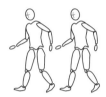

**culture.** The customs, institutions, and achievements of a particular nation, people, or group, including the art works and other embodiments of the intellectual achievements of the group.

**docudrama.** A fictionalized drama based on real events and people.

**drama anthology.** A drama based on a collection of related sources about a particular theme, issue, or person. Both fiction and non-fiction sources may be used (e.g., diary entries, songs, poems, speeches, images, headlines).

**dramatic exploration.** The spontaneous, imaginative use by students of materials and equipment available in the classroom to create drama. The teacher observes and listens while children are exploring, and provides guidance as needed. For example, the teacher may pose a question to prompt deeper thinking, or may introduce new vocabulary.

**dramatic form.** (1) The compositional structure that shapes a drama, as opposed to its theme or content. (2) A broad category of drama that may include within it a number of styles (e.g., puppetry is a form, and different styles of puppetry are characterized by the use of glove puppets or marionettes or shadow puppets; dance drama is a form, and there are different styles of dance drama around the world, such as Kathakali of India and wayang topeng of Bali and Java).

*dramatic play.* Imaginative, pretend play, largely self-directed, that is typical of primary students. The children assume roles, often dressing up and using everyday or found objects to represent objects in their pretend play (e.g., a ruler may represent a magic wand; a structure built of blocks may represent a fort). Students use dramatic play to enact familiar stories, role play real-life scenarios, and create and live through imagined stories and scenarios.

*dramatic works.* In an educational setting, a variety of drama works that are experienced, created, and viewed by students (e.g., plays, improvised drama, short scenes, tableaux, shared drama experiences, reader's theatre scripts).

*elements of drama.* Fundamental components of drama, including the following:

– *character/role.* An actor's portrayal of a character in a drama, developed with attention to background, motivation, speech, and physical traits.

– *focus or emphasis.* The theme, character, problem, event, moment in time, or centre of visual interest (e.g., in a tableau or staging) that gives purpose or impetus to a drama.

– *place and time.* The setting, time period (e.g., past, present, future), duration (e.g., one day), and chronology of the action of a story or drama.

– *relationship(s).* The connection(s) between people, events, or circumstances.

– *tension.* A heightened mental or emotional state resulting from uncertainty about how the conflict or problem in a drama will be resolved.

*empathy/empathize.* The capacity to "step into the shoes" of another and to understand and appreciate that person's experiences and circumstances. Empathy is developed through role play, reflection, writing in role, and viewing and discussing plays, stories, and films. The ability to empathize with characters in drama is a fundamental aspect of building role/character and is essential to skill development.

*farce.* A comic drama that uses ridiculously improbable situations and horseplay, rather than wit, to create humour.

*flashback* and *flash forward.* Conventions used to provide different perspectives on the action in a drama by showing events from an earlier or later time. A *flashback* might be used to explain the causes of an action in the present, a *flash forward* to show an action in the light of its imagined or actual outcome.

*flocking.* A type of improvisation in which students move in groups, with no set pattern or in a diamond formation, following a leader and all doing the same movements simultaneously. This is an extended version of mirroring for three or more people. Participants do not necessarily need to be able to watch each other, as long as they can see the leader.

*form.* See **dramatic form**.

*forum theatre.* A convention in which students collaboratively explore options or possible outcomes in order to shape a dramatic scene. A dramatic situation is improvised by a small group while the rest of the class observes. All students participate in creating the scene – through discussion, by stopping the scene to make suggestions, or by taking over a role. The objective is to create an authentic scene that fits the dramatic context and is satisfying to the whole group.

*four corners.* An activity in which four signs or posters labelled with the possible choices are placed in the four corners of the classroom. Students move to the corner of their choice. Students find a partner in their corner and describe to the partner the reasons for their choice. Students are given three to four minutes to explain the reason(s) for their decision. Each pair then chooses the top two reasons for making their choice. Finally, students write their reasons on the group poster and sign their initials. Students at each of the four corners form a large group and choose a spokesperson. The spokesperson is responsible for presenting a brief summary of their choice and the rationale behind the decisions to the whole class.

*freeze-frame image.* A convention in which students pose to make an image or tableau that communicates an idea or a theme or that depicts a moment in time. Also called a group sculpture or tableau. *See* **tableau**.

*furthering the action.* A group activity in which students build on one another's ideas about how to move the action of the drama forward.

*games/warm-ups.* Activities that help develop a group's readiness for intensive drama work. Such activities can promote group cooperation, trust, risk taking, and listening.

*genres.* The categories into which dramas and other literary works can be grouped. Examples include: thriller, comedy, action, horror, docudrama, melodrama.

*gesture.* A movement of the body or limbs used to express or emphasize a thought, emotion, or idea.

*group role play.* Role playing in which the whole group, including the teacher, acts in role in an imagined context. *See also* **role playing**.

*guided imagery.* A convention used to help a group visualize the setting for a drama. The teacher or a student uses descriptive language to create a word picture of the physical setting and/or historical context in which the action takes place.

*hot seating.* A convention in which students allow themselves to be questioned by the rest of the group. The questioners may speak as themselves or in role (e.g., as reporters).

*improvisation.* An unscripted, unrehearsed drama spontaneously created by a student in response to a prompt or an artefact. *See also* **prepared improvisation**.

*in role.* Acting a part. *See also* **role playing**.

*inner and outer circle.* A convention used for ensemble sharing of contrasting perspectives related to a drama. Students gather in two circles: an inner circle representing one character in the drama and an outer circle representing a second character. (1) *In role:* Students as characters describe their reactions and state of mind at a particular point in the drama. (2) *Out of role:* Students share personal reflections with one another as they are given prompts. Students may speak spontaneously or read from a short passage. Typically, the teacher orchestrates the sharing (e.g., by tapping a student on the shoulder when it is that student's turn to speak), so that the contrasting points of view are highlighted for dramatic effect.

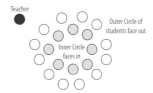

Teacher

Outer Circle of students face out

Inner Circle faces in

*interpretation.* (1) The process of making meaning from stories, images, and poetry and the use of drama conventions to represent or communicate that meaning to others. Students can also interpret drama works that they view at the theatre and on television.

*interviewing.* A convention in which a person or group in the role of "interviewer" asks questions of a student in the role of "expert" to gain information about a particular dramatic situation.

*invented notation.* A form of "picture writing" that students can use in a drama context to explore movement and ideas for drama (e.g., diagrams of blocking to plan movement; symbols to represent aspects of a myth, story, poem, or natural occurrence).

*journal writing.* A means for students to reflect on drama experiences, out of role, by writing and/or drawing in a journal. The teacher may pose questions to guide students' thinking.

*juxtaposition.* The contrast of strikingly different elements to create interest and tension (e.g., differences between characters, settings, moods, the use of space, or the pace of scenes).

*level.* A term used to refer to the position of an actor's body in relation to the vertical. Standing represents a high level, sitting or bending over a medium level, and lying down or crawling a low level.

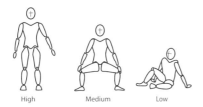

*mantle of the expert.* A convention in which students act in role as "experts" to resolve a problem or challenge. The teacher may also participate, in the role of facilitator.

*mapping.* A convention in which students make maps or diagrams in order to establish the context, build belief in the fictional setting, or reflect on the drama.

*meaning.* (1) The intended message expressed by an actor or by a drama work. (2) A viewer or listener's understanding of the message of a drama work.

*meetings.* A convention in which students and teacher come together in role to hear new information, make decisions, and plan actions or strategies to resolve problems that have emerged in a drama.

*mime.* The use of gesture, movement, and facial expression without words or sounds to communicate actions, character, relationships, or emotion.

*mirroring.* A spontaneous improvisational drama structure used to help students explore characters, themes, issues, or ideas through

movement. Students stand face to face and move their bodies to follow their partner's movements. Variations include a group following a leader's body and/or hand movements.

*monologue.* A long speech by one character in a drama, intended to provide insight into the character.

*mood. See* **atmosphere**.

*narration.* A convention in which a speaker describes the action that is occurring in a drama.

*out of role.* Not acting a part. The term may be used to refer to discussions that take place out of character to further the drama or to plan or discuss artistic choices.

*overheard conversations.* A convention in which the students, role playing in small groups, "listen in" on what is being said by different characters in the drama. A signal is given to freeze all the groups. Then each group in turn is "brought to life" to continue its improvisation while the other groups watch and listen.

*performance.* The presentation of a drama work to an audience.

*picture making.* An activity in which students respond to the drama experience by creating pictures about it, either independently or in groups. The pictures could represent something needed for the drama (e.g., the bridge that connects the two communities on either side of the river).

*place mat.* An activity used to generate ideas. Students record ideas on a piece of paper divided into sections, with a square or circle at the centre representing "common ground". The students generate ideas individually and group ideas they agree on in the "common ground" at the centre.

*play.* A drama work to be read, performed on stage, or broadcast.

*plot.* The sequence of events in a narrative or drama. The sequence can be chronological or presented in a series of flashbacks, flash forwards, and vignettes.

*prepared improvisation.* Improvised enactments of key moments that are central to a drama. Like tableau work – and unlike ordinary improvisations – prepared improvisations require planning and collaboration. Advance preparation includes identifying a suitably significant moment and giving thought to the type of dialogue that would be appropriate in the scene. Limiting the scene to two minutes helps students restrict their scenes to what is essential.

*presentation.* The performance of a dramatic work for an audience.

*process drama.* Unscripted and improvised drama activities. Role play is a key component of process drama, and the activities are intended to promote learning, inquiry, or discovery rather than to create drama for presentation to an audience. The focus is on the exploration and investigation of human dilemmas, challenges, and relationships. *See also* **shared drama experience; role playing**.

*prop.* A portable object used in a drama to support the action or to give authenticity to the setting.

*protagonist.* The main character in a play.

*questioning.* A strategy used to develop students' awareness of universal themes and concepts in the drama that go beyond the basic story line. The teacher asks different types of questions, both in and out of role, to help students broaden their focus. Questions may be designed to elicit information, shape understanding, or stimulate reflection, and may be introduced at any time during the lesson.

*reader's theatre.* A theatre genre in which students: (a) adopt the roles of different characters and of a narrator to read a text; *or* (b) develop scripts based on familiar texts, practise their parts, and present their rehearsed reading to others. Reader's theatre does not involve costumes, sets, props, or movement. The readers generally stand while reading, using their voices to bring the action of the scene to life.

*role on the wall.* A convention in which students represent an important role in picture form "on the wall" (usually on a large sheet of paper) so that information about the role can be collectively referred to or added as the drama progresses. Information may include: the character's inner qualities and external appearance; the community's and/or the family's opinions about the character; the character's view of him or herself; the external and internal forces working for and against the character; known and possible hidden influences on the action or character.

*role playing/role play.* An instructional technique in which a student and/or the teacher acts the part of a character in an imagined situation, usually in order to explore the character's thoughts, feelings, and values. *See also* **group role play; writing in role**.

*scene.* A unit of a play in which the setting is fixed and the time is continuous.

*Seven Grandfather Teachings.* Traditional First Nation teachings about values: honesty – *gwekwaadziwin*; humility – *dbaadendizwin*; truth – *debwewin*; wisdom – *nbaakaawin*; love – *zaagidwin*; respect – *mnaadendmowin*; bravery – *aakdehewin*.

*shared drama experience.* A collaborative classroom exploration of a topic, theme, or issue, using role play and a number of drama conventions to examine multiple perspectives and deepen understanding of the topic, theme, or issue. *See also* **process drama; role playing**.

*side coaching.* A non-disruptive instructional technique used by the teacher to help students working on an exercise or improvisation. As an onlooker, the teacher quietly makes suggestions that the students can use as they develop and shape their drama.

*simulation.* A re-creation of a series of events from real life. Students are assigned roles and provided with background information to help them re-enact the real-life situation. Students work in role in groups to plan their contribution, then negotiate as a class to create a joint product.

*sound and gesture circle.* A group activity in which each student communicates his or her interpretation of an image, concept, or word, using sound accompanied by a gesture. The other students respond as a group by repeating the sound and gesture.

*soundscape/sound collage.* A combination of sounds used to create an atmosphere or to enhance important moments of a scene. Students work as a group to agree on and produce the desired sound effects, using voice and/or instruments. This strategy requires careful listening as well as group cooperation and sensitivity.

*source.* A text, idea, or event that provides the basis for a drama.

*stage areas.* Nine identified sections of the stage, used to help clarify the positions and movements of the actors in stage directions and during rehearsals and performances. The divisions are shown in the diagram below:

*storytelling.* A convention in which storytelling is applied in a drama context. An account of imagined or real people and events is presented through action, dialogue, and/or narration by a teacher or student narrator or by characters within the drama. Storytelling may be done in small groups, large groups, or with the whole class.

*stranger in role.* A convention in which a stranger is introduced into the drama at key moments to refocus the action and/or give it a new direction.

*style.* (1) A particular type of drama within a broader dramatic category (e.g., commedia dell'arte is a type or style of mask comedy). (2) A distinct manner of presenting drama, often associated with a particular historical period, movement, writer, or performer.

*sustaining belief.* Accepting the fictional context of the drama; believing in the imagined world of the drama and thereby convincing the audience of the authenticity of the drama.

*tableau.* A group of silent, motionless figures used to represent a scene, theme, or abstract idea (e.g., peace, joy), or an important moment in a narrative. Tableaux may be presented as stand-alone images to communicate one specific message or may be used to achieve particular effects in a longer drama work. Important features of a tableau include character, space, gesture, facial expressions, and levels.

*tableau cross-over.* A convention in which groups of students form tableaux, after which each student exchanges his or her original tableau position for the position of a partner in the other group's tableau. The convention is used to help students contrast two different but important moments or ideas in a drama (e.g., the effects of a sandstorm on a village years ago before there were trees versus the effects of a sandstorm on the village today). Each tableau should depict a powerful image (e.g., the worst moment during or after the storm).

*talking stick.* A drama strategy named after a ceremonial artefact used in many cultures (e.g., Aboriginal) to ensure that everyone's voice is heard. In Aboriginal tradition, a stick decorated with eagle feathers and crystals was held by a speaker to show that he or she had the right to speak without being interrupted. In drama activities, a stick or other object passed among students can be used to give everyone a turn to speak.

*teacher in role.* A teaching strategy in which the teacher provides input into a drama activity by taking a role in the drama instead of commenting from outside the process.

*technology.* In drama, machinery, including electrical or digital equipment, that is used to help implement or enhance a drama production (e.g., lighting equipment, sound equipment, recording equipment, projector).

*text.* A spoken, written, or media work that communicates meaning to an audience.

*theatre in the round/arena stage.* A type of stage situated in the centre of the space, with the audience facing it from all sides. The placement of the audience quite close to the action creates a feeling of intimacy and involvement.

*theatre work.* A staged drama presentation for viewing, or a script for reading.

*think-pair-share.* A learning strategy in which a student thinks about a topic or idea, works on it with a partner, and then shares the result with the whole group.

*thought tracking.* A strategy in which the teacher circulates, tapping students on the shoulder to prompt them to focus on their inner thoughts and feelings. Thought tracking helps students in role to tap into thoughts and emotions that lie beneath the surface, enabling them to deepen their response and/or contrast outer appearance with inner experience. The strategy can be used effectively with students in tableaux.

*tools.* Equipment (including skills and abilities) used to produce and enhance a drama production. An actor's tools may include vocal skills, movement skills, imagination, and empathy. A director's or producer's tools may include props, costumes, sets, make-up, and special effects.

*turning-on-stage procedure.* A customary practice that calls for an actor to face the audience when turning on stage.

*two stars and a wish.* A method of responding to one's own or another's work by identifying two strengths and one area for improvement (e.g., "I really like… I really like… I wish…").

*visual aids.* Pictures, projections, or objects used to enhance drama performances.

*visual arts extension.* A strategy in which the teacher has students use visual arts to explore drama themes or issues. A visual arts extension should include skill/concept building in both drama and visual arts. Sometimes the created artefact can help provide context for a drama (e.g., masks, murals, books, sets, portraits).

*voice.* The distinctive style of expression of a character, an author, or an individual work conveyed through such things as the use of vocabulary, sentence structure, and imagery, as well as rhythm and pace of speech and tone of voice.

*voices in the head.* A convention used to deepen students' understanding of a conflict or a difficult choice facing a character in the drama. The student representing the character remains silent while others standing behind speak out to express the thoughts and feelings the character might be experiencing at this point. *See also* **corridor of voices**.

*wave.* An improvisational convention in which students stand in a circle or walk in a line, shoulder to shoulder, following a leader, and spontaneously or sequentially drop out of the line to create poses to mirror and then modify an aspect of the shape and/or movement. The shapes can reflect the themes, issues, ideas, or characters being explored.

*writing in role.* Writing done from the point of view of a character in a drama in order to deepen the writer's understanding of the character and create or develop scenes that reflect this understanding. Some examples of forms that may be used include diaries, letters, and reports on specific events that indicate the character's responses to those events.

# MUSIC

*absolute music.* "Abstract" music or music written in specific forms for its own sake – that is, with no connection to a story or other type of "program".

*accent.* An emphasis given to a specific note or tone, often represented by the symbol > as in ♪.

*accidental.* (1) A notational sign indicating a change in pitch: a sharp (♯ – up a half step); a flat (♭ – down a half step); or a natural sign (♮ – restores a note by a half step to its normal pitch in the scale). (2) A sharp or flat that appears in the musical score but is not part of the key signature.

*accompaniment.* A part that supports a voice or an instrument (e.g., a rhythmic pattern; a melodic pattern; a chordal accompaniment, which uses chords to support a melodic line).

*active listening.* The process of listening to music for more than just personal enjoyment; for example, listening to one or more specific elements for a specific purpose, or listening while playing with a focus on specific tasks and effects.

*anacrusis. See* **pick-up note(s).**

*arrange.* Adapt a composition for performance by voice(s) and/or instrument(s) that are different from those of the original version of the composition. The result is often called an arrangement.

*articulation.* The joining or separation of tones, or the way in which musical tones are attacked (e.g., *legato* ♪ – smooth; *staccato* ♪ – detached)

*aural/oral. Aural* relates to hearing and listening. *Oral* relates mainly to singing, but can also include spoken rhymes and chant as well as instrumental music (as in "oral tradition").

*bar.* The notes and rests contained between two bar lines on the musical staff. Also called a measure.

*bar lines.* Vertical lines that divide the five-line musical staff into measures.

*balance.* The blend of voices and/or instruments in a musical work, or the blend and positioning of voices and/or instruments in a performance.

*bass clef.* 𝄢 The clef used for lower-pitched instruments or voices. Also called the F clef.

*beat.* An aspect of the element called duration. A steady pulse. The underlying pulse of many musical forms. In music with a metre, there are strong beats (beats that are often emphasized) and weak beats (unstressed beats). *See also* **rhythm.**

*binary form (AB form).* A musical form that consists of two contrasting sections (A and B). *See also* **form.**

*blues scale.* Usually a six-note scale in which a chromatic half step is added to the pentatonic scale, which gives it the typical blues sound. A flatted note, often the third, fifth, or seventh note, occurs in place of an expected major interval (e.g., C–E♭–F–G♭–G–B♭). *See also* **scale.**

*body percussion.* Sounds produced for different effects by using the body as an instrument (e.g., clapping hands, snapping fingers, patting the thighs).

*bordun.* A repeated pattern using only the tonic and dominant (I and V, or "do" and "so") of the scale as an accompaniment.

*brass instrument.* An instrument that is made of metal and that has a cupped mouthpiece (e.g., trumpet, trombone, tuba).

*breath mark.* ' A symbol placed above the staff indicating when the performer is to take a short breath (for wind instruments) or to lift the bow and play the next note with a downward stroke (for stringed instruments).

*call and response.* (1) A lead-and-follow activity, sometimes also called question and answer. (2) A song or rhythmic pattern consisting of alternating sections of calls sung or played by a leader (solo) and responses sung or played by an individual or a group. The call (question) and response (answer) are different phrases (not echoes). It is a form that is common in many musical traditions. Calls and responses are often improvised. (*Rhythm example:* The teacher claps "ta, ta, ti-ti, ta" and the student claps a response "ti-ti, ti-ti, ta, ta". *Instrumental example:* The teacher and student create a call and response using different notes from a pentatonic scale on a xylophone). *See also* **echo singing**.

*canon.* A piece in which the same melody is repeated exactly by a different voice that begins a short interval after the original voice has started. Canons may also be for more than two voices, and may be sung or performed on instruments. *See also* **round**.

*chant.* The rhythmic speaking or singing of words or sounds, sometimes using only one or two pitches, called reciting tones. Some chants are very simple (e.g., children's chants), whereas others are very complex melodically (e.g., Gregorian chant, which was sung by monks in religious services in the Middle Ages).

*chord.* Several notes, often three or four, played simultaneously, usually containing a root, third, and fifth. Chords of three notes are often called triads. For example, a G-major chord (triad) is made up of the notes G (root), B (third), and D (fifth). Chords are usually described with roman numerals – for example, I for the chord on the first degree of the scale, or tonic; V for the chord on the fifth degree of the scale, or dominant; IV for the chord on the fourth degree of the scale, or subdominant. A commonly used chord progression is therefore written and described as I-IV-V-I.

*chromatic scale.* A scale made up of twelve consecutive notes, each a half step apart.

*coda.* (1) An extra section of music at the end of a piece. (2) A concluding musical section announcing the end of a piece. *See also* **da capo al coda; dal segno al coda**.

*compose.* Create a piece of music (a composition) using the elements of music to convey musical thoughts and meaning.

*compound metre.* A metre in which each main beat in a bar is divided into three (e.g., compound duple: $\frac{6}{8}$; compound triple: $\frac{9}{8}$). *See also* **metre; oral count; time signature**.

*conducting patterns.* Patterns that the conductor uses to indicate the beats in a bar. (At the same time, the conductor indicates tempo, dynamics, and sometimes articulation.)

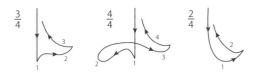

*crescendo.* A common term for a gradual increase in volume, often indicated by the abbreviation "cresc." or the symbol ⟍⟍⟍.

*da capo al coda.* Abbreviated as *D. C. al coda.* Indication to return to the beginning of the piece and play to coda, then play the coda. *See also* **coda**.

*da capo al fine.* Abbreviated as *D. C. al fine.* Indication to return to the beginning of the piece and play to *fine* (the end).

*dal segno al coda.* Abbreviated as *d.s.* (or *D. S.*) *al coda.* Indication to return to the sign 𝄋 and play to *coda* or ⊕, then play the coda. *See also* **coda**.

*dal segno al fine.* Abbreviated as *d.s.* (or *D. S.*) *al fine.* Indication to return to the sign 𝄋 and then play to *fine* (the end).

*decrescendo.* A common term for a gradual decrease in volume, often indicated by the abbreviation "*decresc.*" or by the symbol ⟋⟋⟋. The term *diminuendo* (abbreviation *dim.*) is also commonly used.

*devised notation. See* **non-traditional notation; visual prompts; visual representation**.

*dotted note or rest.* A note or rest to which a dot is added. The dot adds one-half of the note's value. The following are some examples in $\frac{2}{4}$, $\frac{3}{4}$, and $\frac{4}{4}$ time:

– *dotted half note.* A note that is held for three beats.

– *dotted half rest.* Indication of a period of silence lasting three beats.

– *dotted quarter note.* A note that is held for one and one-half beats.

– *dotted quarter rest.* Indication of a period of silence lasting for one and one-half beats.

*See also* **notes and rests**.

*dotted rhythm.* Rhythm in which long notes alternate with one or more short notes. The long notes are dotted. *See also* **dotted note or rest**.

*duple metre. See* **metre; oral count; time signature**.

*duration.* The element of music that relates to time. Fundamental concepts related to it are beat, rhythm, metre, and tempo.

*dynamics.* The element of music relating to the varying degree of volume. Some fundamental concepts related to this element are: *crescendo, decrescendo; forte* (*f* – loud), *fortissimo* (*ff* – very loud), *mezzo forte* (*mf* – moderately loud); *piano* (*p* – soft), *pianissimo* (*pp* – very soft), *mezzo piano* (*mp* – moderately soft).

*echo singing.* (1) A lead-and-follow activity, sometimes also called echoing. (2) A melodic or rhythmic pattern consisting of alternating sections of calls sung or played by a leader (solo) and responses sung or played by the follower(s). The calls and the responses consist of the same melodic or rhythmic phrase, thus "echo". (*Rhythm example:* The teacher claps "ta, ta, ti-ti, ta" and the student claps the response "ta, ta, ti-ti, ta".) *See also* **call and response**.

*elements of music.* Fundamental components of music. They are defined for the purposes of this document as duration (beat, rhythm, metre, tempo), pitch (melody), dynamics, timbre, texture/harmony, and form. *See also* individual entries for these terms.

*ensemble.* A group of singers, or instrumentalists.

*expressive controls.* Particular kinds of emphasis given to notes, using such means as articulation, fermatas, tempo, dynamics, and timbre.

*family of instruments.* A grouping of similar types of musical instruments. In European music, there have traditionally been four families of instruments (i.e., woodwinds, brass, strings, and percussion). Some musicologists now add extra families to include electronic instruments and musical instruments of other parts of the world.

*fermata.* A sign indicating that the performer is to hold a note or pause for longer than its usual value.

*first and second endings.* Signs that indicate the following procedure: at the repeat sign at the end of the first ending , the performer repeats the section just played, then goes on to play the second ending .

*folk song.* A song that is usually transmitted orally over several generations, often related to the daily life of the people in a culture or community.

*form.* The element of music relating to the structure of musical works or pieces. *See also* **binary form (AB form); fusion form; minuet; rondo; ternary form (ABA form); theme and variations; 12-bar blues; verse and chorus**.

*found sounds.* (1) Rhythmic or pitched sounds that can be produced by using everyday objects, such as sticks, combs, pop bottles, shakers, or pots. (2) Environmental sounds, such as the sounds of hammering, traffic, or birds, that can be used in creating a musical composition.

*fusion form.* A musical genre that results from combining aspects of two or more genres; for example, rock music is a fusion of blues, gospel, and country music. *See also* **form**.

*gamelan.* Instrumental music from Indonesia and Malaysia that is characterized by reverberating sounds produced by gongs, chimes, and other tuned metal percussion instruments. Two main gamelan traditions are the Balinese and the Javanese.

*grand staff.* The combination of a staff notated in the treble clef with one notated in the bass clef. This staff is used for notating piano music and music for other keyboard instruments, and is also used to notate vocal works.

*half step.* The smallest interval that is commonly used in Western music (e.g., the interval E–F or C–C♯).

*harmony.* The simultaneous sounding of two or more notes, or pitches. *See also* **chord; texture.**

*head tone.* A sound produced in the upper register of the singing voice. The vibrations of sung head tones are felt in the head rather than in the chest.

*historical periods.* For the purposes of this document, the historical periods for Western classical music are the Middle Ages (ca. 500–ca. 1450), the Renaissance (ca. 1450–1600), the Baroque period (1600–1750), the Classical period (ca. 1750–1820), the Romantic period (ca. 1820–1900), and the twentieth century and beyond (from approximately 1900 on). Classical musical traditions from other parts of the world also have written historical records (e.g., North and South Indian, Arabic, Persian, Chinese).

*homophony (homophonic music).* Music consisting of a single melodic line with chordal accompaniment.

*improvise.* Compose, play, or sing on the spur of the moment without the aid of written music, applying skills learned. *Improvisation* can refer either to the music produced or the activity of improvising.

*interpretation.* (1) Analysis or appreciation of a musical work by a viewer or listener. (2) The particular understanding of a musical work that is communicated by a performer of the work.

*interval.* The distance between two notes (e.g., the interval between two pitches that are one step apart, such as C–D, is called a second). *See* **half step; major interval; minor interval; perfect intervals; skip; step; unison.**

*invented notation. See* **non-traditional notation; visual prompts; visual representation.**

*key signature.* The pattern of sharps (♯) or flats (♭) placed on the staff immediately to the right of the clef to indicate which notes are to be played sharp or flat throughout a piece of music. (Sharps or flats indicated in the key signature can be temporarily cancelled by a natural sign [♮].) The key signature also identifies the key and scale associated with the music. *See* the diagram of key signatures on page 185.

*leap.* Any interval that is larger than a skip, or third (e.g., the interval of a fourth, such as C–F). *See* **interval; skip; step; unison.**

*ledger lines.* Extra, short lines that are added above or below the regular five-line staff to extend the staff in order to notate pitches that fall above or below the staff.

*legato.* Smooth, flowing performance of a phrase.

*major and minor keys.* A major key is based on the notes of the major scale (e.g., C major: C–D–E–F–G–A–B–C), while a minor key is based on the notes of the minor scale (e.g., A minor [harmonic]: A–B–C–D–E–F–G♯–A). *See also* **major scale; minor scales.**

*major interval.* The distance between two notes within the major scale, measured from the first note of a major scale; that is, the major second, major third, major sixth, and major seventh (e.g., the interval F–G is a major second, and C–E is a major third). *See also* **interval; leap; major scale; minor interval; perfect intervals; skip; step; unison.**

*major scale.* A stepwise series of eight notes composed of whole steps and half steps in the following sequence – whole, whole, half, whole, whole, whole, half. In this pattern, a major interval occurs between the first note of the scale and each of the second, the third, the sixth, and the seventh notes of the scale. *See also* **minor scales; scale.**

*manipulatives.* Models, blocks, tiles, and other objects that children can use to explore musical ideas; for example, math cubes to demonstrate the length (duration) of notes: long, long, short short. □□   □□   □   □

*measure.* *See* **bar**.

*melody.* A succession of sounds (pitches) and silences moving through time. Melodies can be thought of as movement in sound by repetition of a pitch, by step, and by skip, or as movement by a series of intervals (unison, step, skip, leap).

*melody map/melodic contour.* A graphic representation that illustrates the movement (rise and fall) of a melodic line. Also called pitch contour.

*metre.* An aspect of the element called duration. The grouping of beats in music using time signatures. Metres are typically simple (e.g., $\frac{2}{4}$, $\frac{3}{4}$, $\frac{4}{4}$), compound (e.g., $\frac{6}{8}$, $\frac{6}{4}$, $\frac{9}{8}$), and irregular (e.g., $\frac{5}{4}$). Duple metres have two main beats in a bar (e.g., $\frac{2}{4}$, $\frac{6}{8}$, $\frac{6}{4}$). Triple metres have three main beats in a bar (e.g., $\frac{3}{4}$, $\frac{9}{8}$). *See also* **oral count; time signature**.

*minor interval.* (1) The distance between two notes within the minor scale, measured from the first note of a minor scale; that is, the minor third, minor sixth, and minor seventh (e.g., a minor sixth is A–F). (2) Any interval that is one half step (or semitone) smaller than a major interval (e.g., a major second is C–D, but the minor second is C–D♭). *See* **interval; leap; major interval; minor scales; perfect intervals; skip; step; unison**.

*minor scales.* (1) In the *natural minor*, there is a stepwise series of eight notes composed of whole steps and half steps in the following sequence – whole, half, whole, whole, whole, half, whole. In this pattern, a minor interval occurs between the first note of the scale and each of the third, the sixth, and the seventh notes of the scale. (2) In the *harmonic minor*, the seventh note is raised. (3) In the *melodic minor*, the sixth and seventh notes are raised going up the scale, and are lowered going down (lowered to the same pitches as those in the natural minor). Common to all three minor scales, ascending and descending, is the minor interval between the first note and the third. *See also* **major scale; scale**.

*minuet.* A musical form in $\frac{3}{4}$ time. It is based on ABA form, but there are many repeats with modifications (usually at the end of a repeated section) and variations of themes used. *See also* **form**.

*monophony (monophonic music).* Music consisting of a single melodic line with no accompaniment. It can be performed by one person (a solo) or by several in unison (e.g., a unison chorus).

*movement.* A relatively independent segment of a larger work that is found in such works as sonatas, symphonies, and concertos.

*musical literacy.* The ability to understand and use the variety of ways in which meaning is communicated through music, including use of the elements, aural skills (in listening and performing), reading and writing skills (use of notation, symbols, terminology), and interpretative performance skills.

*musicianship.* The knowledge, skills, and artistic sensitivity necessary for interpreting music through performance and conveying understanding of feelings and ideas in the music.

*non-pitched percussion instruments.* Percussion instruments that sound only one pitch (e.g., snare drum, cow bell, cymbals, tambourines, wood blocks). Also can be called unpitched or untuned percussion instruments.

*non-traditional notation.* A way of writing music that is not standard notation, such as rhythmic or stick notation, graphic notation, a melody map, depiction of melodic contour, notation using icons, or a visual representation. Sometimes referred to as devised or invented notation. *See also* **melody map/melodic contour; oral prompts; solfège; visual prompts; visual representation**.

*notation.* A way of indicating pitch and rhythm in written form; for example, standard notation, tablature, and percussion notation, as well as written forms of oral syllables, such as the syllables used in the Indian tabla tradition and the Griot tradition of Africa. *See also* **non-traditional notation; oral prompts; solfège**.

*notation software.* A computer application used to compose, arrange, and publish musical compositions. Most notation software is able to receive information from, and send information to, a MIDI-capable keyboard or synthesizer.

*note.* A musical sound or the symbol used to write it down.

*notes and rests.* The following are the standard symbols for common notes and rests. The values given here are samples in simple time ($\frac{2}{4}$, $\frac{3}{4}$, and/or $\frac{4}{4}$).

– *whole note.* ○ A note that is held for four beats.

– *whole rest.* ▬ Indication of a period of silence lasting four beats.

– *half note.* ♩ A note that is held for two beats.

– *half rest.* ▬ Indication of a period of silence lasting two beats.

– *quarter note.* ♩ A note that is held for one beat.

– *quarter rest.* ♩ Indication of a period of silence lasting one beat.

– *eighth note.* ♪ A note that is held for one-half of a beat. Beams can connect sequential eighth notes: ♫

– *eighth rest.* ♪ Indication of a period of silence lasting one-half of a beat.

– *sixteenth note.* ♬ A note that is held for one-quarter of a beat.

– *sixteenth rest.* ♬ Indication of a period of silence lasting one-quarter of a beat.

– *multi-measure rest.* ▬ Indication of the number of measures of silence, which is used to conserve space. This convention requires the performer to count carefully.

*See also* **notation; oral prompts**.

*numbers for notation (scales).* In scales, the names of notes are usually used (e.g., C, D, E, F, G, A, and B), but the notes are sometimes assigned numbers (1, 2, 3, 4, 5, 6, and 7) or syllables (do, re, mi, fa, so, la, and ti) for purposes of instruction. For example, it is helpful to use numbers to refer to notes when having students play a scale together on band instru-

ments, because, in several instances, the same sound/pitch is referred to by a different name for different instruments (e.g., a B♭ on an oboe is the same pitch as a C on a clarinet). *See also* **chord; chromatic scale; major scale; minor scales; pentatonic scale; scale; solfège**.

*one-line staff.* A "staff" of one line on which the up-and-down nature of pitch progression can be indicated in relationship to a reference point (the line). It can be used to teach young children to read music. The number of lines can be increased to two, three, and finally five. *See also* **notation**.

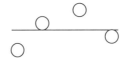

*oral count.* Use of words to indicate beats and divisions of beats; for example, in $\frac{3}{4}$ time, "one and two and three and" to indicate quarter and eighth notes. Also called counting aloud. *See* the chart on page 185 showing a way of counting aloud for various metres. *See also* **metre; time signature**.

*oral prompts.* Syllables derived from the Kodály method of teaching music. *See* the chart on page 186 for oral prompts and their equivalents in standard and rhythmic (stick) notation.

*ostinato.* A continuous repeated rhythmic or melodic pattern (e.g., bordun). An example of a simple rhythmic ostinato might be "ta, ta, ti-ti, ta". A melodic ostinato might include a word from a song that is repeated using the melodic pattern of "so–so–la–la–so–so–mi". *See also* **oral prompts; rhythmic pattern; solfège**.

*partner song.* A song that results when two different songs are sung together that have melodies that fit together well when they are performed simultaneously (e.g., "Fish and Chips and Vinegar" sung with "Rufus Rustus Johnson Brown"). It is a form of polyphony.

*pentatonic scale.* A musical scale of five pitches or notes (e.g., C–D–E–G–A, or do–re–mi–so–la). The pentatonic scale plays a significant role in music education, particularly in Orff-based methodologies that place a heavy emphasis on developing creativity through improvisation. Orff instruments (e.g., xylophones) use wooden bars that the teacher can remove, leaving only those bars that correspond to the pentatonic scale. Because of the nature of the pentatonic scale, it was found that it was impossible for a child to make any real harmonic mistakes when using it. *See also* **scale**.

*percussion instrument.* An instrument that one has to hit, scrape, or rattle in order to make a sound. Percussion instruments are typically classified as pitched (e.g., xylophone) and non-pitched (e.g., maracas).

*perfect intervals.* The perfect 4th (e.g., the interval C–F or F–B♭), perfect 5th (e.g., the interval C–G or F–C), octave (e.g., the interval from C to the next C, ) and unison. In Western music, perfect intervals have been considered to be the most harmonious.

*perform.* In elementary school, share work in progress to get feedback from peers and the teacher (e.g., sing a song), or share a finished product with another individual or a group of people in either an informal or a formal context (e.g., play an instrumental piece for a classroom audience).

*phrase.* (1) A group of sounds that has a beginning, a middle, and an end. (2) A musical sentence that is both rhythmic and melodic (often four to eight measures long).

*pick-up note(s).* One or more unstressed notes that lead in to the downbeat, or strong beat. Also called an anacrusis.

*pitch.* The element of music relating to the highness or lowness of a tone.

*pitched percussion instruments.* Percussion instruments that produce more than one pitch (e.g., xylophone, metalophones, piano, orchestral bells).

*pitch matching.* Singing or playing, in tune, exactly the same pitch as another person, after hearing it sung or played.

*polyphony (polyphonic music).* Music consisting of two or more melodic lines that are performed simultaneously. Also called counterpoint. *See also* **partner song**.

*program music.* Music that depicts a story, scene, or emotion.

*question and answer. See* **call and response**.

*recorder.* A woodwind instrument consisting of a wooden or plastic tube, at the top of which is a whistle-like mouthpiece. The recorder has a softer tone than the flute, and is held vertically, not horizontally.

*repeat.* A symbol used to enclose a passage that is to be played more than once. If there is no left repeat sign, and the performer encounters a right repeat sign, he or she goes back to the beginning of the piece and plays it again. *See also* **first and second endings**.

*rest. See* **notes and rests**.

*rhythm.* An aspect of the element called duration. The pattern of long and short sounds or silences. Patterns can be created by both musical sounds and lyrics or words. Rhythm differs from beat; for example, the rhythm at the beginning of a song might be "ta, ti-ti, tika-tika, ta", whereas the beat is the underlying steady pulse of "ta, ta, ta, ta". *See also* **beat**.

*rhythmic (or stick) notation. See* **oral prompts**.

*rhythmic pattern.* A short, repeated pattern using two or more note values (e.g., quarter note and eighth note). A sample of such a pattern is "ta, ti-ti, ta, ta".

*rhythm syllables. See* **oral prompts**.

*roman numerals. See* **chord**.

*rondo.* A form of music in which the main theme alternates with contrasting themes. It often consists of five sections, of which the first, third, and fifth are the same or almost the same (ABACA or ABABA). *See also* **form**.

*round.* A piece for three or more voices or instruments in which each sings or plays the same melodic material but starts one after the other at a set point (e.g., "Row, Row, Row Your Boat", "Frère Jacques"). It is a kind of canon.

*scale.* A series of notes that go up or down stepwise. Names of notes are usually used (e.g., C, D, E, F, G, A, and B), but the notes are sometimes assigned numbers or syllables for purposes of instruction. Chords based on the notes of the scale are referred to with roman numerals. *See also* **chord; chromatic scale; major scale; minor scales; numbers for notation (scales); pentatonic scale; solfège.**

*section.* A part of a larger composition that is longer than a phrase (e.g., an introduction, a verse, a chorus, a coda). Musical forms, such as binary and ternary, are built from smaller musical units called sections.

*sforzando (sfz).* A sudden and very forceful emphasis, often on a whole chord.

*sight reading.* Singing or playing notated music that one has not seen before.

*skip.* Any interval that is larger than a step, or second (e.g., the interval of a third, such as C–E, which is the distance between notes either a line or a space apart on the staff). *See also* **interval; leap.**

*slur.* A curved line connecting notes on a score to indicate that they are to be played or sung smoothly (*legato,* or without separation). For example, for a violin, a slur encompasses more than one note in a single bow stroke; brass and woodwind players should tongue only the first note of a slur group; in guitar music, slurs are commonly known as "hammer-ons" and "pull-offs".

*solfège.* A technique for teaching sight singing and ear training in which each note is sung to a special syllable, called a solfège syllable (or sol-fa syllable). The syllables do, re, mi, fa, so, la, and ti represent the pitches of the scale. Various kinds of syllables are used in oral traditions around the world for learning music or for reciting

(e.g., Indian, Balinese, Chinese, Korean traditions). In some cases, music is notated using oral syllables (e.g., Indian drum notation). *See* the drawings of the hand signs on page 186 that indicate the solfège syllables. *See also* **visual prompts.**

*soundscape.* A piece of music that, through sound, depicts a picture or an event or creates a mood or an atmosphere. It can, for example, contain a structured or shaped sequence of musical and found sounds.

*staccato.* Short and detached, indicated by a dot above or below the note head.

*staff.* The five lines and four spaces on which the symbols of standard notation of music are written.

*standard notation.* The system of written symbols conventionally used to represent the sounds of a composition. This includes the five-line staff, notes, key signatures, time signatures, and indications of tempo, dynamics, and articulation. *See also* **notation; solfège.**

*step.* The interval between a note that is on a line and a note on the adjacent space, or vice versa (e.g., the interval C–D or E–F♯). Also called the interval of a second, a whole step, or a tone. There are two half steps (semitones) in a step.

*stick (or rhythmic) notation. See* **oral prompts.**

*stringed instrument.* An instrument that has strings and that is played with a bow or plucked (e.g., violin, viola, violoncello, double bass, guitar, lute).

*style.* Characteristic use of the elements of music by musicians of particular traditions. Often refers to music of a specific historical period (e.g., Baroque style). Knowledge of aspects of the style of a particular time or tradition is essential for proper interpretation and performance of works in that style.

*syllables. See* **oral prompts; solfège.**

*symbols.* Conventional marks, signs, or characters indicating how to perform musical notes.

*syncopation.* The displacement of beats or accents so that emphasis is placed on weak beats rather than on strong beats.

*tablature.* A form of notation used for guitar and other plucked instruments, such as the lute. In the example below, notation is given for a solid A minor chord that is followed by some individual notes. The lines represent the strings (not a staff) and the numbers represent the frets (not fingering). *See also* **notation**.

*technology.* Electronic instruments and interfaces, as well as compositional hardware and software, used for composing music and altering and recording sound.

*tempo.* An aspect of the element called duration. The speed of a piece. Some common tempo indications are: *allegro* (quickly and in a lively way), *moderato* (at a moderate speed), *andante* (somewhat slowly, at a walking pace), *largo* (slowly), *adagio* (slowly and gracefully), and *vivace* (briskly, quickly, brightly).

*ternary form (ABA form).* A musical form that consists of three sections – a first section, a contrasting section, and a third section that is a repetition of the first. *See also* **form**.

*texture.* The relationship between the "horizontal" aspect of music (i.e., a single line such as a melody) and the "vertical" (i.e., some type of accompaniment such as harmony). For example, texture that is mainly vertical is homophonic (i.e., it consists of a melody with chordal accompaniment), and texture that is mainly horizontal is polyphonic (i.e., it consists of two or more melodies sung or played together). Texture may also be created by a group of percussion instruments playing music that is not primarily melodic, such as the Balinese gamelan.

*theme and variations.* A form of music in which a melody or section of music constitutes the basis (the theme) for a series of variations (A, A1, A2, A3…). The variations often result from changes in the key, metre, rhythm, harmony, speed, and/or mood of the theme. *See also* **form**.

*tie.* A symbol that links two adjacent notes of the same pitch, indicating that the first note is to be held for the total time value of the two notes. A tie can also extend over two or more measures.

*timbre.* The element of music relating to the unique quality of sounds that allows us to distinguish between them (e.g., the characteristic sound of a trumpet versus a clarinet, or a male versus a female voice). Also called tone colour.

*time signature.* A numerical indication showing the number of beats in a bar and the value of the note that gets one beat. The following are some common examples:

– $\frac{2}{4}$ *time.* Indication that there are two beats to a bar and the quarter note gets one beat. Also called *simple duple.*

– $\frac{3}{4}$ *time.* Indication that there are three beats to a bar and the quarter note gets one beat. Also called *simple triple.*

– $\frac{4}{4}$ *time.* Also represented by ¢. Indication that there are four beats to a bar and the quarter note gets one beat. Also called *simple quadruple* or *common time.*

– $\frac{5}{4}$ *time.* Indication that there are five beats to a bar and the quarter note gets one beat. Also called *irregular compound.*

– $\frac{6}{4}$ *time.* Indication that there are six beats to a bar and the quarter note gets one beat. Also called *compound duple,* since there are really two main beats to a bar, each divided into three.

– $\frac{6}{8}$ *time.* Indication that there are six beats to a bar and the eighth note gets one beat. Also called *compound duple,* since there are really two main beats to a bar, each divided into three.

– $\frac{9}{8}$ *time.* Indication that there are nine beats to a bar and the eighth note gets one beat. Also called *compound triple,* since there are really three main beats to a bar, each divided into three.

*See also* **compound metre; metre; oral count; time signature**.

*treble clef.* 𝄞 The clef used for higher-pitched instruments or voices. Also called the G clef.

*triad. See* **chord**.

*triple metre. See* **compound metre; metre; oral count; time signature**.

*triplet.* A grouping of three notes that takes the same amount of time that two notes of the same value would normally take in a specific piece. A small numeral "3" is placed above the triplet. Heard in succession, triplets produce a gently swinging motion.

*tone colour.* The quality of a particular musical sound. Also referred to as timbre. Words that are sometimes used to describe the tone colour or timbre of an instrument or the tone colour(s) of a musical work might be *rich, bright, mellow*, or *piercing.*

*12-bar blues.* One of the most popular forms in the blues and in other popular music. The 12-bar blues has a distinctive structure both musically and in its lyrics. The typical 12-bar blues chord progression is a version of the I-IV-V-I chord progression (e.g., G-C D⁷-G or A-D-E⁷-A). This chord progression forms the basis of thousands of songs, not only blues songs such as "Shake, Rattle, and Roll" and "Hound Dog", but also jazz classics such as "Night Train" and pop and rock songs, such as the Clash's "Should I Stay or Should I Go?". Lyrics are typically in three lines, and the first two lines are almost the same with slight differences in phrasing and interjections. *See also* **form**.

*two-line staff. See* **one-line staff**.

*unison.* (1) The sound produced when two or more instruments or voices play or sing the same pitch. (2) The interval that occurs when two melodic parts (voices or instruments) join to produce the same sound.

*verse and chorus.* A musical form in which a verse part and a chorus part alternate. The chorus is usually repeated relatively unchanged, whereas the verses are not usually exactly alike. Sometimes there is an introduction, or the chorus may be repeated without an intervening verse. *See also* **form**.

*visual prompts.* Pre-reading representations, such as hearts, to represent the beat, or sticks, to represent note values (see illustration below). Visual prompts facilitate the learning of notation at early stages. Other forms of visual prompts are solfège hand signs; visual placement of solfège hand signs higher and lower in space or placement of solfège letters (e.g., S, S, M, S) on the blackboard to indicate melodic movement up and down; placement of solfège letters or simple circles on a staff; or indication of pitches and rhythm by using solfège letters with rhythmic (stick) notation (with or without a staff). *See also* **melody map/melodic contour; non-traditional notation; oral prompts; solfège; visual representation**.

*visual representation.* Use of symbols visually to reflect pitches and/or rhythms heard. For example, the size of the visual symbols used can provide an indication of the volume or duration of the sounds (e.g., a large object could indicate a loud or long sound). Also called graphic response. *See also* **melody map/melodic contour; non-traditional notation; visual prompts**.

*whole step. See* **step**.

*wind instrument.* An instrument in which the sound is produced by a column of air (e.g., flute, clarinet, oboe, trumpet, trombone, tuba).

*woodwind instrument.* An instrument, usually made of wood, that one has to blow into in order to make a sound (e.g., clarinet, oboe, English horn, flute, recorder, bassoon). Despite the name, some woodwind instruments are made of metal – for example, flutes, saxophones, and some clarinets.

## Illustrations of Some Musical Concepts

### Key signatures

The following chart shows the number of sharps and flats in key signatures. (Lower-case letters indicate minor keys.)

| Number of ♭'s or ♯'s in Key | Names of Keys With Flats | | Names of Keys With Sharps | |
|---|---|---|---|---|
| | Major keys | Minor keys | Major keys | Minor keys |
| 0 | C, a | | | |
| 1 | F | d | G | e |
| 2 | B♭ | g | D | b |
| 3 | E♭ | c | A | f♯ |
| 4 | A♭ | f | E | c♯ |
| 5 | D♭ | b♭ | B | g♯ |
| 6 | G♭ | e♭ | F♯ | d♯ |
| 7 | C♭ | a♭ | C♯ | a♯ |

### Oral count

In the following chart, illustrations are provided to show how one might count aloud in some commonly used metres. Only the main beats and main divisions of beats are indicated. Primary emphasis is indicated with bold type and secondary emphasis with bold italic. (*See also* **notes and rests** and **time signature** for the specific meaning of the time signatures and note values.)

| Time Signature | Metre | Count |
|---|---|---|
| $\frac{2}{4}$ | simple duple | **one**-and-*two*-and |
| $\frac{3}{4}$ | simple triple | **one**-and-*two*-and-*three*-and |
| $\frac{4}{4}$ | simple quadruple | **one**-and-*two*-and-***three***-and-*four*-and |
| $\frac{5}{4}$ | irregular compound | **one**-*two*-*three*-**one**-*two* or **one**-*two*-*three*-**four**-*five* |
| $\frac{6}{8}$ | compound duple | **one**-and-a-*two*-and-a |
| $\frac{6}{4}$ | compound duple | **one**-*two*-*three*-**four**-*five*-*six* |
| $\frac{9}{8}$ | compound triple | **one**-and-a-*two*-and-a-*three*-and-a |

*Continued on next page*

### Oral prompts with rhythmic and standard notation

The oral syllables and the equivalents in rhythmic notation and standard notation are given in the chart below. Rhythmic notation, often called stick notation, which is a simplified form of standard notation, is often used in conjunction with oral prompts.

| Oral Prompt | Rhythmic (or Stick) Notation | Standard Notation |
|---|---|---|
| ta | | |
| ti | | |
| ti-ti | | |
| tika-tika | | |
| ta-ah | | |
| ta-ah-ah-ah | | |
| ti-tika | | |
| tika-ti | | |
| tum-ti | | |
| syn-co-pa | | |
| tim-ka | | |
| shh (or "rest") | | |

### Solfège hand signs

For instructional purposes, the solfège hand signs are usually posted from bottom to top (as in the illustration below), so that students will associate the rise in pitch with the rising of their hands in the air as they sing and use the hand signs.

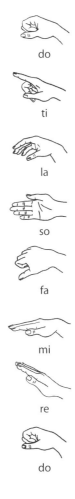

do

ti

la

so

fa

mi

re

do

# VISUAL ARTS

*abstraction.* A technique of depicting observable phenomena such as figures, places, or objects in a simplified or modified form (e.g., as geometric shapes, stick figures, shapes and spaces composed of tonal areas). Below is an example of abstraction of musical instruments and symbols. *See also* **style: abstract art; style: non-objective art**.

*advancing colour.* Colour that appears to come forward in the picture plane and forward from the surface (e.g., a warm colour or a vivid colour).

*allegory.* The use of symbolic figures, events, or actions to represent abstract ideas.

*analogous colours.* Two or more colours that are next to each other on the colour wheel, such as red, red-orange, and orange. Also called adjacent colours. *See also* **colour**.

*angle of view. See* **point of view (visual)**.

*animation.* The process of creating the illusion of movement through a series of images (e.g., drawings, digital images, paper cut-outs, photographs, puppets, sculpted figures) that show slight, progressive changes sequentially in time using various techniques (e.g., claymation, cut-out/collage animation, flipbook, thaumatrope, pixilation, rotoscope, stop motion, digital processes).

*appropriation.* The taking or borrowing of elements to recontextualize them or create new works. The borrowed elements may include images, forms, or styles from art history or from popular culture, or materials and techniques from non-art contexts (e.g., everyday objects). The audience or viewer may or may not be aware of the intertextuality of the imagery.

*art analysis strategy.* A method for analysing visual art works. Types of strategies include the following:

– *artist journal (in role).* The student synthesizes biographical information about an artist and compositional information about the art work by writing a journal, in role, as an artist. A variation is writing letters in role.

– *image improv(isation).* A cooperative strategy. Students in small groups discuss an art work to determine what could be happening and/or the relationships among the people, animals, or objects in it. Students then explore their analysis of the image through various drama conventions and improvisation.

– *pop master.* Students select an Old Master painting and create an abstract painting in response to it, using contemporary figures, settings, or issues. Students generalize the shapes in the painting as either geometric, hard-edged shapes or organic, free-flowing shapes. The placement of objects in the composition should match the original image. Students test out their shape abstractions with rough sketches, then select a warm, cool, or limited colour scheme to work with (choosing a colour scheme that contrasts with the original colour scheme would increase the "abstract" effect). Students then discuss how their new composition and colour choices affect the viewer and change the meaning/interpretation of the original art work.

– *word and image match.* A cooperative strategy. Students match printed words to postcard-size or large reproductions of art images. The words can be in different sets (e.g., emotions, moods, adjectives, nouns, verbs, adverbs). Students then discuss their choices.

– *word association in image interpretation.*
A cooperative strategy. The teacher presents students with paired images in a variety of art forms (e.g., paintings, sculpture, photographs) along with two words that are not related to visual arts (e.g., flip, flop). The students decide, according to their own criteria and direct observation, which image suits which word. A wide variety of interpretations are acceptable as long as visual support can be found in the selected images.

*See also* **artist interview; artist's statement; classifying images; image round-table**.

*artist interview.* A cooperative art-analysis strategy in which one student takes on the role of an artist and is interviewed by a student or students. The interview is used to explore ideas and to gain personal and practical information from the "artist". Interviews help to focus on significant information, ideas, or experiences that yield new learning, and can teach students how to probe and use follow-up questions to extend understanding.

*artist's statement.* A concise summary in which the artist reflects on and/or analyses what he or she has done, in order to help the viewer understand his or her purpose, priorities, and techniques.

*artist trading cards (ATCs).* Miniature art works (65 by 90 mm; 2½ by 3½ in.) created by artists to trade with other artists. They may be unique works or limited editions of prints. The art on the cards may be done in any medium.

*assemblage.* A three-dimensional work of art that combines a variety of materials such as textiles and found objects or parts of objects.

*asymmetry.* Inequality in size, shape, and/or position between parts or elements or objects. An asymmetrical arrangement may still produce a balanced visual effect or weight.

*automotion.* A technique in which a figure or object is drawn in motion in a series but within one frame or within a single image.

*background. See* **ground plane**.

*balance.* A principle of design. A feeling of balance results when the elements of design are arranged symmetrically or asymmetrically to create the impression of equality in weight or importance or harmony of design and proportion. Forms and figures acquire greater weight the farther away they are positioned from the centre axis of the image.

*blending.* The drawing and painting technique of mixing two or more colours. It may be used to create gradations of colour so that two hues or values merge imperceptibly. There are a variety of techniques for blending in each of the different media.

*block print. See* **relief printing**.

*camera angles.* Various positions of the camera with respect to the subject being photographed, each giving a different viewpoint and perspective. *See also* **point of view (visual)**.

*camera shot.* (1) The view that is seen or filmed through a camera's viewfinder. (2) The composition of key elements within a frame used to support the story or idea indicated in a storyboard. Different types of shots include the following:

– *close-up.* The camera is placed close to an object or person to focus attention on details (e.g., to display emotions and reveal what the character is thinking). In these shots, the subject will dominate the frame.

– *medium shot.* The camera is placed so there is a relatively equal balance between subject and setting in order to demonstrate relationships (e.g., of the subject to others or to the environment) and body language. When the subject of this shot is a human body, its field of view will include the knees or waist up to the head. The subject of this type of shot will take up about as much space as the background.

– *tracking shot.* The camera follows a character as he or she moves.

– *wide shot.* The camera is positioned to observe simultaneously everyone and everything present in the scene. Wide shots establish the setting or location and background detail. Individual characters are not the main focus in this composition or view.

*caricature.* A representation, especially pictorial or literary, in which the subject's distinctive features or peculiarities are deliberately exaggerated to produce a comic or grotesque effect.

*cast shadow.* The dark area that appears on a surface when an object intervenes between the light source and the surface.

*ceramics.* (1) Objects made of clay and fired in a kiln. The term refers to functional and decorative objects, as well as sculpture made from clay. (2) The art of making ceramic objects. *See also* **hand building (clay)**.

*characterization.* In art, a technique in which features or qualities of an inanimate object are exaggerated and given human qualities. Also known as personification or anthropomorphism.

*chine collé. See* **printmaking**.

*classifying images.* A critical-thinking art-analysis strategy in which students collect, sort, display, and interpret images according to established or student-generated criteria in order to identify a variety of relationships among the images or parts of the images.

*close-up. See* **camera shot**.

*clustering.* In design, creating a focal point by grouping different objects or shapes together.

*collage.* A form of art in which a variety of materials (e.g., photographs, fabric, found objects, bits and pieces of originally unrelated images including commercial images) are arranged and attached to a flat background, often in combination with painted or drawn areas. Also known as découpage. *See also* **composite image**.

*collograph.* A print made from a surface that has been constructed as a collage of objects and textures. The surface requires low-relief texture in order to print.

*colour.* An element of design. The particular wavelength of light seen by the eye when an object reflects or emits light. The four characteristics of colour are hue (name), value (lightness and darkness), intensity (saturation, or amount of pigment), and temperature (warm and cool). *See also* **cool colours; hue; intensity; neutral colours; primary colours; secondary colours; tertiary colours; value; warm colours**.

*colour wheel.* A tool for creating and organizing colours and representing relationships among colours. *See also* **complementary colours**.

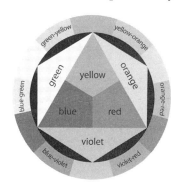

comic. A graphic art form in which images and words are used to tell a story. The images are the main focus and are presented in strip or page layout. Dialogue and necessary information are enclosed in speech balloons and boxes. Panels, layout, gutters, and zip ribbons help indicate the flow of the story. Ideas in a comic are organized into a series of "shots", like the storyboards for a film. A related form is the graphic novel. *See also* **camera shot; point of view (visual); pose**.

complementary colours. Colours that are directly opposite each other on the colour wheel (e.g., red and green, blue and orange, yellow and violet). A secondary colour's complement is always the primary colour that is not used to create it (e.g., red and yellow make orange; the only primary not used to create orange is blue, therefore blue is the complementary colour or opposite of orange).

composite image. An image made from a variety of materials and methods (e.g., a mixed-media print made up of text, images, and other materials). *See also* **collage; photo montage**.

composition. The organization of the elements of design in an art work, following certain principles of design (e.g., balance of positive and negative spaces; variety of shapes, textures, and values; off-centre placement of the focal point; division of the area into several areas of interest; overlapping of objects of various sizes; placement), as well as other layout considerations such as the rule of thirds and compositional triangles.

conceptual art. A work of art that is regarded as a vehicle for the communication of ideas, which may be drawn from disciplines such as philosophy or film studies or from the agendas of social justice advocacy and political activism.

construction. A type of sculpture in which the form is built by adding on material (e.g., a sculpture built with scrap wood blocks). Also called additive sculpture.

conté (crayon). A drawing medium consisting of natural pigments such as fine charcoal and clay mixed with a waxy material to create a hard stick. Conté crayons can create sharp lines and very dark tones.

contemporary art. Art created in the present by living artists.

content. The meaning of an image beyond its overt subject matter, including the emotional, intellectual, symbolic, thematic, and narrative connotations. *See also* **subject matter**.

continuity. In design, the arrangement of shapes so that the line or edge of one shape leads into another (a technique used to achieve unity in a composition).

contour drawing. An outline drawing that represents the edge of a form. In "blind" contour drawing, the artist slowly draws each bump and curve on the edges of an object without looking at the paper.

contour lines. Lines that define the edges, ridges, or outline of a shape or form.

contrast. A principle of design. The juxtaposition of different elements of design (e.g., complementary colours such as red and green, textures such as rough and smooth, values such as dark and light) in order to highlight their differences and/or create balance, visual interest, or a focal point.

I will make exciting art.
I will make exciting art.
I will make exciting art.
I will make exciting art.
I will make exciting art.
I will make exciting art.
I will make exciting art.
I will make exciting art.
I will make exciting art.
I will make exciting art.

I'M A REAL ARTIST

**cool colours.** Colours that suggest coolness (e.g., blue, green, purple). Cool colours often appear to recede into the background or distance.

**critique.** A review of a finished art work, or constructive feedback that can be used by the artist for further revision of an art work in progress.

**cropping.** The trimming or cutting away of unnecessary or unwanted edges of a picture, or the reframing of an area of an image to create a stronger composition. A viewfinder may be used to help determine the best composition before cropping. *See also* **viewfinder**.

**crossed creatures.** A drawing technique in which the features, characteristics, shapes, or forms from two different creatures (e.g., an elephant and an ant) are combined into a single image.

**cross-hatching.** A drawing technique for shading using numerous crossed sets of parallel lines, and usually resulting in darker values. The darker values are created by frequency rather than thickness of line: fewer lines create a light image, while more lines, closely spaced, create a darker image. *See also* **hatching**.

**cubist technique.** The technique of reducing and fragmenting the form of an object from multiple points of view into geometric shapes and planes of the cone, cube, and sphere. Colour plays a secondary role. In graphic design, the technique develops simplified, flat shapes. Cubist art depicts real objects although it may appear abstract or geometric. *See also* **style: cubism**.

**current media technologies.** Technologies that are used to create art. Examples include digital photography, animation, interactive video and time-based displays, installations incorporating new media, and software-based and web-based art.

**design.** *See* **composition**.

**design process.** A problem-solving model that involves the concrete manipulation of images, materials, and technology for the purpose of solving a design problem. The technical design process can be open ended when the student designs all the steps, or it can be teacher directed to varying degrees.

**dimension.** An object's extent in space. A two-dimensional object has length and width. A three-dimensional object has length, width, and depth.

**directional lines.** Edges of objects, such as roads, trees, folds in clothing, or even people's line of sight, that cause the viewer's gaze to follow a particular path. The eye tends to follow lines towards the centre of a picture and/or towards areas of greatest contrast. However, since the eye also follows arrow-type shapes, images need to be carefully composed to avoid leading the eye away from the focal point. *See also* **line; movement**.

**dominant element.** The element in a work of art that is noticed first (elements noticed later are subordinate).

**drawing.** The process of marking a surface by applying pressure on a tool (e.g., pencil, marker, computer drawing tablet) and moving it across the surface to record observations, thoughts, feelings, and ideas, or to explore the artistic possibilities of the drawing material(s). Dry drawing materials include charcoal, conté, crayon, ink, marker, pastel, pencil, scratchboard, software, and watercolour pencils. Wet drawing materials include black or coloured ink applied with a pen, soft brush, nib, or other stylus. *See also* **cross-hatching; hatching; scumbling (drawing)**.

*drawing pencil.* A drawing tool made from graphite. The graphite used in drawing pencils is relatively soft and malleable. Shading pencils in the B to 6B range provide dark, even tones and values. Primary printing pencils contain soft graphite or lead and are a substitute for drawing pencils in classroom settings.

*elaboration.* A technique in which the shapes or forms are decorated with additional features such as lines, dots, circles, and patterns. Also called mark making.

*elements of design.* Fundamental components of art works. They include colour, form, line, shape, space, texture, and value.

*emphasis.* A principle of design. Special attention or importance given to one part or element in an art work (e.g., a shape of darker value in a light composition). Emphasis can be achieved through placement, contrast, colour, size, and repetition, among other means.

*etching (dry point).* A dry (non-acid) printmaking process in which a design is scratched (etched) into the surface of a soft metal or plexiglass plate. When ink is applied to the plate and wiped off, the etched lines retain the ink, which is then transferred to (printed on) paper pressed against the plate. Also called dry-point engraving.

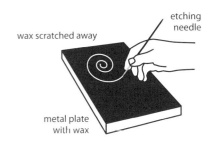

wax scratched away
etching needle
metal plate with wax

*exaggeration.* A technique of increasing, distorting, or enlarging an element, object, or figure.

*expressionism. See* **style**.

*facial proportions (standard).* Generalizations about the relative position of the features of the human face. For example, the eyes are about halfway between the top of the head and the chin; the bottom of the nose is halfway between the eyes and the chin; the mouth is halfway between the nose and the chin; the outer corners of the mouth line up with the centres of the eyes; the tops of the ears line up just above the eyes; the bottoms of the ears line up with the bottom of the nose. In both men and women, the front of the neck is lower than the back; however, a woman's neck is usually longer and more rounded than a man's, while a man's neck is wider.

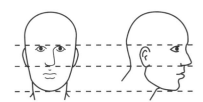

*figurative art.* (1) Drawings and paintings of the human figure. (2) Art that depicts recognizable subjects such as landscapes, still lifes, portraits, and figures.

*flipbook.* A book of pictures in which the sequential images vary slightly from one page to the next. When the pages are turned (flipped) rapidly, the sequence of changes in the pictures simulates motion. Persistence of vision creates the illusion that continuous motion is being seen rather than a series of discontinuous images.

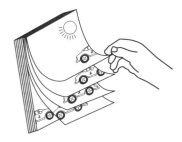

*focal point.* The centre of interest in an art work (i.e., the elements or area in an art work on which the viewer's attention is focused). The artist directs the viewer's eye using a variety of means, including directional lines, contrast, location, isolation, convergence, and the unusual (e.g., areas that are light in value, or bright in colour, or highly detailed).

*foreground. See* **ground plane**.

*foreshortening.* A form of perspective where the nearest parts of an object or form are enlarged so that the rest of the form appears to be farther back in space.

*form.* (1) An element of design. The compositional style, design, and arrangement of the visual elements within an art work. (2) The physical shape and dimensions of an object within an art work. (3) A particular field or genre within the visual arts (e.g., painting, printmaking).

*framing. See* **camera shot; point of view (visual); viewfinder.**

*gallery walk.* An instructional technique in which students rotate around the classroom looking at art work, composing answers to questions, and reflecting on and reacting to the answers given by other groups. The technique is used to encourage active engagement by students in synthesizing important concepts, building consensus, writing, and speaking.

*genre.* A style or category of art that has a tradition or history and is identifiable by specific characteristics (e.g., portrait, landscape, still life, abstract painting).

*geometric shape.* A shape that is based on geometric figures (e.g., square, circle, triangle).

*gesture drawing.* A drawing done quickly to capture the action and movement of the subject. It is most concerned with the essence of the pose and economy of means in representing it rather than careful depiction of anatomy or form. Artists use gesture drawing as a warm-up of the full arm, to prepare themselves mentally and physically for a figure-drawing session.

*glue-line printing.* A relief or block printing technique in which a raised image is created by drawing with thick beads of white glue or a low-temperature glue gun on a printing plate. Once the glue drawing is dry, ink is rolled onto the raised surfaces with a brayer, for printing onto paper.

*gradation.* In a drawing or painting, a small, subtle change from one shade, tone, or colour to another.

*ground plane.* The perceived space of a composition. Its parts are classified as follows:

– *background.* The part of a composition that appears to be farthest from the viewer or behind the other objects.

– *foreground.* The area of a picture that appears to be closest to the viewer and in front of the other objects. It is often at the bottom of the picture plane.

– *middle ground.* The part of a composition that appears to be in the middle of the picture plane.

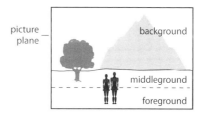

*hand building (clay).* The creation of ceramic pieces using only the hands and simple tools (as opposed to a potter's wheel) by coiling, moulding, pinching, pulling up from a mound of clay, slabbing, or combinations of these techniques. Terms used in ceramic work include the following:

– *clay types.* Clays may be classified according to the temperature at which they harden or vitrify in the kiln. Earthenware clay is fired at relatively low temperatures, while stoneware clay and porcelain clay require higher temperatures. Clay also comes in many colours based on its mineral content.

– *coiling.* Building ceramic forms by rolling out coils or ropes of clay and joining them together with the fingers or a tool.

– *kiln.* A furnace designed to gradually and safely reach high temperatures for firing clay.

– *leather-hard clay.* Unfired air-dried clay. The surface is still soft enough to be carved.

– *moulding.* Flat slabs of clay are draped over forms or pressed into moulds in order to create various shapes or forms.

– *pinching.* The thumb of one hand is inserted into the clay, and the clay is lightly pinched with the thumb and fingers. The ball of clay is slowly rotated in the palm of the other hand as the clay is shaped.

– *score and slip.* A method of joining two pieces of clay together. Scratches are scored (e.g., with a fine-toothed scraper or old toothbrush) in the surfaces that will be sticking

together. The surfaces are then wetted with slip (liquid clay), and the two pieces are pressed together. Leather-hard clay should be used in this process to prevent the pieces from popping apart when they are fired.

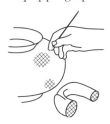

– *sgraffito.* A method of decorating clay. Leather-hard clay is coated with a slip (made from clay of a contrasting colour but of the same clay type), and a pattern or picture is created by carving through, incising, or scraping off the air-dried slip to reveal the clay underneath.

– *slabbing.* Building ceramic forms by rolling out a flat piece of clay.

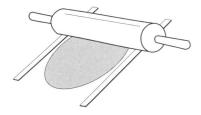

– *slip.* A muddy solution of liquid clay, usually made by dissolving a small piece of clay into a shallow cup of water, and used to coat clay shapes during various ceramics processes. The slip should be of the same clay type as the piece it will be applied to and the consistency of thick cream.

– *slip trailing.* A method for drawing on the surface of a piece. Slip (liquid clay) is applied to a dry piece (greenware) through a tube or nozzle. The slip should be made from the same type of clay but may be in a contrasting colour.

– *stages of dryness.* Degrees of moistness or dryness that determine the malleability of clay. The three basic stages of dryness are wet, leather-hard, and bone-dry (greenware).

– *stamping.* Pressing forms (e.g., shells, lace) into wet clay to add surface detail, texture, and decorative effects.

*handmade paper.* Paper made using water and shredded fibres, or scrap (recycled) papers, beaten and turned into a soupy pulp (slurry), which is usually scooped into a mould or a screened frame, drained, and then dried on blank newsprint or felt into individual sheets.

*harmony.* A principle of design. The combination of elements so as to highlight their similarities and produce a unified composition.

*hatching.* A drawing technique used to create a sense of depth or three-dimensionality on a flat surface. Areas of darker value and shading are created by using numerous repeated strokes of an art tool (e.g., pencil, marker) to produce clustered lines. The lines are usually parallel, but may also be curved to follow the shape of the object. Fewer lines create a lighter image, while more lines, closely spaced, create a darker image, since less white paper shows. *See also* **cross-hatching**.

*horizon line.* The "line" at which the sky and the earth appear to meet. *See also* **perspective**.

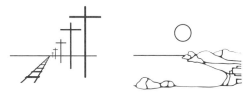

*hue.* The common name of a colour (e.g., red). Also referred to as pigment. *See also* **colour**.

*hybrid art.* Art in which genres, styles, concepts, materials, media, and cultural forms are combined to create new forms. Hybridization is the technique used in creating hybrid works, and is often associated with postmodernism in popular culture and contemporary art. *See also* **style: postmodernism**.

*icon.* A symbol, image, motif, emblem, or object that is generally recognized as representative of a person, place, era, or culture.

*illusory texture. See* **texture**.

*illustration.* An art practice, usually commercial in character, that stresses anecdotes or story situations and focuses on subject more than form.

*image round-table.* A cooperative image-analysis strategy. Students move around the classroom between art reproductions. Beside each image is a piece of paper on which students answer a question about the image. Students then fold the paper so that their answer is no longer visible and move to the next image. After responding to several images, students return to their starting point and read the accumulated statements about their image. Students use some or all of the words to describe the image, in poetry or prose, then paint or draw a response to the image and the ideas generated about it.

*implied line.* A line that is not drawn but suggested by the way elements have been combined in an art work.

*impressionism. See* **style**.

*imprint.* An image or pattern created by pressing an object onto a wet surface or by coating the object with paint and pressing it onto a dry surface. Objects with raised or textured surfaces produce the clearest images.

*ink. See* **printing ink**.

*installation.* A two-dimensional, three-dimensional, or time-based art work (or a combination of these) made specifically for a chosen site or environment, arranged in place either by the artist or to the artist's specifications, and often involving interaction between the work, its audience, and the site. Installations are relatively large, and may be temporary or permanent and created for indoor or outdoor settings.

*intensity.* The saturation (amount of pigment), strength, or purity of a colour. A vivid colour is of high intensity, a dull colour of low intensity. Visual intensity can be enhanced by placing complementary colours next to each other in an image or reduced by mixing in a small amount of the colour's complement (e.g., a small amount of yellow mixed into violet neutralizes and dulls the colour). *See also* **colour**.

*juxtaposition.* The placing of items in an image close to one another to reveal some contrast or similarity that conveys a message.

*kinetic art.* Any work of art that includes natural or mechanical movement as one of its defining properties or as part of its intended expression.

*landscape.* (1) A painting or drawing in which rural scenery is the main feature. Cityscapes, streetscapes, and seascapes are variants of the landscape genre. (2) The physical orientation of a two-dimensional art work, where the width is greater than the height.

*layering.* A technique of applying one layer of opaque or transparent material (e.g., tissue paper, paint, glaze) on top of another.

*layout.* The arrangement and positioning in a design of text, illustrations, photographs, and/or diagrams.

*limited palette.* A restricted range of colours. As a problem-solving exercise, students may be required to work with only a few specific colours for particular assignments.

*line.* An element of design. The visual path left by a moving point; also, a mark, guide, or boundary that leads the eye in an art work. Differences in the type, orientation, and/or quality of lines can be used to suggest a variety of ideas, states, or moods. For example, horizontal and curving lines can feel restful or inactive, and vertical and diagonal lines can imply movement or action; combinations of horizontal and vertical lines can suggest stability.

*linoleum.* A material made of a pressed mixture of heated linseed oil, powdered cork, and pigments on a burlap or canvas backing. Linoleum can be used for block printing. The image is cut into the surface. *See also* **softoleum**.

*logo.* A typographic or graphic form or image used as an emblem to identify an individual, club, organization, project, or product. Also called a logotype.

*magnification.* A technique in which a small detail of an object is enlarged. In art, this technique can be used to create a form of abstraction. Below is an example of abstraction through magnification (part of the torso of a bug). *See also* **abstraction**.

*materials.* The substances out of which something is or can be made, including media (e.g., wax, crayons, modelling clay), substrate or surface (e.g., canvas, paper, wood), and found objects (e.g., leaves, shells, wire).

*matte.* Non-glossy; having a dull surface appearance.

*media production.* The use of a variety of technological and media tools to create a work that conveys information or represents a student's culminating performance or project. Tools used in media production include cameras, video or digital editing equipment, televisions, video players, audio recorders and players, projectors, computers, and the appropriate software required to use these tools. Media production provides the opportunity to integrate and present text, graphics, sound, video, and animation in new ways.

*medium (plural: media).* (1) The material(s) used by an artist to produce a work of art. A medium may be two-dimensional (e.g., graphite, ink, paint, photographic paper, canvas), three-dimensional (e.g., fibre, clay, wood, metal, glass, plastic), or time-based (e.g., animation, video), and may have wet properties (e.g., paint, ink, dye, wash) or dry properties (e.g., pencil, charcoal, conté, crayon). (2) A clear polymer or acrylic gel or emulsion used for glazing or varnishing in painting, in image transfer processes, or as an adhesive in collage. (3) The liquid with which powdered pigments are mixed to make paint (e.g., in oil paints, linseed oil is the medium). *See also* **mixed-media work; wet and dry materials**.

*medium shot. See* **camera shot**.

*metamorphosis.* A change in form or nature. Artists may create forms and images showing such change (e.g., a letter becoming an object, a flower becoming a dancer) to communicate a variety of ideas.

*middle ground. See* **ground plane**.

*mixed-media work.* An art work in which more than one medium is used (e.g., acrylic paint, collage, and oil pastels, in combination).

*model (noun).* (1) A small-scale preliminary work made as a "trial run" in preparation for a larger sculpture or architectural work. Also called a maquette. (2) A person who poses for an art work.

*model (verb).* (1) To shape and manipulate malleable sculptural materials such as clay. (2) To simulate light and shadow on a flat surface in order to create the appearance of depth or three-dimensionality in two-dimensional art.

*model making.* A thinking strategy involving the creation of two- or three-dimensional constructions to represent ideas and interpretations and demonstrate knowledge and understanding. It emphasizes the importance of information carried by visual, tactile, or concrete features and often attempts to represent ideas and mental constructs of the universe through physical details, shape, dimension, and scale. Model making is a process activity that can be used in all subject areas.

*modernism. See* **style**.

*modulation.* A drawing technique for depicting levels of darkness on paper by applying a medium (e.g., pencil) more densely or with a darker shade for darker areas, and less densely or with a lighter shade for lighter areas. Hand control of pressure rather than smudging is used to create smooth transitions between different degrees of darkness.

*monochromatic colour scheme.* A colour scheme in which only one hue is used, along with its tints (i.e., the hue plus white) and shades (i.e., the hue plus black).

*mosaic.* An art work made with small pieces of a material, such as coloured stone, glass, paper, or tile.

*motif.* A design or theme that may be repeated in a larger overall design (e.g., in a two-dimensional or three-dimensional art work) or a time-based art work (e.g., video) for decorative or narrative purposes.

*movement.* A principle of design. The way in which the elements of design are organized so that the viewer's eye is led through the work of art in a systematic way, often to the focal area. Movement can be directed along lines, edges, shapes, colours, and similar values within the work. *See also* **directional lines; line**.

*multimedia applications.* Computer software programs that combine a variety of elements such as sound, animation, text, and graphics into a multimedia production. Multimedia applications that provide hypertext links among elements such as computer text, visual material, and sound files are called hypermedia applications. Multimedia applications may be non-linear. They allow students to compose, communicate, and create new knowledge in innovative ways.

*narrative art.* An art work that tells a story, or in which a story line is a prominent feature.

*negative space/shapes.* The empty or open areas within or around an object or form (in two-dimensional and three-dimensional art work). When these areas have boundaries, they also function as design shapes in the total structure. *See also* **positive space/shapes**.

*neutral colours.* Colours such as black and grey that are created by mixing equal proportions of complementary colours. The proportions may be altered to create variable colours such as blue-grey, green-grey, or purple-grey or red-brown, yellow-brown, or green-brown.

*non-objective art. See* **style**.

*opaque.* A material or colour that does not let light pass through. Strong opacity will prevent the colour below from showing through. The opposite of transparent.

*op art. See* **style**.

*organic shapes or forms.* Non-geometric, irregular, or free-flowing shapes or forms that are based on shapes or forms found in nature. Also referred to as free-form shapes.

*original art work.* An art work created by hand using techniques such as drawing, printmaking, painting, and sculpture, singly or in combination.

*painting.* The process of marking a surface by applying pigments suspended in a liquid medium to record observations, thoughts, feelings, and ideas or to explore the possibilities of the materials. Materials include acrylic, block and liquid tempera, food colour, liquid ink, gouache, and watercolour.

*painting techniques.* The following are some examples of commonly used techniques:

– *blocking in.* The process of establishing the main shapes and areas of colour or tone in a painting by filling in large areas with thin layers of paint, starting with the background. The technique helps organize shapes and values before colour details are added. Also called underpainting.

– *broken colour.* The use of small separate strokes of pure colour, which, when viewed from a distance, mix optically to form the impression of blended colour.

– *dry brush.* A technique using thick paint on a dry brush that produces a textured or "scratched" appearance. *See also* **watercolour techniques**.

– *glazing.* The process of superimposing transparent washes of paint over other washes that have dried, creating a glowing effect similar to stained glass.

– *impasto.* The process of applying oil paint in thick, solid masses, producing a textured surface.

– *scraping.* The process of scraping paint off the surface of a painting to show the layers or material below, as in sgraffito. When the paint is wet it can be scraped away with a palette knife, the back end of a paintbrush, or a fingernail. In watercolour, a blade or sandpaper may be used to produce white highlights.

– *scumbling.* Applying fairly dry paint with an irregular scrubbing motion in order to place an uneven layer of colour over an already dry underlayer. The paint may be applied using a variety of implements (e.g., brush, rag, sponge, paper towel). The technique is useful for representing weathered or irregular textures such as rocks or bushes. *See also* **scumbling (drawing)**.

– *spattering.* The process of flicking spots of colour onto a horizontal surface from a brush held above it to create a random pattern of dots.

– *stippling.* The use of small dots of pure colour placed close together, which, when viewed from a distance, mix optically to form the impression of blended colour. The unmixed colours are vibrant, and the dots create a shimmering effect. Sometimes the colour is applied with a stiff brush or a sponge as a faster method than painting each dot with a brush. Also called pointillism. *See also* **stippling (drawing)**.

*paint resist.* A technique in which colour is drawn or rubbed onto paper with wax crayons or oil pastels, followed by the application of a water-based wash (e.g., food colour, tempera, watercolour block). The water-based colour wash is absorbed by the paper but not the wax or oil.

*palette.* (1) A board or surface (e.g., wax paper, polystyrene, plastic) on which colours are blended and mixed, allowing the painter to experiment with mixtures of colour while leaving pure, unmixed colour in the paint tubes. (2) The range of colours that an artist uses.

*papier mâché.* A sculptural technique using paper pulp or paper strips mixed with glue or paste (e.g., wheat paste, boiled cornstarch paste) built up on an armature of cardboard, rolled newspaper, or plastic bags stuffed with crumpled paper. The surface can be painted after it has dried.

*pastel.* (1) A drawing medium consisting of pigment compressed into a stick. The following are some examples:

– *chalk pastel.* Chalk is the medium for the pigment. It can be smudged.

– *oil pastel.* Oil is the medium for the pigment. It smudges less easily than chalk pastel.

(2) An art work created using pastels. (3) A descriptive word for certain soft, light shades of colour. *See also* **conté (crayon)**.

*path (of movement).* The path along which the viewer's eye moves from one part of an art work to another.

*pattern.* (1) A principle of design. A regular arrangement or sequence of alternated or repeated elements (shapes, lines, colours) or motifs. (2) A template, model, or guide for making something.

*performance art.* A series of events performed or staged by an artist for an audience.

*perspective.* The representation of space and three-dimensional objects on a two-dimensional surface so as to convey the impression of height, width, depth, and relative distance. The illusion of depth, distance, and so on, is created through methods such as the depiction of far-away objects as smaller in scale and positioned closer to the top of the art paper and the use of overlapping objects, vertical placement, diminishing size, and shadows and shading. Ways of characterizing and/or creating perspective include the following:

– *atmospheric perspective.* The intensity of colour and the distinctness of detail are gradually lessened to indicate an increase in the distance between objects and the viewer, The technique is based on how atmosphere affects the appearance of distant objects (e.g., dust and other substances in the air make background elements less distinct than the same things close to us). Also referred to as aerial perspective.

– *diminishing perspective.* Objects are depicted as smaller in size as their distance from the viewer increases.

– *linear perspective.* The parallel lines of buildings and rectangular shapes or objects are drawn so as to converge at a point on the horizon or eye-level line called the vanishing point. There can be as many vanishing points in a painting as there are sets of converging parallel lines. In *one-point linear perspective* (see first illustration below), parallel lines converge at a single point on the horizon or eye-level line. In *two-point linear perspective* (see second illustration below), parallel lines converge at two vanishing points on the horizon or eye-level line.

 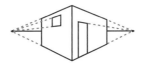

*photography.* The process of creating still or moving pictures (e.g., photographs, video, animation) usually through a photographic lens in a traditional or digital camera, but also using a simple pinhole camera (made with a sheet of film in a light-tight can such as a coffee can). Pictures produced with photographic materials but without a camera, called photograms, are created by exposing light-sensitive paper to sunlight. Objects placed between the light-sensitive paper and the light appear on the paper as silhouettes. *See also* **camera shot; viewfinder**.

*photo montage.* A form of collage in which photographs are used to create a composition. The subject matter and arrangement of the individual photographs combine to express a new meaning conceived by the artist. Assembly can be done through cut and paste or digitally. *See* **collage; composite image**.

*plaster bandage.* A sculpture material made of a cloth similar to cheesecloth that has been saturated with plaster of Paris.

*point of view (literary).* A social, political, economic, intellectual, or emotional position or opinion expressed by an artist through an art work.

*point of view (visual).* The angle from which the viewer sees the objects or scene. Also called angle of view. The following are two examples:

– *bird's eye or aerial view.* A downward perspective that gives the viewer a feeling of elevation in relation to the subject or art work.

– *worm's eye or low view.* An upward perspective that gives the viewer a feeling of seeing from the floor or the surface of the earth in relation to the subject or art work.

*popular culture.* Art, objects, images, artefacts, literature, music, fashion, and so on, intended for, consumed by, or representing the taste of the general public.

*portrait.* (1) An art work that depicts a person. Portraits may be life size, or smaller or larger than life, and may depict heads, torsos, or full-length figures. They may be abstract or realistic and executed in a variety of media. A self-portrait is an artist's depiction of him- or herself. (2) The physical orientation of a two-dimensional art work, where the height is greater than the width.

*pose.* The position of a figure. The artist may position a subject to suggest the subject's mental attitude or a physical movement or action.

*positive space/shapes.* Shapes or forms on a two-dimensional surface. *See also* **negative space/shapes**.

*poster.* (1) A mass-produced digital or photo-mechanical reproduction of an original art work. (2) A combination of image and text produced to convey a message to a specific audience, using graphic design considerations such as backgrounds, colour, spacing, legible text, concise message, and graphics. *See also* **print**.

*primary colours.* Red, yellow, and blue. These are colours that cannot be created by mixing other colours but that can be mixed to produce all the other colours.

*primary printing pencil. See* **drawing pencil**.

*principles of design.* Generally accepted ideas about the qualities that contribute to the effectiveness of an art work that are used as guidelines in composing an image and analysing how viewers are likely to perceive it. The qualities include but are not limited to the following: balance, emphasis, harmony, movement, proportion, rhythm, unity, variety. *See* individual entries for these terms.

*print.* An image created and reproduced by hand, on paper, fabric, or other support, using a printmaking technique (e.g., etching, woodcut, silk screen, lino cut). *See also* **etching; poster; printmaking**.

*printing ink.* Thick ink, used specifically for relief or block printing, that produces complete, even coverage on raised surfaces, including linoleum, wood, and flexible printing plates such as softoleum or polystyrene. (Water-based inks are recommended for elementary classrooms.)

*printing plate.* A surface, used in the process of making relief or block prints, into which the image to be printed is incised (e.g., wood, linoleum, or polystyrene in block printing; low-relief collage in collograph printing). The image is then transferred to another surface (e.g., paper or fabric) after a colour medium

(e.g., ink) is applied. *See also* **collograph; relief printing**.

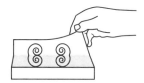

*printmaking.* An artistic method or process that uses a printing plate, screen, stamp, or stencil to create one or a series of prints. Printmaking processes include collograph, embossing, and glue-line printing. Materials include linoleum, silk screen, softoleum, stamps, stencils, and polystyrene. Other tools and processes used in printmaking include the following:

– *bench hook.* An aid used by printmakers to steady the printing block during cutting. It is made from a wooden baseboard with one strip of wood along the top edge to hold the block in place and another underneath to hook the board against the edge of the table. Also known as a side hook. A clamp can be used for the same purpose.

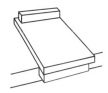

– *brayer.* A rubber roller that is used to roll out printing ink on an ink slab and then apply the ink to the raised surface of a block printing plate.

– *chine collé.* A process used for printing on thin paper. Thin paper (e.g., tissue or kozo paper) is placed on an inked printing plate, glue is applied to the other side of the paper, and the plate and paper are placed on a dampened piece of some backing material. The whole is then run through a printing press or a set of rollers so that the ink adheres to the paper and the paper to the backing. The backing provides support that prevents the thin paper from tearing.

– *lino cutter.* A tool with a metal blade used to cut into a linoleum or softoleum printing block.

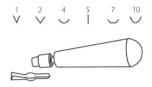

– *monoprint.* A one-of-a-kind print that cannot be duplicated, made by pressing paper onto the wet paint or ink of an image on another surface (e.g., pressing paper onto a finger-painted image on plexiglass).

– *polystyrene plate.* A thin, polystyrene sheet on which the slightest pressure (e.g., with a pencil) can create an incised impression, eliminating the need for sharp, pointed tools that might be hazardous for younger students.

– *screen printing.* A process in which a stencil is attached to a taut fabric screen, which is placed over paper. Ink is wiped over the screen with a rubber blade or squeegee, forcing the ink through the mesh fabric onto the paper while leaving the area beneath the stencil white (without ink).

*proportion.* A principle of design. The relationship between objects with respect to size, number, and so on, including the relation between parts of a whole. *See also* **proportions (figure)**.

*proportions (figure).* The average human height in drawing is eight heads high (nine in fashion drawing). This measure may be used as a reference for locating the main points of the body. On a vertical line the height of the figure, the halfway point is the hip, the one-quarter point is at the bottom of the knees, the three-quarters point is the chest, and the

seven-eighths point is the bottom of the head. These proportions can be adapted to drawing children, depending on their age: a three-year-old is, on average, five heads high; the neck is less developed than in adults and the face and body are rounder. A teenager could be seven heads high with a smaller head and less rounded face than a child. *See also* **proportion**.

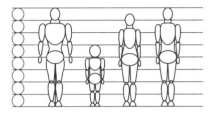

*radial design.* A composition that has the major images or design parts emanating from a central point or location. If the radiating parts are equal in size and/or shape, the composition would have radial symmetry (also called a balance pattern). *See also* **symmetry**.

*realism. See* **style**.

*real texture. See* **texture**.

*reflected colour.* Colour that bounces off nearby objects and affects the perceived colour of the objects (e.g., the red of a cup on a desk may bounce off the surface of the desk, making a faint area of visual redness on the surface of the desk).

*relief printing.* Any method of printmaking where the surface to be inked is raised ("in relief"). The printing plate (e.g., woodblock, polystyrene, glue line, linoleum, softoleum) is adapted, cut, incised, or built up to create a low-relief image, and the image is then transferred to a surface (e.g., paper or fabric) after a colour medium (e.g., ink) is applied. Also called block printing. *See also* **printing plate; relief sculpture**.

*relief sculpture.* A type of carving or sculpture in which the form projects from a background (e.g., high relief, low relief/bas-relief, sunken relief). Unlike other types of sculpture, relief sculpture is intended to be viewed from one side. *See also* **relief printing; sculpture**.

*repetition.* A principle of design. The repeated use of similar elements and visual effects in a composition. Repetition may produce the dominance of one visual idea, a feeling of harmonious relationship or unity, a pattern, or a rhythmic movement of the viewer's eye (e.g., a repeated pattern of similar colours, brushstrokes, and textures can lead the eye through the art work).

*representational art.* Art that depicts the physical appearance of recognizable images from "real" life.

*reproduction.* A copy of a work of art. *See also* **poster**.

*resist. See* **paint resist**.

*rhythm.* A principle of design. The use of recurring elements to direct the movement of the viewer's eye through the art work and give a sense of unity to the composition. There are five kinds of rhythm: random, regular, alternating, progressive, and flowing.

*rubbing.* (1) The technique of placing paper over a textured surface, then rubbing the surface of the paper with a pencil, pastel, or crayon, causing the appearance of the texture to be reproduced on the surface of the paper. Also called frottage. (2) An image produced by the use of the rubbing technique.

*rubbing plate.* A tool for exploring texture that may be created by building up a low-relief texture on a surface (e.g., cardboard). The low relief may be created as conscious exploration of line or pattern using materials such as beads of glue or random or found elements such as lace or mesh bags. Rubbing plates may also be themed (e.g., using fossils or shells).

*rule of thirds.* A compositional rule of thumb that advocates dividing an image space into thirds, both horizontally and vertically, and positioning important elements in the composition at or near the imagined dividing lines or near the points at which the lines would intersect. The rationale is that the use of off-centre rather

than centred elements gives tension, energy, and interest to the composition.

*scoring.* A sculpting technique. In paper sculpture, the use of a semi-sharp object to crease paper for easy folding. In clay sculpture, the process of abrading or scraping surfaces before joining pieces, for improved adhesion.

*sculpture.* (1) A work of art in three dimensions (i.e., with height, width, and depth), usually intended to be viewed from all sides. (2) The technique of creating three-dimensional forms or figures by carving, cutting, hewing, casting, moulding, welding, or assembling materials. Materials may include clay, found objects, papier mâché, plaster bandages, plasticine, wire, and wood. Types of sculpture include the following:

– *found-object sculpture.* A type of sculpture made of materials and objects found in the environment. The materials and objects are reorganized and reassembled into a new form with or without surface decoration.

– *free-standing sculpture.* A self-supporting three-dimensional form surrounded by space and designed to be viewed from all sides. Also called sculpture in the round.

*scumbling (drawing).* A drawing technique that uses layers of small, calligraphic, scribbled marks to build up value and texture.

*secondary colours.* Colours that are created by mixing two primary colours (e.g., orange is made my mixing red and yellow; green is made by mixing blue and yellow; violet is made by mixing blue and red).

*self-portrait. See* **portrait**.

*sequential images.* Images organized into a series to tell a story. They are an important component used in some forms of narrative art, such as animation, comics, graphic novels, and historical tapestries.

*shade.* (1) A dark value of a colour, made by adding black. (2) A drawing and painting method for adding darker values to an image using a variety of techniques such as modulation, stippling, or hatching.

*shape.* An element of design. The external form or outline of an image produced by the use of line, value, colour, and/or texture. Shape may be geometric or organic, positive or negative. Shapes have two dimensions, length and width.

*sign.* An image used to represent or point to something (e.g., a concept or object) other than itself.

*sketch.* A quick drawing that may be a reference or plan for composition or later work. A figure sketch designed to capture proportions and body language may be highly stylized, with very little detail. *See also* **thumbnail sketch**.

*sketchbook.* A book of drawing paper in which artists record things they see or imagine. It may include sketches, completed work, rough plans, notes, images, and clippings.

*softoleum.* A soft, grey, rubber-like material designed to be easily and safely cut or incised, for use in block printing.

*space.* An element of design. The area around, within, or between images or elements. The appearance of space can be created on a two-

dimensional surface by means of techniques such as the overlapping of objects, the varying of object size or placement, the varying of colour intensity and value, and the use of detail and diagonal lines.

*stamp.* (1) A piece of clay, rubber, polystyrene, or similar material on which a design has been carved or incised. When its surface is inked it can be used to print the design onto another surface (e.g., paper, fabric). (2) A created or found texture tool (e.g., shells, lace, textured rolling pins) with a raised, low-relief surface used to impress a design onto the surface of clay.

*stencil.* Thick paper, cardboard, or other stiff material with a cut-out design used as a template in printmaking. The stencil is held above a surface, and paint or ink is brushed over it to reproduce the design on the surface below.

*still life.* An art work depicting a grouping of inanimate objects.

*stippling (drawing).* A drawing technique that uses patterns of dots to create shadows, values, and value gradations. Darker tones are created by using more dots close together rather than larger dots. *See also* **drawing; painting techniques**.

*storyboard.* A visual planning tool for organizing ideas for an animated work, story, video, or comic book into a sequence of sketches, images, or "shots". Each item (frame) in the sequence depicts scenes or figures and includes commentary that describes details of how the image should look and how it fits into the story. *See also* **camera shot**.

*style.* The way of creating art that is characteristic of a particular person, culture, historical period, or group. In an art work, the type and use of materials, methods of work, subject matter, and so on, may reflect a particular style. The following are some major artistic styles:

– *abstract art.* Art that achieves its effect by simplifying the visual elements (e.g., line, shape, colour) of images. Though people and things may not be recognizable as such in abstract art, they are the inspiration behind the simplified shapes and forms. *See also* **abstraction**.

– *cubism.* A non-objective school of painting and sculpture developed in Paris in the early twentieth century. Its practitioners often depicted objects as fragmented assemblages of geometric planes. *See also* **cubist technique**.

– *expressionism.* (1) Art in which emotion or feeling is paramount, often characterized by distortion or exaggeration and the emotive use of colour. (2) A movement in the arts during the early part of the twentieth century that emphasized subjective expression of the artist's inner experiences.

– *impressionism.* A style or technique of art that is concerned with depicting the visual impression of the moment, especially the shifting effect of light, by the use of unmixed primary colours and small strokes to simulate actual reflected light; the theory and style of impressionism originated and developed in France during the 1870s.

– *modernism.* (1) Art in which the images are focused not on traditional subject matter but on elements of design (e.g., form, colour). (2) A general term used for most of the artistic work from the late nineteenth century until approximately the 1970s, loosely signifying art that repudiates traditional forms or ideas.

– *naturalism. See* **style: realism**.

– *non-objective art.* Art that achieves its effect by using the elements of line, shape, and colour in a non-representational way rather than to depict recognizable objects or figures. It is often focused on exploring colour, form, and texture as formal concepts or shapes and forms produced from the imagination. *See also* **style: abstract art**.

– *op art (optical art).* Art that emerged in the 1960s and that uses line and colour interactions to create optical illusions, causing the viewer to see the work as pulsating, flickering, or moving.

– *postmodernism.* Art that is opposed to the modernist preoccupation with form and technique and that encourages the fusion of genres, ideas, media, technologies, and forms to promote parody, humour, irony, and criticism. This style often features words as a central artistic element, and uses collage, simplification, current technologies, performance art, and elements from works of the past or from consumer and popular culture arranged in new combinations.

– *realism.* (1) Art in which objects, figures, or scenes are drawn or painted as they appear in nature or in real life. Also called naturalism. (2) A style of art, developed in nineteenth-century France and influenced by the advent of photography, that based its depictions on direct observation of reality without the addition of personal emotion associated with romanticism.

– *surrealism.* Art associated with a twentieth-century artistic movement that attempts to express the workings of the subconscious mind and that is characterized by the use of fantastic imagery and incongruous juxtapositions of subject matter. Surrealist art works often feature imaginary creatures formed from collections of everyday objects, and unnerving and illogical scenes depicted with photographic precision.

*subject matter.* The ideas, objects, figures, feelings, and understandings represented in a work of art. *See also* **content**.

*substitution.* A technique in which the qualities of an object are changed to create an incongruous effect (e.g., a furry teacup, a brick patterned couch).

*symbolism.* The use of something (e.g., an object) to represent something else (e.g., an idea or person). In art, a style that uses symbolic images to suggest abstract ideas or intangible things or states.

*symmetry.* Equality in size, shape, and/or position between parts or elements or objects.

*technique.* A method or procedure of using a tool or material to produce a work of art or achieve an expressive effect (e.g., using the side of a pencil to shade light and dark tones; using the point of a pencil to create a fine line). *See also* **drawing; painting techniques**.

*tertiary colours.* Colours made from combinations of all three primary colours (red, yellow, and blue). (*Tertiary* means third in order or level.) For example, a colour made by combining orange and blue is a tertiary colour because orange (secondary colour) is made up of the two primary colours red and yellow, with blue as the third primary colour. In traditional painting, the term *tertiary colour* is used loosely to signify a colour made from the combination of a primary colour and a secondary colour.

*texture.* An element of design. The feel, appearance, thickness, or stickiness of a surface or substance. Subcategories of *texture* include the following:

– *illusory texture.* A visual effect in which the eye is tricked into seeing three-dimensional materials (e.g., wood, fur, glass, metal, fabric) on a two-dimensional surface. Also called simulated texture or the illusion of texture.

– *real texture.* The three-dimensionality of surfaces and materials that is perceptible by touch as well as sight (e.g., smooth, rough, silky, furry).

*thumbnail sketch.* A small, quick sketch that records ideas and very basic information. Thumbnail sketches are often used as examples of possible layouts, showing combinations of pictorial elements of various heights and widths, different vertical and horizontal treatments, and/or close-ups and distant views. *See also* **sketch**.

*tint.* A light value of a colour, created by adding white.

*tone.* A dark value of a colour, created by adding black.

*transfer (acrylic).* A process for transferring an image or colour from one surface to another. Acrylic gel is brushed onto the surface (e.g., inkjet transparency, photocopy) holding the image, and the gel-soaked surface is pressed firmly onto a new surface. Once the gel is dry, the original paper is moistened and rubbed with a sponge until all of the paper fibres are gone and the new surface holds only the image embedded in a layer of clear acrylic. For a process for transferring texture, *see* **rubbing**.

*transformation.* A change in structure, appearance, character, or function.

*unity.* A principle of design. The arrangement of elements to give the viewer the feeling that all the parts of the piece form a coherent whole.

*value.* An element of design that describes the lightness or darkness of a colour and/or the gradual changes in the lightness or darkness of an art work even when colour is absent.

*value scale.* A tool for showing a range of values, consisting of a series of spaces filled with the shades of one colour from lightest to darkest.

*variation.* A representation (e.g., of an object) that is changed in some way from an earlier representation of the same thing (e.g., through magnification, distortion, changes in texture or pattern, and so on).

*variety.* A principle of design. The quality of being diverse or incorporating a number of different or contrasting elements. Variety may be achieved by opposing, changing, elaborating, or contrasting the elements of design.

*video.* A recording of moving images and sound on an electronic medium such as videotape, a hard disk, or streaming media, or the process of making such a recording.

*viewfinder.* (1) A cardboard frame used as a tool to select images, or to compose an image, by cropping out unwanted perimeters (edges). (2) A device on a camera used to frame what is to appear in the picture. *See also* **cropping**.

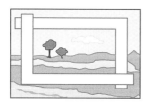

*warm colours.* Colours that suggest warmth (e.g., red, yellow, orange). Warm colours usually appear to advance into the foreground.

*watercolour paint.* Transparent, water-soluble paint available in solid cakes or in semi-liquid form in tubes.

*watercolour techniques.* Painting techniques using water-soluble paint. Types of watercolour techniques include the following:

– *dry brush.* A technique that involves the use of thick paint and little water on the brush. The relative dryness causes the brush to skip on the surface of the paper, producing a broken or textured appearance.

– *salt resist.* A technique that involves sprinkling coarse salt on washes of damp, water-based paint. The salt crystals gradually take up the pigment, creating a multiplicity of light, starlike shapes on the surface of the paper.

– *wash.* A technique that involves broadly applying thin layers of diluted pigment to a surface, producing an almost transparent effect.

– *wet on dry.* A technique that involves letting each layer dry before applying another layer of colour on top.

– *wet on wet.* A technique that involves applying wet paint to a wet surface so that the paints bleed and blend into one another.

*wet and dry materials.* Art-making media with wet properties (e.g., paint, ink, dyes, washes) or dry properties (e.g., pencil, charcoal, conté, crayon).

*wide shot. See* **camera shot**.

The Ministry of Education wishes to acknowledge
the contribution of the many individuals, groups, and
organizations that participated in the development
and refinement of this curriculum policy document.